GENTLEMAN GERRY

A Contender in the Ring, a Champion in Recovery

Gerry Cooney
John Grady

ROWMAN & LITT
Lanham • Boulder • New

D1197909

Published by Rowman & Littlefield
An imprint of The Rowman & Littlefield Publishing Group, Inc.
4501 Forbes Boulevard, Suite 200, Lanham, Maryland 20706
www.rowman.com

6 Tinworth Street, London SE11 5AL

British Library Cataloguing in Publication Information Available

Library of Congress Cataloging-in-Publication Data

Names: Cooney, Gerry, 1956–, author. | Grady, John, 1976–, author.
Title: Gentleman Gerry : a contender in the ring, a champion in recovery / Gerry Cooney, John
    Grady.
Description: Lanham : Rowman & Littlefield, [2019] | Includes bibliographical references and index.
Identifiers: LCCN 2018054444 (print) | LCCN 2019000352 (ebook) | ISBN 9781538111017 (elec-
    tronic) | ISBN 9781538111000 (cloth : alk. paper)
Subjects: LCSH: Cooney, Gerry, 1956–. | Boxers (Sports)—United States—Biography. | Alcohol-
    ics—United States—Biography.
Classification: LCC GV1132.C668 (ebook) | LCC GV1132.C668 A3 2019 (print) | DDC 796.83092
    [B]—dc23
LC record available at https://lccn.loc.gov/2018054444

∞ ™ The paper used in this publication meets the minimum requirements of
American National Standard for Information Sciences Permanence of Paper for
Printed Library Materials, ANSI/NISO Z39.48-1992.

Printed in the United States of America

In memory of my parents, my friend and great teacher
Victor Valle, and my siblings. Thank you for always
being there for me.

—Gerry Cooney

To all my loved ones, each contributed to my life in
unique and meaningful ways—but especially Mom,
forever my guardian angel.

—John Grady

CONTENTS

FOREWORD

Randy "Commish" Gordon

I saw him win his first championship in the New York Golden Gloves as a tall, skinny middleweight; I saw him lose as a taller, still-skinny light heavyweight; and I saw him win the tournament again as a still-growing heavyweight the year after. But it wasn't until I saw him in a USA vs. Russia meet in 1975 that I knew Gerry Cooney had arrived.

Team USA had chosen many of its best boxers to face the then world-dominant and always rough Russian squad. The man chosen by Team Russia to face Cooney was at least five inches shorter than the Long Island native. However, the Russian was an explosive puncher with both hands. One of his specialties was beating much-taller heavyweights. One of his victims was legendary Cuban star Teófilo Stevenson. The Russians had studied films of Cooney and put in a call to their "giant killer."

"No problem," was Cooney's feeling about the fight. He was right. It *was* no problem. A booming left hook to the jaw put the Russian to sleep in the very first round.

With the Olympics less than a year away, Cooney turned his attention to Montreal, the site of the XXI Olympiad. However, when Cooney's dad, Tony, fell ill and then died in 1976, Cooney needed to reset his focus. There would be no Olympics for him. He would take his vaunted power and turn pro, guided by two Long Island businessmen.

When Cooney made his pro debut on February 15, 1977, I was ringside, covering for both *World Boxing* and *International Boxing* magazines, where I was the assistant editor. I was ringside for all but two of Cooney's first twenty-six fights, missing his match against Eddie "the

Animal" Lopez in Las Vegas, a bout Cooney won by third round knock-out, and his comeback fight in September 1984 against Eddie Gregg.

In the summer of 1979, I became the editor in chief of *The Ring* magazine. My change in business address also saw a change in Cooney's attitude toward me. At postfight interviews, Cooney always answered my questions, but he did so with short, abrupt answers. To other reporters, he'd smile, answer their questions, and even joke around. I wondered why he was nicer to them than me and thought there must be a specific reason for his affection for other sports journalists. After trying from 1980 to 1981—through Cooney's power-packed victories over Jimmy Young, Ron Lyle, and Ken Norton—I gave up trying to make Cooney like or even respect me. For whatever reason, he felt neither for me.

In late 1981, when a title fight between Larry Holmes and Gerry Cooney was imminent, I received a call from one of the two participants. The caller wasn't Gerry Cooney.

"Randy, would you know of any tall heavyweights I can use as a sparring partner as I train for Gerry Cooney?" asked Larry Holmes, with whom I had developed the kind of relationship I also wanted to have—but didn't—with Cooney. Instantly, I knew of one. His name was Mitch Green, a six-foot, five-inch right-hander from Brooklyn. His nickname was Blood. I called Mitch Green's manager, Shelly Finkel, and he agreed to have his heavyweight join Holmes's camp as a sparring partner. Green became an integral part of Holmes's preparation for Cooney.

On June 11, 1982, Holmes stopped Cooney in a classic heavyweight title fight. In victory, Holmes proved—again—what a great champion he was. In defeat, Cooney showed championship heart, skill, and courage. However, Cooney didn't look at it that way. Disappointed with himself, he disappeared from view for the next twenty-seven months.

At the press conference in the summer of 1984 announcing his come-back in September against undefeated Eddie Gregg, I waited until the veteran boxing writers were done interviewing Cooney. I then walked up to him and said hello. With little expression, he nodded. It was the perfect time to ask him a personal question.

"Why don't you like me?" I asked him. "You have been indifferent to me for the last five years. Why?"

Cooney looked at me. There was anger in his eyes.

"You've been writing bad things about me for years," he said, his stare piercing my soul.

"What?" I said. "I've been writing bad things about you?"

Nothing could have been further from the truth. If anything, I had consistently made glowing remarks about him in *World Boxing* and *International Boxing*, *The Ring* magazine, and on ESPN and USA Network.

"Where have I said or written bad things?" I asked.

Looking embarrassed, Cooney said, "My managers told me you were writing bad things."

I thought for a moment and then said, "Gerry, I'll tell you what. How about I meet you anywhere you want for lunch tomorrow. I will bring every issue of *The Ring* with me since I became editor in 1979. If you find one bad thing—just one—I will buy lunch. If you can't find anything, you buy! Fair enough?"

"Fair enough," he said. He then picked a restaurant in a popular Long Island shopping center for us to meet.

I came with a suitcase filled with magazines. He perused many of them. This is what he found: "The hardest hook in boxing." "A pulverizing jab." "Cooney is destined for boxing greatness."

Cooney bought lunch, and we have been friends ever since.

Ironically, I announced his final fight. It was on January 15, 1990, in Atlantic City against George Foreman. Although dejected after losing the fight, there was no more hiding, no more solitary confinement. Gerry Cooney had beaten his demons in many ways, including beating a long-standing problem with substance abuse.

In 2010, SiriusXM's president, Scott Greenstein, walked past me in the hall one day. I was then hosting a mixed martial arts show called *Fight Club*.

"Randy, do you know Gerry Cooney?" Scott asked.

I nodded.

"Do you think you can get him to come up and have lunch with me? I have always wanted to meet him. Tell him I will send a car to pick him up."

I called Gerry and told him my boss wanted to meet him. "Why not?" he said.

A few days later, Cooney was in Greenstein's office, and I was invited to sit in. A few stories in, Greenstein said, "Guys, how would you like to do a boxing show together?"

Cooney and I looked at each other in surprise. Then we looked at Greenstein.

"A boxing show," he repeated. "A talk show. You guys will host it together."

A short time later, we were sitting across from each other on *At the Fights*.

Going into the SiriusXM studios with my good friend and sitting ringside all over the country with him has become a special part of my life.

He is as warm, thoughtful, and compassionate to everyone he meets outside the ring as he was vicious, destructive, and pulverizing in the ring. He is one of the select number of big-name fighters who have successfully transitioned from a world-class athlete into a world-class citizen. His charity work is endless, and his compassion for others is genuinely seen, felt, and heard. I have seen him take private phone calls from listeners who beg him for help with their addiction problems.

To Gerry Cooney, it's no longer about living in the fast lane and self-indulgence.

It's about going the distance.

ACKNOWLEDGMENTS

The information contained in this literary effort was derived from count-less sources. In addition to the recollections and self-disclosures of the author, Gerry Cooney, other resources include interviews with Gerry's peers, friends, and noted boxing professionals. Contemporary periodicals of each time period, too, were utilized to generate discussion questions and to provide background data.

The authors are most grateful for the following list of contributors, all of whom shared stories, experiences, expert analysis, and insights that bolstered the book's quality: Steve Petramale, renowned boxing and mixed martial arts fighter; Jerry Izenberg, legendary sports journalist; and Randy "Commish" Gordon, former chairman of the New York State Athletic Commission (1988–1995).

* * *

With enduringly grateful hearts, we thank Lisa Tansey for editing our work with professionalism and enthusiasm that exceeded our most lofty expectations. Thank you.

We also thank the legendary photographer Joe DiMaggio (http://joedi-maggiophoto.com) for providing all of the photos found in our book. Your professionalism, support, and contributions are cherished—and your friendship even more so.

PROLOGUE

May 11, 1981. Madison Square Garden. The historic mecca of boxing was alive with the palpable sense of impending destruction. It was an intoxicating feeling for fight fans—and unique to significant heavyweight fights.

The much-anticipated bout featured what many considered to be a rising star's most significant battle to date. This dominant contender had efficiently catapulted to the upper echelon of the rankings, but now he would finally encounter a force capable of challenging him. For the esteemed opponent, nearing the latter days of his sensational run as a top heavyweight in the sport's most competitive era, this title-elimination contest was a platform to ultimately compete on the world championship stage once again.

The contender, "Gentleman" Gerry Cooney, was primed to conquer his foe. Ken Norton, tasked with spoiling the meteoric rise of the much-discussed destroyer, was a physically imposing figure. Many experts, including *The Ring* magazine's then–associate editor Randy Gordon, thought that Norton was in the best shape of his illustrious career. Champion Larry Holmes expected Norton to win. After all, the veteran warrior boasted the same muscular, sculpted torso that he used to author his Hall of Fame career. Norton had also just handed Randall "Tex" Cobb, the World Boxing Council's (WBC) ninth-ranked heavyweight coming off a stoppage victory against the formidable Earnie Shavers, his first loss.

Norton's résumé included numerous accomplishments. The future Hall of Famer became only the second man to defeat the great Muhammad Ali. During that bout, Norton fractured Ali's jaw—the same one that withstood the powerful blows of George Foreman and Joe Frazier—en route to a split-decision victory. Only three years removed from his momentous battle with the great Holmes, the highly regarded Norton was expected to present a formidable challenge to his much-heralded opponent.

Although in only the fourth year of his professional fighting career, Gerry was already considered by many to be the top contender to Holmes's crown. He was also an awesome physical specimen. Standing six feet, six inches tall, "Gentleman" Gerry easily towered over all of his foes. And he was ready for Norton. A warrior's spirit fueled Gerry's drive to encounter, fight, and overcome. A primal rage amplified his already prodigious punching power. Boxing was the outlet for him to express himself, to feel alive, to *be* alive. The bigger the fight, the more electrifying the process felt.

It was almost fight time.

* * *

Fear grips all fighters. It is a necessary reality. Fear keeps them alert and primed. The emotion served as fuel to Gerry's keen focus on the upcoming battle. The thrill of combat—of competition, playing chess in the ring, changing his opponent's facial expression—was more intoxicating than any chemical created by humankind. The time was near. Gerry's mind zeroed in on destroying Norton's body, employing his offensive arsenal, and knocking out the legend who would soon be in front of him.

The bell chimed, signaling round one.

Bouncing lightly on the canvas as the bell rung, Gerry swiftly met Norton in the ring's center. After a brief feeling-out period that featured jabs from both gladiators, Gerry landed the fight's first meaningful blow. A right hand noticeably buckled Norton's knees. Like a predator sensing a prey's weakness, the aspiring heavyweight champion unleashed a furious, brutal attack that first stunned, then overwhelmed, and finally devastated the former WBC world champion. Focused rage powered Gerry's onslaught. Within mere moments, his attack to Norton's body and jaw quickly drove the future Hall of Famer to an alarmingly prolonged state of unconscious.

It was a historically quick conquest.

Fifty-four seconds into the most meaningful bout of his promising career, Gerry emphatically solidified his place as the world's top challenger to the most prestigious individual title in sports. He had matched Lee "the Battling Bartender" Savold's record for quickest knockout in a Madison Square Garden main event, one that had lasted for more than three decades. The new standard would remain for more than a quarter century. Joy flooded Gerry's veins.

He was atop the boxing world.

* * *

History views Gerry's victory as one of the most disturbingly brutal knockouts the sport has ever seen. The frightening annihilation of Norton swiftly sent the legend into retirement. Ecstatic fans soon began spirited debates regarding the inevitable contest between Gerry and the reigning champion, "the Easton Assassin" Larry Holmes. Boxing authorities, too, engaged in educated discussions regarding the factors that would determine the fight's outcome. The dream match would eventually occur. It would become one of the most glaring and historically significant stages in sports—an epic battle that will forever be remembered and revisited by boxing enthusiasts.

But on this night, a heavyweight contender had evolved into a boxing legend.

Part One

A Survivor Evolves into a Fighter

I had a great career, had a lotta fun, a lotta troubles. I want to talk about what happened . . . and maybe change some things for today's fighters, hopefully help some people out along the way.—Gerry Cooney

I

THE EARLIEST DAYS

The sun smiled on the Long Island, New York, household. It was the mid-'60s, a time of conflict and change. The early September air was crisp enough to flood even the sleepiest soul with energy. A little boy tiptoed his way outside his home. He closed the door slowly, carefully, with educated levels of stealth. Every precaution had to be taken. Dad wasn't working today, the boy knew, but the workingman's body clock made it easy for him to wake with little prompting—even after a night of hard drinking, which, the boy sadly understood, was almost every night.

Though lying quietly in bed was his best protection, seeing his friend was worth the risk. The boy was almost there. He could see him. The dog's compromised condition belied the natural power that, paradoxically, was clearly evident. The boy understood that precious creature. Domino was his name. A bit haggard, the middle-aged German shepherd somehow looked regal despite being tied to the slowly decaying backyard fence. The leash was only four feet long, enough to stand up and pace a bit. Its eyes were hopeful as it gazed upon the benevolent presence slowly moving toward him. Inner strength radiated from his canine frame. He, too, was a survivor.

A fighter.

The little boy, Gerry Cooney, felt a fleeting sensation of fear evaporate as he tiptoed toward his favorite friend. It was a familiar feeling but it only fueled his resolve, his power. His mind clear again, Gerry was fully living the unfolding experience. The aging canine's slow but happy rise

to all fours brought joy to the boy's existence. The increasingly enthusiastic wag of Domino's tail made Gerry's world a perfect one.

A heartbeat later, fear returned, as it often did. It was a consistent
cycle when his father was home. Gerry's conditioned mind recentered on
the doom that was rarely predictable and always impending.

Was he awake?

*Where can I hide? If I go in now, I can make it to the basement
corner. . . .*

I'm no good, don't deserve anything.

The boy found himself wincing as much from imagining Arthur
Cooney's condemnations as he would from his father's powerful blows.
Those messages were internalized. Then he pushed the negative messages
away, pushed the fear away, and kept moving forward. This effort, too,
was part of the process. The process of surviving, moving forward, and
overcoming.

Nature and animals always had a healing effect on the boy. Gerry felt
safe despite having endured a near fatal attack from his previous dog,
Fury, a few years earlier. Fury's bite was an eighth of an inch from the
boy's jugular vein. Gerry had to wait for a taxicab to go to the hospital
because the family had no running car, only a motorcycle. But that was a
different time. Gerry survived that threat, just as he had every threat
before and since.

For the moment, there was neither future nor past, just the unfolding
events of the moment—one that produced a euphoria so profound that it
erased all of life's worries or concerns.

Just like boxing would, one day.

* * *

The future contender for the sport's greatest prize, the heavyweight
championship of the world, was born on August 24, 1956. Unlike many
professional boxers, Gerry was not raised in a poverty-stricken neighbor-
hood. Huntington Station, Long Island, consisted mainly of working-
class households less than forty miles from New York City. Gerry's home
was a red Cape Cod house on Holland Street. He was the third of six
children born to Eileen and Arthur "Tony" Cooney. The family consisted
of four boys: Gerry, Thomas, Michael, and Stephen—and two girls, Eileen and Madeleine. But although the fundamental necessities were not a
persistent focus for the future fighter, survival was nevertheless a con-

stant concern. The menacing force in his life was the same that should have protected a child from such emotion—his father, Tony Cooney.

Surviving early abuse challenged—but ultimately empowered—the future heavyweight contender. Becoming familiar with struggle, and the process of overcoming it, was perhaps his life's greatest teacher. Gerry instinctively survived an alcoholic household with a warrior's heart. He fought for identity, to establish independence, to be happy—a journey similar to most, but one that also included the fight to endure a chaotic and unsafe household.

Survival in the Cooney household—much like a prizefight—depended on effective planning for anticipated attacks. A great defense. Like preparing for an upcoming opponent, Gerry's child's mind had to manage his fears and read his father—his state of mind—and respond to his words in ways that would avoid attacks. Just like fighting the offense of Muhammad Ali in his prime, Tony Cooney's moods and complicated repertoire of attacks were frequently unpredictable. The abuses had damaging consequences. Gerry fought persistent feelings of unworthiness. Even so, the same experiences that produced emotional scars ultimately educated the future fighter and added depth to his emotional strength.

The elder Cooney economically sustained his large family. His trade as an ironworker contributed to the many Manhattan buildings being erected. Like most men of his era, Tony's emotional wounds—bred from suffering his own childhood abuses—were not discussed or acknowledged. This may have added to his brutality, secrecy, and continual focus on self-sufficiency. After all, hurt people hurt (other) people. Many abusers and alcoholics create similar household conditions: Keep the drinking a family secret. Keep the abuses a secret. Keep everything a secret.

Trust no one.

* * *

Secrecy would ultimately include Gerry's own alcohol abuse, which, for many years, was not known even to himself. That is almost always the case with those afflicted with the disease. Given his genetics and the power of his addiction symptoms, Gerry's addiction was activated upon his first introduction to chemicals. The first drink is a landmark one for the alcoholic. It is a time when experimentation—with the user unaware of the horrific consequences to be paid—unites genetics, social learning behaviors, and the brain-changing processes to manifest the disease of addiction. It is a self-activated illness, but no one signs up for a drinking problem.

Experimentation is common among children and adolescents. The twelve-year-old Gerry couldn't possibly understand how significant the act would be, as is the case with virtually all children and adolescents. Even if there were warnings from aware adults, a boy of that age would likely disregard them. Most adolescents and adults would, too. After all, negative consequences happened to other people, and a young person's comprehension of his or her own mortality can range from limited to nonexistent.

The preadolescent came across Boone's Farm Apple Wine at a party and readily ingested it. The experience was not like any before in his young life. The chemical affected parts of Gerry's brain in ways that produced feelings and sensations that were instantly appealing. He felt attractive, funny, liked by people. Good feelings became great. Fear evaporated. Even though he became physically sick—terribly sick—Gerry's brain didn't register this part of the experience for long. Soon, he remembered only the great parts. The process of remembering only the good parts would be the core of his relationship with alcohol.

However, Gerry's teen years would feature an introduction to the greatest and most important outlet of his life: boxing.

* * *

Before the sport of boxing was introduced to Gerry's life, first came street fighting. When he saw injustice, he would fight. Defend others. Gerry couldn't protect anyone in his father's dictatorship, so helping others nourished his soul and filled many voids. Fighting also forced him into the moment. The threat of impending harm sharpened his focus. The feel of connecting with a foe and seeing him fall—threat managed and disposed of—produced a sense of accomplishment. He didn't look to fight but readily did so when it was justified. It was the only problem-solving skill that seemed to work.

The fighting process resonated with the adolescent, who would bring his boxing gloves to the bus stop and spar with whomever was available and willing. These contests allowed Gerry to express himself and to hone a gift that would ultimately take him to one of the most viewed stages in boxing history. It was his playing ground. A fair playing ground. The opposite of the household produced by his father's abuses. Life had introduced Gerry to a new world—one that provided him with the ability to express his pain and his potential. To feel joy. To fully experience the moment.

* * *

Tony saw his son's skills and sensed his potential. Potential enough to live his own dreams through his son. So he "trained" Gerry. Gerry's days began before the sun rose. The adolescent frequently awoke to sadistic acts: his hair being pulled or a splash of ice-cold water. The shock and pain ignited the young fighter's adrenaline, instantly waking him up. Intense running drills were conducted before venturing off to school, which served as a relative brief respite from his arduous training routines. After school, Gerry was coerced to return to roadwork and other endeavors while his friends were busy enjoying the fruits of youth. Finger push-ups, rope climbing, and ascending trees without shoes were all used to improve conditioning, but the threatening manner in which they were directed made them an extension of Tony Cooney's abusive tactics.

The elder Cooney, with a six-foot, three-inch frame that supported 220 pounds, eventually created a makeshift ring in the backyard. Four poles were planted in the dirt with ropes draped around them. The simple design served as the sparring ground for the Cooney men. Hopefully, it was meant to train Gerry, to toughen him up. But most certainly, Tony wanted to live out his own unrealized dream of being a fighter.

Even as an adolescent, Gerry packed a tremendous punch. Yet, something held him back when fighting his father. He always felt something— sometimes irrational guilt and sometimes fear of the repercussions—even as the elder Cooney taunted him to unload. Gerry was pragmatic. He knew how Tony would react to being humbled. More abuse. This fear transcended Gerry's joy of combat, of competition, of hitting and getting hit, of expressing himself in a fair environment. Tony may or may not have been trying to instill discipline, to create goals, to generate toughness in his son, but he was certainly not the man to train Gerry.

Professional guidance would ignite the inferno of potential in the future boxing legend.

* * *

Gerry survived one day at a time. It is more manageable that way. Physical wounds healed even while some emotional ones remained. The boy's survival skills were sharpened as he found inspiration that sustained him. Gerry's older brother, Tommy, was a prominent motivator in his young life, as most older brothers are to their younger siblings. Tommy represented realistic hope to the adolescent, one who wanted to experience freedom. Tommy, three years Gerry's senior, left the house at age fifteen. He was always a little different than the other family members—a bit more distant, perhaps—and this attribute likely helped him to escape Tony's control early in life.

Tommy was also a fighter. A boxer. A good one, too. Gerry admired his older brother, followed him around as much as he could, and was most thrilled to see him train in an actual boxing gym. The relationship provided special moments for Gerry—there was a feeling that everything will eventually be okay, even though Gerry didn't know how that would happen. Such is the power of an older brother's presence upon a younger one.

Gerry's journey as a fighter would lead him to a more professional setting: the Huntington Athletic Club. Here, Gerry's world came alive with meaning and realistic hope. On some level, Gerry knew that he had a gift—the power in his fists, after all, ended most of his street fights—and he intuitively understood that he was on his best life path. Like an enduring light shining at the end of a dark and foreboding tunnel, this understanding carried Gerry through his most difficult moments.

* * *

Walking up the now-familiar stairs to Huntington Athletic Club, Gerry felt almost numb with excitement. His school days at Huntington Station, New York's Walt Whitman High School, went by so quickly these days. The teenager knew that training would commence not long after that last school bell rang. And Mr. Capobianco—John Capobianco Sr., a trainer introducing Gerry to this new world—was proving to be an important figure in Gerry's development.

The young man thirsted for guidance and, although his advancement was quicker than could be expected, Gerry overcame a tough beginning to his boxing life. The teenager was not unlike an adolescent stallion whose young body had grown a bit quicker than his brain and nervous system. Already taller than his peers and long limbed, Gerry sometimes lumbered awkwardly and had some trouble coordinating his legs to follow his mind's instructions. The young man's athletic potential was clear, especially to the expert eyes of any athletic authority who worked with young people, but it would take time before Gerry's skills matured—but not much.

Like a teenager who suddenly hits a growth spurt, Gerry's dormant fighting abilities prospered significantly when challenged with live combat nurtured by professional guidance and fueled by a passion for the sport. The thrill of combat and allure of his burgeoning mastery was often intoxicating to the improving adolescent. Boxing was making him a somebody—somebody who mattered.

Formal training allowed Gerry to fully explore his potential. The trainers and fighters were tough, professional, and disciplined. Gerry could unleash on the bags and fellow pugilists in a way that he could never against his father. Gerry's natural skill, power, and resiliency led him to enjoy near-immediate success in the ring. Quality sparring sessions and training translated into amateur victories and validation. Boxing created intense purpose and meaning in the young man's spirit.

The young fighter was flourishing.

* * *

Although he had structured outlets for his fighting energies, Gerry still fought outside the squared circle when needed. Sometimes, the opponents were unexpected. The school's football coach, a big strong adult, repeatedly taunted Gerry regarding his boxing prowess. The adult thought he was a tough guy by antagonizing the biggest student in class. Gerry's status as a boxer was unique in his high school, making him a target to some. Eventually, the coach challenged Gerry to bring in gloves.

Gerry did so the next day.

The adult and adolescent stepped into the private confines of the wrestling room. Educators and peers alike gathered to witness the conflict rather than derail it. The contest was not competitive. The trained adolescent jabbed and toyed with the adult tough guy. The encounter became part of Gerry's high school legacy. In some ways, it was as memorable as his amateur accomplishments.

There were, of course, bumps in the road as Gerry faced new adversities and honed in on his ever-developing skills. Gerry's unusual height provided more body for his foes to hit, but his uncommon hand speed enabled him to keep adversaries at bay. His progress was astounding. The gym had become Gerry's safe haven. The best version of himself materialized in the ring, where he could fully express himself. Now, he would do so in front of the masses.

A mere half year after his training began, Gerry was empowered to truly explore his talents and entered the New York State Golden Gloves

Middleweight Championship at Madison Square Garden in New York City.

2

THE SURVIVOR FIGHTS BACK

After only five months of training, the teenage Gerry entered the 1973 subnovice 160-pound New York Golden Gloves and ultimately advanced to the finals. It was an astonishing irony: the boy who once hid in the basement corner to escape his abusive father, whose quest to simply survive forced him to adopt the life strategy that he couldn't be hurt if he couldn't be seen, would soon be under the spotlight of the world's most famous arena. He would be in a situation in which facing pain was inevitable but experiencing the immense joys of competition was a certainty.

The Golden Gloves tournament included Gerry's first championship stage. It proved to be a vital learning experience for the sixteen-year-old on myriad levels. The sport challenges one's very soul, pushing the body, mind, and spirit far beyond the limit of one's comfort zone. This is where resiliency is accessed and growth is realized. Boxing places its fighters in position to access the courage needed to fight through adversity, an important process that can be generalized to many life events.

For Gerry, boxing also led to some incredible encounters with sports legends.

* * *

Gerry found himself in the Felt Forum, a small theater inside Madison Square Garden (MSG), preparing for the middleweight semifinals of the New York State Golden Gloves. Focused on the battle before him, Gerry—like all athletes—had moments of overvaluing outcomes. Win. Loss. Knockout. Decision. Such moments produce pressure. Some pressure is essential for peak performance, but too much can decrease productivity.

Distraction can help ease tension by producing a natural reprieve from excessive focus on a competition's consequences.

On this significant day, the natural nerves associated with impending combat made Gerry come alive. But these energies flirted with transforming excitement into anxiety. Nerves serve as a double-edged sword, but the negative aspect was soon largely negated by a team of New York sports legends strolling toward their own version of sports combat.

The 1973 New York Knicks, who had played the Los Angeles Lakers in the NBA Finals the year before, were celebrities throughout the sports world. They transcended the sport in their home state and city. The '72 to '73 season would witness their avenging the previous year's loss to the Lakers en route to earning the championship. These Knickerbocker athletes were champions. They had won the championship in 1970, too, and were accustomed to success. Many had swagger, most had the compelling confidence of elite athletes in their prime, and all had the scent of a championship mentality.

It was surreal for Gerry to see great athletes like Walt "Clyde" Frazier, Willis Reed, and Dave Debusschere confidently stride into the locker room. Frazier's presence was particularly influential. Clad in his outlandishly stylish fur coats and brimming with confidence, the basketball great was nothing short of mesmerizing. Quiet by nature despite a ferocious, competitive heart, Gerry gravitated toward outspoken athletes. He loved Muhammad Ali then and to this day. Witnessing the great Frazier and his teammates—in real life and in ways most would never enjoy—immediately became cherished memories forever imprinted in Gerry's mind. Even now, the two sports legends talk about this experience.

The naturally humble Gerry, sometimes prone to diminished self-esteem due to years of abuse, fed off the swagger of the seemingly innately confident Frazier. A part of Gerry shared such confidence. A big part. Gerry smiled as he absorbed the experience. That part of him that knew he was worthy, knew that he was an elite athlete, was emboldened. It was a significant moment for the young prospect—one that fueled him forward.

* * *

Gerry excelled in his first Golden Gloves tourney. The experience forced Gerry to directly face his demons. He won by consistently fighting through adversity, both external (provided by his foes) and internal (provided by his father's abuses). In those days, it took five or six wins to earn the championship and elevated concentration and endurance to even be competitive. With each fight, Gerry's focus overcame his father's mantra that Gerry would never amount to anything. The challenges and internal conflicts were continuous, beginning well before his first bout.

Two weeks prior to the tourney, Gerry arrived for his physical. The entire experience was new. He never before had been in New York City. He was one of twenty-five hundred fighters. After hours of waiting, Gerry finally reached the doctor's office. The door opened, and a spectacularly built fighter emerged and declared, "Anybody at 160 novice may as well go home because I'm going to win it this year!" Gerry's life passed before his eyes. Incredibly and ironically, this fighter was Gerry's opponent in his first match. After throwing up in his corner due to nerves, Gerry fought hard and earned a tough win.

Gerry's first three fights ended in victories. They included a one-round knockout and a bout against fellow Irishman Chris Flynn, which went the distance. Gerry thought he would knock out the skinny competitor, but Flynn was much tougher than Gerry anticipated. Gerry got tired in the second and third rounds. Fighting through fatigue is among the worst experiences in sports, but it provides the adversity needed for wisdom and growth. Gerry tapped into his reservoir of resiliency, persevered, and learned the developmental process for personal evolution, earning a place in the semifinals against Eleby Frazier.

Frazier, twenty-four, was much older than Gerry. He was a taxi driver built like a tank. Standing across from his foe in the hallway, Gerry thought that he really deserved the finals if he beat this fighter. The teenager had to access his courage, yet again, to face this imposing figure. This was a normal process for Gerry by now. Years later, a dear friend, Bob Lewis, offered Gerry this insight: no matter how terrible his father had treated Gerry, his upbringing instilled something powerful in him, something that empowered Gerry to get into that ring, to feel fear, but to move forward anyway and achieve success. Gerry went on to knock Frazier out cold, a victory that sent him on to the back page of the *Daily News* and into the finals with Larry Derrick.

It was the most validating event of Gerry's young life.

* * *

So close to the treasured goal of becoming a champion, the prodigy walked up the four steps of the battleground. Gerry was responsible for a sold-out MSG event—twenty-one thousand people, lights off, and the spotlight was on him. It all hit Gerry at once. His brief life flashed before him. He was the underdog. But there was no time for thinking about how others viewed his chances—he had to fight. Gerry was just listening for the bell to ring.

He just wanted to fight.

First, the prefight rituals needed to be completed and soon after the announcements commenced. Gerry paced slightly, periodically bouncing up and down to keep his body warm. The boxer's fight, flight, or freeze mechanisms unfolded. He was there to fight. Gerry's alertness expanded, his focus narrowed, and his body produced the adrenaline needed for combat. Fear was increasingly redirected into excitement and strength.

As the ring announcer's work concluded, Gerry's concentration sharpened on the task at hand. He had to fight. He needed to survive. Any concerns about being exposed as inferior to the whole world under MSG's spotlight were now nonexistent. Such thoughts were reserved for contemplative periods, not when one is about to be put into a dangerous environment. The fighter's focus was also empowered by disciplined preparation, which had produced comprehensive muscle memory sharpened by countless hours of training.

The prodigy was primed to fight and, on some level, he knew it.

* * *

The first round was an encouraging one for the lanky Long Island pugilist. Towering over his foe at six feet, four inches tall, Gerry's long limbs made him something of an Irish American version of Thomas "the Hitman" Hearns. The future "Gentleman" would use his natural size and heart to overcome his relative lack of experience and physical awkwardness. Gerry dropped Derrick twice, much to the appreciation of the crowd. The spirited contest excited the knockout-seeking audience. Such is the allure of a heavy puncher—one never knows when the highlight reel knockout will occur. It can happen at any second. This was a spell that Gerry's abilities would cast upon the boxing world throughout his career, much like a home run hitter captures the imagination of fans with each at bat. It was with him even at this, the earliest stage of his career.

The bout highlighted several educational experiences for the future contender. Gerry was still learning to use his leverage optimally. Stamina, too, was not yet fully established. But he wasn't alone on this night. Both young men were tired by the middle of the second round, which ended with another knockdown from Gerry's vicious left hook and a respectful slap of the gloves at round's end. The third and final round began with both fighters clearly fatigued but with Derrick the worse for wear.

Gerry transcended his physical weariness and hurt Derrick, who clinched Gerry noticeably after the referee separated them. The compromised finalist received a standing eight count. The referee called off the fight with no protest from the runner-up. Gerry had earned a technical knockout victory! He leapt toward the sky as the crowd roared its approval, then hugged his trainer in a manner that hoisted the tall champion high above the ring.

On the day before St. Patrick's Day, the famously Irish Gerry Cooney became a Golden Gloves champion. He had proven his father wrong—Gerry was somebody!

Interestingly, Gerry's future stablemate, fellow Long Island native Howard Davis Jr., won his first of four Golden Gloves titles by decisioning Carlos Gonzalez for the 126-pound subnovice championship. Both Gerry and Howard would go on to achieve historically significant boxing careers. However, this night of shared success was the most compelling of each fighter's career up to that point.

Gerry and boxer Johnny Turner won Fighter of the Year, the equivalent to the most valuable fighter of the tournament. Jack Dempsey, among the most legendary fighters of all time, presented the duo with the award. Dempsey *was* boxing to Gerry. Their interaction was magical for the young man. Boxing remained relatively new to Gerry, yet here he was being presented an award by one of the sport's most historic figures. Gerry, after years of guarding family secrets due to fears of abuse, was now happily sharing his whole life with people. He had a good life; he had purpose.

And his boxing journey was only just beginning.

* * *

The Golden Gloves victory put Gerry's picture in the paper and provided him with the pride and recognition that were unavailable in Tony Cooney's household. Yet, even amid his young life's greatest moments, many of Gerry's thoughts had been on his brother, Tommy. All through the tournament, the sixteen-year-old had prayed that if only one of the brothers could win, "Please, God, make Tommy the victor." The elder sibling was always in the gym but hadn't trained optimally for the big fight. He didn't do enough roadwork. The younger Cooney had been concerned that this would translate into a loss. Although Tommy, likewise, possessed excellent power at the Golden Gloves level, even prodigious talents must be well prepared.

Gerry's prayers and bargaining were not answered. God hears all prayers, Gerry would one day learn, but sometimes the answer is no. The youngster's sense of urgency was based, consciously or otherwise, on the belief that a loss would derail Tommy from his dreams of becoming a professional fighter. Tommy lost a decision to Eric George. Unfortunately, history would show that Gerry's fears were prophetic. Tommy had more potential than Gerry ever possessed but didn't pursue the sport as Gerry did. He didn't fully explore where it could take him, and his energies soon became focused in other directions.

The joy derived from the victory was fleeting in many ways. Tony's demands made his son's victories more of a relief than cause for celebration. Plus, there were the normal challenges of all kids his age. Gerry was confused as to what to do with his life. Most of his peers were going to college or on track for traditional jobs. Gerry was on a unique path that was lonely but also exceptional. Boxing was providing him some hope—real hope. Gerry was different, but the positives clearly outweighed the negatives. Gerry was in the spotlight, and boxing provided him validation.

The fighter was finding his own way.

* * *

Gerry's prodigious power was budding and clearly compensated for the awkwardness that comes with learning how to utilize increasingly long limbs, something every adolescent body experiences, though perhaps not as much as men the size of power forwards. The teenaged Gerry's journey continued to produce unique and treasured memories. It would also feature many unexpected challenges that directly led to personal growth.

Boxing was like a microcosm of life; it produced many life lessons in short periods of time.

Gerry's physical size made him a likely candidate to be a bully, but his compassion naturally led him to be protective of others. Deferential and kind, as well. Sometimes overly so. Gerry was a gentle giant who also wanted to avoid conflict. His trainer, John Capobianco, supported and worked well with Gerry in most ways, but he also had sons who fought in the gym. Not wanting to cause any trouble, Gerry would hesitate when sparring with these particular peers. Gerry, when fighting one of the coach's sons, held back enough to avoid problems, just like at home, his domineering father's home.

Despite his mounting amateur successes, Gerry had yet to unleash the fury and potential that dwelled within. He still didn't really know it was there—or at least the extent to which it existed. Punching bags allowed Gerry to let go of some anger and actual bouts permitted a terrific outlet for more anger and pain. They also provided a sense of self, a connection to others, and accomplishment. He wasn't what his father said he was— Gerry was, in fact, something special. But he had yet to truly open up in the gym—his fear of conflict was simply too much to fully overcome, at least when it came to the coach's son.

One day, after the latest rough sparring session, another trainer—Otto Gianvinello—came over to the tall Irish fighter. "Fight those guys," he bluntly stated. "Fight back against those guys! Go ahead. Open up, Gerry—don't let them do that to you!" Otto had been Gerry's guide. Starving for a nurturing father figure, Otto filled that role—albeit too briefly—and his encouragement fed and inspired the young fighter.

An authority figure had given Gerry permission to explore his talents, and it was all that he needed. He wasn't alone. Someone had his back. Otto encouraged Gerry's fighting spirit to emerge and be sustained. The desire to fight back became increasingly present. Now, Gerry was given authority to fully express himself in the ring regardless of the foe.

Not long after, Gerry sparred with the coach's son once more. Gerry was a different young man. His talents were allowed full expression. Gerry had significantly evolved mentally and as a warrior. He increasingly centered himself in the moment. His skills were expressed. He was competitive, calculating every move. The teenager had grown to more than six feet tall and effectively used every inch. He seemed even taller, given that he had only 155 pounds covering his frame. Most importantly, Gerry fully embraced his safety zone—the boxing ring was his domain.

The trainer's son, used to imposing his will on Gerry, was suddenly facing a fighter fully battling back. During these moments of combat, Gerry had a voice in what occurred. His intentions and needs mattered. And he had the power to manifest them—something he could never have done in his home, not with Tony Cooney's presence. The act of boxing fueled and fed the young fighter.

The sparring session concluded with Gerry feeling proud of himself. He had truly explored his abilities, had felt the impact of transcending self-imposed limitations, and he liked it. It was an exhilarating emotion that compelled him to fight. The reveries of the experience produced a welcomed collection of surreal moments for Gerry.

Then John Capobianco Sr.'s powerful hand gripped Gerry's elongated neck, briefly picking him off the ground before throwing him against the wall. He threatened to smash Gerry. Just like his father. The frustrated trainer was not accustomed to seeing his son challenged so comprehensively, especially in his own gym. Otto wasn't there that day—he would have intervened if he had been, as he was an incredible and honorable guy. Gerry was all alone and once again facing violence from an adult.

Gerry faced the conflict alone. He had to figure it out. It was a hard process, but one in which he was well experienced. The event was precisely the type of scenario that Gerry had dreaded. But he had been given the green light to fight. Sparring required the participants to fight hard. Holding back was not productive for anyone involved. The coach's reaction wasn't fair, but it was real. Gerry's fears had been realized.

And he survived it.

* * *

That message—surviving adversity—would prove to be an enduring one. But there was something more, too. Gerry was now thriving even when confronted with old, self-imposed obstacles to success. The entire event—beginning with Otto's encouragement and ending with Capobianco's frustrations with Gerry—proved to be a monumental one for the young man. He had moved forward, despite the anticipated threat of harm from an adult male.

Walking home, Gerry knew that he couldn't tell his father about the altercation with the coach. Tony couldn't help; he wasn't supportive. It would be a nightmare. It was better to handle it himself. Still, difficult emotions and realizations manifested in the young man's mind. Mr. Capobianco had been a father figure to Gerry, but like nearly all of Gerry's father figures, he disappointed him. This cycle of gravitating toward father figures, whose flaws would eventually hurt or disappoint Gerry, would continue to varying degrees for the next three decades. But living through each episode added to his resiliency and developed his coping mechanisms.

Gerry was finding his own way, one meaningful step at a time.

* * *

The night was quickly evolving into day. Gerry could feel the fear welling inside as he voyaged home. It was nearly 5:00 am, but it wasn't the beginning of a new day for Gerry, but rather the end of his evening. He had snuck out at 10:00 pm the previous night to go out with his friends. His father's strict rules had been violated, and if caught, the consequences would be severe.

Gerry rounded the corner and neared the outskirts of his family's property. He mechanically and nearly silently negotiated the backyard's aging fence. He quietly approached his home, each step a deliberate one. The bathroom was nearby. If Tony happened to be in it, then his son would be badly beaten for leaving the home. It was always treacherous to escape the home and even more dangerous to return.

Gerry eyed an old picnic table that had, on other such rebellious nights, served as his canopy. This morning's earliest hours offered a decent atmosphere for sleeping outside. The door was most assuredly locked, so Gerry couldn't get to the makeshift bed on the concrete floor and walled basement. The picnic table would have to be his canopy. Settling in, the safe confines of sleep overcame him.

Gerry knew what would happen if and when he got caught, and he understood the realistic consequences of beatings but went out anyway.

A few hours later, Gerry found that the back door was open. The teenager's height was becoming immense, but he negotiated the path to the basement with great stealth. One learns to move quietly in alcoholic households. Soon he was downstairs, and his bed was within reach. His body was long enough to challenge the bed's ability to fit his lanky frame, but it was better than the ground. He was tired and eager to rest.

Gerry stopped and observed the middle of each of the room's four walls as the morning light spilled into the basement. The heavy bag hung motionless at the far end. The young man breathed deeply, quelling the emotional distress that unknowingly had been rising in his heart.

Courage took its place—a fighter's courage.

That heavy bag was Gerry's first real outlet for the fear and rage that existed where hope and a father's love should have resided. He was grateful for that bag and the sport that had provided his life's purpose and meaning. It was providing him an identity, putting the fighter in position for meaningful encounters with others. Starved for validation, each positive encounter with fans, fellow fighters, trainers, and media professionals fed Gerry and kept him alive.

Quite symbolically, the heavy bag was set up near Gerry's most favored hiding place as a child. In the first area, his rage was funneled into
explosive power, where aggression and openness to combat was pure.
Yet a short distance away lay the other end of the spectrum: a fifteen-foot
strip consisting of a dark pathway surrounded by boxes and a sewer pipe.
Leaning against the warm pipe often comforted Gerry's tense body and
anxious mind. The dank corner provided an essential outlet to the fearful
aspect of Gerry's psyche. The piles of boxes and items was a perfect
hiding place, a haven of respite from the abuse. If he couldn't be seen, he
couldn't be hurt. This was the only strategy the child version of Gerry
could employ.

But the fighter was no longer a child. The fear could evolve quickly
into anger and rage. Oftentimes, it manifested into a strong desire to fully
live. This primal energy fueled his fighting capacity and power. Fighting
provided outlets for his negative emotions. It even transformed them.
Boxing was saving his life, giving it purpose, and providing an outlet for
his pain and emotional angst.

Gerry shook his head and returned to the moment. He noticed that his
hands were cold, palms sweaty, and the muscles in his legs and arms were
tense. Gerry became aware, too, that his field of vision had been narrow,
focusing alternatively on the heavy bag and the corner, and now it seemed
like his eyes were permitting more data to flow in. The house was quiet.
No footsteps were falling on the floor above, which meant that his father
was still sleeping. Or that he was at the dining room table drinking,
reading the paper, or something else that required little movement. His
ears were alert to signs of danger—the shifting of a chair, heavy footsteps—all of which indicated that his father was present.

Gerry was safe for now.

Taking a deep breath, Gerry's racing heart slowed as he neared his
corner. It was getting harder to fold his long limbs and torso into his safe
haven, but he could still do so. The part of him that wanted love from his
father was easily thwarted by the reality that his father couldn't provide it.
Tony was unavailable. He didn't have that love inside. One cannot give
what one does not possess. The best that Gerry could hope for was peace,
safety, and sleep. Gerry lay down on the worn mattress. It was frequently
a trigger for calm, and within several heartbeats, he was engulfed in the
safe confines of slumber.

* * *

The survivor was increasingly fighting back. Boxing created the environment for Gerry to fight for a life—a great life, one that was triggered by his efforts and not dictated by his domineering father. The sport demanded the tunnel vision needed for a complete reprieve from life outside the ring—most notably, his abusive household, but it also included Gerry's own demons: self-loathing and negativity. Boxing forced him to be thoughtful, creative, and to find ways to persevere and win. And he had the ability to do exactly that—to win. He had control over his condition, unlike his home. The process was incredibly compelling, providing life, validation, and purpose for the young man.

Changing the expressions on the faces of his foes as Gerry's punches connected became the positive reinforcement that drove Gerry's devotion to the sport. Problem solving, something that his brain was used to in order to avoid his father's abuses, was an acutely needed skill in the boxing ring. Reading his foes' eyes for evidence of the fight leaving them, Gerry found ways to break boxers down by figuring out their strategies and thwarting them. Fighting commanded Gerry's attention, provided him clear obstacles to overcome, and he found that he could do it time and again. He could read the landscape, see himself increasingly progress toward victory, and swim in his own resiliency as he took shots and fought back harder. The entire process made Gerry feel relevant. Like a somebody.

Gerry's in-the-moment analytics had been honed since his earliest memory. Surviving an abusive household required a keen mind. But in the ring, he could not only survive, but also fight back—and win. Boxing provided a vacation from the sometimes-horrific symptoms of unhealed trauma, a vehicle to assuage his anger and anxieties, and a method to secure the validation so elusive at home. His victories accumulated despite brief exposure to formal training, and the stages he fought on were becoming brighter and brighter.

Quite suddenly, Gerry was on his way to national acclaim.

3

FROM PROSPECT TO NATIONAL SENSATION

The accolades, victories, and experiences were accumulating with terrific frequency. Boxing was providing Gerry an outlet for the anger, much of which was produced by the profound psychological wounds from his father's abuse. Anger, when channeled effectively, was also empowering Gerry to fight harder. Each contest was a specific challenge for Gerry to face, and the consequences—both positive and negative—were very clear. If he won, he would face the next best guy. If he lost, he'd have to earn his way back up the ladder. The system was simple, fair, and predictable.

Gerry lost in the quarterfinals of the 1974 Light Heavyweight Open to defending champion and future stablemate, Eddie Davis. The older fighter was a polished and talented amateur by this time in his young career. Davis would go on to author an impressive professional career that was highlighted by competing for Michael Spinks's World Boxing Council (WBC), World Boxing Association (WBA), and International Boxing Federation (IBF) light heavyweight crowns. This bout occurred about a year and a half after his younger brother, Johnny, lost via technical knockout (TKO) to Spinks for the WBA light heavyweight championship. Overall, Eddie would construct a 34–6–1 record with twenty knockouts. The Davis brothers also shared another Hall of Fame opponent, Dwight Muhammad Qawi, with Eddie losing to Qawi with the WBC light heavyweight championship on the line.

Gerry later avenged his loss to Eddie Davis and prevented the fighter from adding another championship to his expansive resume. Gerry, the 1973 Golden Gloves 160-pound subnovice middleweight champion, once again found himself on the championship stage in 1975. This time, Gerry's frame had filled out a bit more, and he competed in the 175-pound open division. His finals opponent would be Eddie's young brother, Johnny. At roughly five feet, ten inches tall, Davis was much shorter than his heralded opponent. He fought out of the Time Out Club in Hempstead, Long Island. The two fighters—hailing from similar geographic locations—added to both the brotherhood and competitiveness. The tournament also featured Kevin Rooney, who would later train a young Mike Tyson, emerging as the 147-pound champion over West Point cadet Kevin Higgins.

As Gerry focused on his latest championship match, he continually dealt with negative forces from his father. For example, Tony insisted that he be provided a ticket to the Golden Gloves final, even though Gerry wanted his girlfriend to attend. Despite the negative influences of Tony's controlling antics, Gerry entered the bout with a great deal of confidence, due in part to his defeat of the older and more established Davis brother. Yet Johnny avenged his older brother's loss in a competitive bout against his larger foe. The result was a stunning one. Gerry would have to wait another year for a chance to recapture another Golden Gloves championship.

Not accustomed to losing, Gerry endured the harsh criticisms of his inner demons, which echoed his father's debilitating and emotionally abusive words. Gerry's brain was already conditioned to berate himself in times of defeat and to minimize his efforts in times of victory. His father also contributed his demoralizing influence on a seemingly daily basis. Tony demanded that Gerry drop weight and avenge the defeat. Gerry had just won second place in a prestigious tournament, but the honor felt like a defeat.

At this stage of competition, most of Gerry's opponents were especially skilled and would soon author excellent careers. Johnny Davis's resume includes two New York Golden Gloves championships, one that he shared with a relative (Willie Stallings). Johnny would go on to hand Hall of Famer Dwight Muhammad Qawi—then known as Dwight Braxton prior to his conversion to Islam—his first professional loss (which was later avenged via ten-round decision and, in a rubber match, a split-decision battle). He would also challenge Michael Spinks for the WBA world light heavyweight championship (TKO by 9). Johnny was a gifted fighter, and his defeat of Gerry was a highlight in his young career.

As with most setbacks, the loss was an opportunity to learn and grow.

* * *

Gerry's personal growth included realizing his independence. He couldn't take living in his household anymore. The seventeen-year-old felt that it might be better for his mother if he left, since he was the problem. This mind-set happens in abusive households—survivors often blame themselves for the family discord. So Gerry packed his bags to move in with his brother. He left at 5:00 at night, the time when his father would be coming home. A part of Gerry wanted his father to ask him to stay. This part, the one that wanted a father's love, always hoped that "it would be different this time." But Tony didn't come home. Again, a father figure—his real father in this case—disappointed him.

Challenges continued to confront Gerry, yet they seemed to place him on his best path. His apartment was condemned, and Gerry was given no time to find new living quarters. His friend Janet Sullivan invited him to stay with her family. Although her parents did not know the young boxer, they welcomed him with warmth and compassion. The family's patriarch, Ed Sullivan, embraced Gerry and did what he could to guide him. He encouraged Gerry to receive counseling and empowered him to address his problems.

Gerry found some direction. Ed educated Gerry in many ways. The older man had open-heart surgery and explained that this changes life expectancy. He taught Gerry about life. Although the lessons were sometimes lost in Gerry's young mind, seeds were planted. Ed's kindness resonated with the fighter on deeply meaningful levels. It was the first time in his life that someone authentically cared for Gerry, looked out for him, without an ulterior motive. These caring efforts would prove to the bedrock upon which Gerry's future recovery, many years later, would be built.

At this time in his life, however, there wasn't much time for Gerry to get lost in any negatives or to fully work on his personal demons. His life became a whirlwind of activity; 1976 witnessed the fighter flying around the world, competing in—and winning—tournaments in foreign lands such as Wales, England, and Scotland. These victories set Gerry up for perhaps the most important event of his amateur career.

The battle would occur at a now-familiar setting—Madison Square Garden (MSG)—perhaps the most famous sports arena on earth. Shortly before the 1976 Golden Gloves, Gerry fought in MSG as the youngest member of the American team against their Russian counterparts. A few days earlier, Gerry had split his nose while clowning around with his friends. The cut was bad enough that his trainer feared it might impact his ability to fight. The future contender competed anyway. Gerry was the underdog. Even so, talking to commentator John Condon, Gerry expressed confidence that he would knock out the much more experienced Russian.

And he did.

Nikolai Aksyonov was an esteemed Soviet heavyweight, eight pounds heavier than his 190-pound counterpart. The Cold War was still sizzling, and Gerry found himself fighting for his country. He took a solid shot from the favorite that—instead of demoralizing the young fighter—instigated Gerry's focus and fury. And he fought like it. A right hand—something critics throughout his professional career would claim that he didn't have, despite many examples of its devastating effects—knocked his foe out in the first round. The dominant performance contributed to the 6–4 U.S. victory over the Soviet Union. The victory was a magnificent one for the young Gerry, one that would rank among the most revered in the future contender's heart for decades to come.

Sometime during this time period, Gerry's moniker—which would be attached to his name for the rest of his life—was established. Working in a gas station, Gerry was labeled "Gentleman" by his boss, Harry Bolhoeffer. He was a nice man and a kind influence in Gerry's life. Harry would invite Gerry to dinner with his family. These were nice experiences for the young fighter that provided glimpses of healthy family dynamics. Gerry worked through some awkwardness as he became more experienced with positive male role models.

Gerry reminded Harry of "Gentleman" Jim Corbett. The father of modern boxing, Corbett has been credited for the evolution of prizefighting from brawling to its paradoxical status as both a science and art form. The empowering message resonated with the young man. An older male provided Gerry with encouragement. Such acts of kindness were permanently embraced. Gerry would go on to cherish a picture featuring him hugging Harry in the aftermath of Gerry's career-defining victory over Ken Norton. Gerry would go on to use this picture for signing photographs for many years—a tribute to the man who provided compassion for the care-starved young fighter.

* * *

Four months after Gerry's victory over the celebrated Russian amateur, the 1976 Golden Gloves Open Heavyweight Championship housed a sold-out audience at MSG. It boasted sensational talent. The tourney included future professional fighters such as Howard Davis Jr., who would win his fourth Golden Gloves championship—this time in the 135-pound open class—setting the tone for an exciting night. Also competing were Juan LaPorte, a future WBC featherweight champion, and Davey Moore, a future four-time New York Golden Gloves champion who would win the WBA light middleweight championship in only his ninth professional fight. Moore would also combat legend Roberto Duran as a five-to-two favorite but lose via a brutal TKO in eight. Mitch "Blood" Green also emerged as a subnovice heavyweight champion in 1976. The talent produced by the New York Golden Gloves has long been elite, with 1976 among its most prolific years.

Gerry resumed his quest to secure another Golden Gloves championship. The nineteen-year-old earned his shot yet again, this time battling Earlous Tripp in the Open Heavyweight finals. Hall of Fame fighter Floyd Patterson and John Condon served as the announcers. For the first time in his son's career, Tony Cooney would not be present. He was simply too sick with cancer to attend. Father and son would watch the contest on television, however, when the event was broadcast.

Gerry remained in denial of his father's fatal condition. Gerry also didn't have time to dwell on the new experience of fighting without his father's domineering presence. A fighter is unlike most athletes. His or her sporting environment is also, literally, a battleground. Although other athletes describe "going to war" and employ no less intensity and effort in their chosen sports, they are not literally fighting to survive. Fighters do just that. Their level of focus is often amplified by the most primal mechanisms of the mind. Distractions can prove fatal to a fighter, as the fighting process will likely expose those who are not adequately focused.

The finals was an important battle for Gerry on multiple levels. He wanted to be a champion once again. He also needed to rebound from his defeat by Davis the previous year. The year 1976 witnessed Gerry's authoring of an important life chapter—a finals victory would cap a phenomenal amateur career. Also, Gerry was no longer simply a prospect. He was an established amateur fighter who was expected to win most fights. The role change was a dramatic one filled with additional pressure. This can be challenging, of course, but such pressure places one outside one's comfort zone, in a place in which growth can occur.

Gerry's road to the finals had included two knockouts and a decision victory. He had grown to roughly six feet, four inches tall at this point and towered over the fast moving, sleek Tripp. Both fighters had to wait almost five hours to fight. Tripp, a young man who found work as a grocery clerk, was a good boxer who could also punch. He had engineered two knockouts and a bye en route to the finals. He was also an educated fighter who persistently moved. Tripp's quickness and balanced skill sets made him a dangerous and talented foe.

The Garden crowd remained for the finals despite the event's late start at 11:00 pm. The bout was between a pair of great young talents with knockout power—two factors that made for an anticipated main event. The fight was a competitive one that featured Gerry's power in both hands. It also witnessed Gerry employing his boxing skills, jabbing regularly, and intelligently using his size by leaning on Tripp, tiring his foe.

While fighting a disciplined fight on this championship stage, Gerry's primal instincts sometimes may have overcome his allegiance to his game plan. He abandoned his jab at times and began to fight back with semi-controlled rage. It is sometimes difficult for young fighters with power to trust and patiently employ their trainers' strategies. As Joe Louis once famously stated (and Mike Tyson later paraphrased), "Everyone has a plan until they've been hit." Further, guys usually fell when Gerry hit them, an intoxicatingly rewarding experience that could conceivably happen at any time for fighters with Gerry's power.

Both fighters were bloodied before the competitive bout's final moment passed. A clear victor, a grateful Gerry met Tripp in the middle of the ring to respectfully embrace his foe. Tripp, in the throes of the immediate aftermath of a tough fight, pushed Gerry's arms away. Gerry then went over and hugged his cornermen. Tripp was consoled and treated by his own supporters. Heartbeats later, Gerry walked over to Tripp to, again, attempt a respectful connection. The disappointed Tripp was more welcoming of his former foe. It wasn't long before Gerry was declared the winner. Tripp immediately shook the hands of Gerry's team, a classy gesture from a tough fighter.

Gerry found joy in his victory. It was the product of myriad hours of preparation. Yet in the immediate moments of victory, he wanted to connect with his adversary. Despite codependency features, which include the belief that one is responsible for (or largely responsible for) other people's emotions and behavior, Gerry wasn't offended by Tripp's initial distancing behavior. He was too caught up in the moment. As was his instinct, Gerry was focused on reassuring his vanquished opponent and encouraging him. Years later, when Tripp fell on difficult times, he found friendship in the giant heavyweight contender.

Such is the bond that is solidified through battles between warriors.

* * *

The papers featured Gerry's victory with such back-page headlines as "A Tripp to the Canvas." Happiness swelled Gerry's heart. The day after his Golden Gloves triumph, Gerry watched the finals with his ailing father on television. The young man did not feel as though his father was proud of him, even at that moment, but rather that he was living through Gerry's experiences. This perception contrasted with those of Tony Cooney's work peers, who later said that Gerry's father bragged about his son's exploits. Sometimes, positive emotions are challenging to express directly to loved ones, especially for those—like Tony—who endured abuses.

Even in the intoxicating reservoir of emotions following a significant victory, Gerry never felt an authentically positive connection with his father. Tony's intensity and sternness were never accompanied by underlying love. Even as Gerry watched his most significant victory alongside his father, the adolescent could not feel close to the dying man. Although it was a natural consequence of the elder's abuses, this unfortunate reality would haunt Gerry—and put him in position to access his resiliency and strength for decades to come.

THE WRITING PROCESS

A Fan Meets a Boxing Legend

Early spring 2011. The morning sun gently blanketed the dining establishment's well-maintained patio, providing a welcomed balance to the cool, invigorating breeze that persistently greeted the diners. Taking a prolonged breath, I focused on the precisely typed notes and expanded question list that rested on my trusted—but glaringly well-worn—attaché case. I tried to "act as if"—an established therapeutic technique in which one pretends to naturally behave in the manner he or she wishes. On this particular day, that meant I was mimicking a calm, tranquil man who normally meets with legendary boxing figures.

As brains will tend to do, mine kept focusing on the future, the past, and fantasyland. "I don't think he's going to show," I thought. "Maybe I have the wrong place or time," my anxiety screamed. By paying attention to possible consequences—both negative and positive—my mind generated a great number of emotions that were not all helpful. For both better and worse, I was deeply contemplating my great fortune, which I was about to experience—an in-depth conversation with a heavyweight boxing legend, one who fought two of the greatest fighters in history.

A few moments passed, moving the clock close to our proposed meeting time. "Now I really don't think he's going to show," I thought.

A few forced deep breaths later, I soon felt the remaining anxious energy transform entirely to its healthy counterpart—excitement. After two decades of reading and observing professional boxing from afar, I was about to have breakfast with an authentic historic sports figure who, by all accounts, was kind and engaging. I should have fun and enjoy each moment to the best of my ability. These thoughts, along with simple prayers of gratitude and for guidance, permitted me to settle deeply into confidence and hope.

Just in time, too.

Peering through the glass doors, I knew that the fighter had arrived. He was quite distinguishable. Gerry Cooney's massive six-foot, six-inch frame stood imposingly in the diner's anteroom, immediately command-ing attention from citizens of the small New Jersey town. His mouth was moving noticeably—in this day and age of Bluetooth technology, it is sometimes difficult to know when a person is engaged in conversation with others or oneself—so I elected to politely wait until he seemed available.

Mildly animated hand gestures and frequent jaw movements indicated that, even at such an early hour, the fighter was on an important phone call. I would later come to learn that such communications were frequent in the boxing legend's life. They ranged from business deals, to setting up charity appearances, to helping friends and other recovering persons. Mo-ments later, the giant man strode out to the patio, where I rose and stood awkwardly, waiting for Gerry's phone call to end. My mind began to race:

This man fought the great Larry Holmes, put forth a phenomenal performance in one of the most historically significant fights of all time! He battled George Foreman, another all-time great—and I get to talk with him! How about that?

Another well-practiced, deep calming breath later, and I was centered once more. It would take many such efforts to contain my enthusiasm during the forthcoming conversation.

Several heartbeats later, the heavyweight legend ended his discussion and shook hands with his would-be biographer. "Wouldn't it be better to go inside? The wind, you know, wouldn't it mess up the tape recorder?" Having framed the observation in the form of a question, Gerry saved his amateur biographer his pride. Nodding like a bobblehead doll, I immedi-ately agreed and followed Gerry into the building.

After asking for a secluded table in the corner of the backroom, Gerry promptly arrived at the primary topic. "People have come to me before about doing something like this, but it never felt right. Seemed to me that they wanted to sensationalize everything, you know, about the Holmes fight." Gerry's authenticity shone through his nonverbal behavior, most notably his facial expressions, which communicated sincere disappointment in the media's focus on the racial divides associated with the historic event.

Again, I silently shamed both my professional and personal intuition, as my proposal had featured this very topic. Of course, my motivation was different. I wanted to chronicle how Gerry and Holmes transcended their racially charged prizefight to become dedicated friends rather than to detail the uncomfortable happenings that occurred prior to their legendary contest. Gerry didn't know me, after all, and had every reason to assume my focus would be the same as every other author he had encountered.

My fears soon dissipated entirely as I absorbed Gerry's transparent straightforwardness—if he had an issue with the proposed ideas I suggested, he would directly address them. In addition, our conversation was already quite fluid. It was going well. I didn't have time to think too much, which was a good thing.

I asked whether Gerry would be comfortable discussing his most challenging demons—and the awful life experiences that manufactured them. After all, our project's primary goal was to discuss Gerry's inspirational life journey, and to do so would include processing some extremely difficult emotions. "It is all activating events for me, but it's healing, too." Gerry paused meaningfully, apparently gathering his thoughts as he considered the question. "I made mistakes, had some successes. . . . You know, pain is repeating mistakes over and over again, sort of like that definition of insanity. I think my way out of doing that. I want to talk about it and maybe help out a few people. It's been a great life. I wanna give back, it's all about giving back, you know what I mean?"

The focus was made clear: if Gerry agreed to work with me, this book would be an extension of Gerry's commitment to be of service to others, a view that I very much appreciated and embraced.

Part Two

EXPLORING POTENTIAL

A Fighter Becomes an Elite Pugilist

Fighters have a very short window of time when they can perfect their career and become really good at it. A lot of guys get distracted. This hurts them. They have to stay focused and work very hard at boxing. You got to work very hard at life.—Gerry Cooney

4

FROM PRODIGY TO PRO

Top athletes—or elite professionals in any industry—tend to objectively identify their flaws and seek to correct them. It is also a natural component to many personalities who find themselves in leadership positions or in upper echelon competitive atmospheres. Yet the energy fueling Gerry's productive introspection was often tainted with authentic shame for not being perfect. Anything less was not only unacceptable, but an indication of his lack of self-worth. This exaggerated conclusion was fueled by the condemnations and trauma produced by his father. It transformed healthy levels of self-reflection regarding flaws and areas in need of improvement into moods and obstacles for optimal improvement.

But although Gerry's victories were not always enough to capture his own admiration for long, they certainly were for those who witnessed them. Legendary trainer Gil Clancy, who would train Gerry in his final fight against George Foreman many years later, believed that Gerry could evolve into a top fighter—and he wasn't the only person to take note of Gerry's displayed abilities and the depth of skill they suggested that he could attain.

Gerry's performance in the Golden Gloves—and, perhaps even more prominently, the crowd's reactions to his in-ring efforts—caught the eye of Dennis Rappaport and Mike Jones. Although far from experts on boxing talent, the duo had finely honed business intuition that frequently resulted in quality products. They saw that Gerry's natural charisma, power, and talent resonated with the audience. The businessmen's intuition alerted them to an opportunity. Whereas land was the product in real estate, fighters were the products in boxing. The processes of business can be generalized across myriad enterprises from agriculture to sport to zoological scientific pursuits.

The youthful Gerry, still developing fundamental coping skills for his powerful emotions and not yet possessing much business savvy, was being courted by multiple business managers. Rappaport and Jones were just one team of businessmen interested in signing Gerry. At the same time, the youth was dealing with his father's aggressive cancer and the prospects of competing for a spot on his nation's Olympic team. Life was a whirlwind of extreme, conflicting emotions.

Gerry would ultimately elect not to fight for a spot on the Olympic squad. The impending death of his father produced many conflicting and powerful emotions. This was enough for the warrior spirit inside Gerry to not have the final say in the decision to compete for Olympic status. It was, perhaps, the future legend's greatest regret. In his later years, Gerry would use the term "taking shots"—taking chances and being okay with making mistakes. Yet his younger self was less receptive to such a philosophy—the impending doom of ridicule, abuse, or his father's condemnations was often too much to consider.

Sometimes, just living through the day was tough enough, and dreams were set aside—if only for a while.

* * *

Fifty-five-year-old Tony Cooney's cancer had suddenly progressed. It was a shock to all who knew him. The Cooney patriarch was virtually never sick—he would wear short sleeves amid freezing temperatures—he was the toughest of men. Yet the ailment vigorously assaulted his body. It had been nine years since his last drink, but after years of working with asbestos, cancer had formed and plagued the ironworker's lungs.

It was a horrific era for Gerry and his household. His beloved mother absorbed most of the challenges of caring for the declining alcoholic and abuser, but the whole family wrestled with conflicting feelings associated with tending to their tormentor. This is a difficult task for any abuse survivor. Further, the prospect of losing a dominant personality for a person without the life skills that are normally generated through more stable home environments left the young man in need of guidance. By this time, Gerry had moved in with his brother Mike, paying $10 per week. But Gerry needed to drive his father to the hospital for chemotherapy, so he was frequently at his father's home, doing what he could to care for him.

Despite his compromised condition—or because of it—Tony Cooney's control issues escalated. Now that he couldn't dominate his son physically, he had to rely entirely on emotional abuse—most notably, shame. One episode featuring Tony's efforts to maintain control remains clear in Gerry's mind, despite the passing of multiple decades.

It centered on Gerry's hair—though if it wasn't his hair, it would have been something else—and how the fighter had not cut it to his liking. Tony stated that if Gerry couldn't live under his roof, get his hair cut, and come home on time, he'd rather crawl to the hospital on his hands and knees than have Gerry drive him to chemotherapy. Rage and self-righteousness fueled Tony's voice. The future heavyweight contender's unhealed trauma had conditioned his brain to respond with the primitive forces of fight or flight whenever he heard his father's angry tones or anything similar. Simply communicating with Tony required the management of myriad emotions. Somehow, Gerry managed it, but on this particular day, it was too much.

The natural rebelliousness of his teenage brain also factored into Gerry's mind-set. Confusion set in. Gerry briefly looked in his ailing father's eyes. This was a challenging act on myriad levels for Gerry, whose chief survival strategy throughout his young life had been to avoid detection from those eyes. Gerry then shifted his focus to the kitchen. There, his mother was busy washing the dishes. It seemed to be Mom's escape from the chaos that, if not active at the moment, was persistently on the verge of unfolding.

At the moment Gerry glanced at her, Eileen Cooney looked up to find her son's eyes. Nothing was communicated, yet at the same time, everything was understood. A heartbeat later, Gerry went outside and jumped over the fence, leaving his father's rage and shame tactics behind his physical body, even as their echoes resonated increasingly loudly in his mind with each retreating step.

It would be the last time Gerry would see his father alive.

* * *

Two months after Gerry's Golden Gloves victory, Tony Cooney succumbed to his illness at the age of fifty-five. Gerry's grief, a natural reaction to a father's death, was complicated by the years of abuse manufactured by Tony's hands and words. The atrocities had served as an obstacle to Gerry manifesting quality coping mechanisms. They also slowed or delayed his ability to grieve. Rage, manifested from his abuse, was in conflict with the natural need to mourn one's father.

It would be years before Gerry could understand Tony Cooney's own torment—hurt people, after all, hurt (other) people—and forgive his father. At this point in his life, Gerry simply struggled to feel his emotions, like any other son would at such moments. He lamented that he expressed love for his father only once, toward the end. Yet the expression was never modeled. His father never communicated love either verbally or through any actions, save for working hard to financially provide for the family. Understanding how to effectively feel and manage emotions was not possible for Gerry, who was now accustomed to assuming excessive responsibility for his life path and virtually all of its happenings.

Death can empower an individual to develop a more acute appreciation of life. Each interaction can, conceivably, be our last with another person. Despite hoping and expecting that it will be only one of many more, that knowledge can create a healthy sense of urgency and appreciation needed to live without regrets. Such was not the case for the young version of Gerry. He was simply trying to survive his powerful and confusing emotions. Life had knocked him down, and he was struggling at times to survive the round.

The boxing ring remained Gerry's sole escape from the torment engineered by his powerful and conflicting feelings. Even so, a schoolteacher advised Gerry that he needed to stay home and assist his mother through her loss. His dream of reaching his pugilistic potential would have to be put on hold. To the confused and sometimes insecure giant boxer, the teacher's perspective offered an authentically honorable excuse to disengage from the event of Gerry's lifetime thus far: to compete as an American Olympian.

* * *

Gerry's opportunity to fight for placement on the 1976 Olympic team—perhaps the most prestigious in our county's history—came at an inopportune time. His father's illness and relatively sudden death occurred shortly before the finals were held. Future professional and Olympic bronze medalist John Tate was likely to be Gerry's top competition to represent the United States. Gerry's skills were flourishing, and he had a legitimate chance to become an Olympian.

However, Gerry's upbringing did not produce the coping skills necessary to handle the death of a parent. Children of abusive alcoholics often have extremely powerful emotions regarding the impending and actual death of their abuser. The natural sadness that is associated with the event is at odds with the difficulty of feeling compassion and love for the person primarily responsible for the child's torment. The Golden Gloves heavyweight champion at age nineteen, Gerry qualified for the Olympic Trials Finals, but he couldn't put himself on this stage, at least not yet.

Gerry's self-doubt, which throughout his boxing career was reliably overwhelmed by his thrill of competition, was amplified by his father's passing. It rendered the fighter susceptible to trusting his fears rather than his realistic hopes. The fire to prove his father wrong and to release his anger, too, was temporarily stifled. No one could question the young man's decision against fighting for the honor. Family responsibilities are respected by all.

Gerry forfeited his chance to fight on the U.S. Olympic Team.

Although tending to his family's understandable needs was his public reasoning, additional factors contributed to this decision. Fear of failure, of looking silly, led Gerry to cite his father's illness as the reason he couldn't compete. He didn't feel like he deserved a shot. In his complicated grief, it made sense to immerse himself in the negative. He wouldn't try; he wouldn't take the shot.

The older version of the fighter regrets this decision perhaps more than any other, labeling his father's declining health as an excuse—rather than an explanation—for not trying. The compassionate mental health clinician might cite the young fighter's raw emotional wounds and insufficient coping skills as true obstacles to his overcoming the normal pressures associated with Olympic tryouts. It was only natural for a traumatized young man to be unable to process the impending, and then actual, death of his abusive father—the innate love for one's parent simply conflicted terribly with the torment of his abuses.

Gerry's amateur career—which included winning an outstanding fifty-five of fifty-eight fights—was over.

* * *

As is typical with addictive thinking, Gerry sometimes engaged in all-or-nothing thinking. He disengaged from fighting to work with a construction crew building swimming pools. He eventually stopped working altogether and stayed at home. The idleness was difficult for the adolescent in many ways. Gerry missed his lone positive outlet for his emotional anguish. Once the Olympic trials concluded, he was in a better position to return to the ring.

Humor always soothed the gentle giant. Making others laugh fueled Gerry's spirit as much as boxing. Once on the Long Island Railroad, Gerry saw his old friend, Janet Sullivan. She waved and smiled, but Gerry kept an angry expression on his face. Getting up and leaving his seat on the congested train, he made his way to Janet, stopping in the middle of the aisle. Attention was on the huge young man, since no one could pass. After a few moments of buildup, Gerry loudly exclaimed that Janet would need to choose between him and her husband before venturing off, leaving Janet to absorb the stares of her fellow passengers. In an era in which such events were not common, the mortified Janet began to explain to a train full of strangers that the departed Gerry was her friend and that she was not even married. The prank was recalled with great humor more than forty years later—such is the impact of Gerry's humorous antics.

Time passed without a return to serious formal training. However, Gerry's hiatus from boxing did not mean that this period was uneventful. There were many career developments. Managers, businessmen, and agents continued to contact Gerry on a near-daily basis. It was great to have options, but it still was challenging for the young man. Gerry's father was gone, and his siblings and mother offered what guidance they could. Inner conflict remained and Gerry was dealing with the thrills of stardom even while, at times, putting forth enormous amounts of energy convincing himself that he didn't deserve it. Or he focused excessively on helping others to the point where he felt responsible for their emotions and life conditions. When a mind is used to a chaotic environment, it tends to manifest it, even when there are no storms to weather.

A year passed, and Gerry was pressed in a corner—he needed to fight his way out.

* * *

By this time, Mike Jones and Dennis Rappaport had created a secure footing in the boxing world. The two had met at a poker game where their backgrounds as real estate agents and boxing fanatics connected the unlikely pair. Jones was a family man, Rappaport a bachelor. Jones was conservative in mind and style; Rappaport enjoyed flashing gold. Both grew up in Brooklyn, and each harbored a love for boxing. Their passions were invested in the business world where, if championships were awarded to successful entrepreneurs, Jones and Rappaport would have earned multiple world titles. The two men, united with a shared interest in boxing and generating massive amounts of profits, soon threw their hats into the prizefighting business.

This union would prove to be chaotic, if also financially successful.

* * *

With a brain wired to assume unhealthy interpersonal roles, it was almost inevitable that the young man would be approached by the pair of Long Island real estate tycoons, Jones and Rappaport. Relatively new to the boxing world, the duo would earn the moniker "the Wacko Twins" due to their highly creative methods of promotion. They were also mistrustful of one another, and the resulting tumultuous environment felt natural to Gerry. It was what he knew. Although Gerry wasn't directing himself consciously toward another unhealthy relationship, he was virtually destined to gravitate toward what he knew even if it was unhealthy. Such is human nature, for many.

Jones and Rappaport boasted excellent business success for both themselves and their fighters. The duo had guided Howard Davis to an unprecedented and creative contract with CBS Television. Although they had not yet established relationships with the sport's premier power brokers, they benefitted from not having tainted any alliances. The managers also had the finances to entice the professionals required to nurture their fighters' skill sets.

Aside from the prospect of joining a stable centerpiece with an Olympic star, one whose amateur journey included four consecutive Golden Gloves championships and decision wins over future Hall of Famers Tommy "the Hitman" Hearns and Aaron "the Hawk" Pryor, Gerry was comfortable and friendly with Davis. The Olympic champion was emotionally tough—his mother had passed days prior to his first Olympic bout—and he was a good person. He grew up with Gerry in the amateurs, was about the same age, started boxing a little later than other fighters, and they won Golden Gloves together and both were Long Island natives. Gerry hoped to travel a similar trail that Davis was blazing and to create his own incredible career path. With the same management team, Gerry reasoned that he could realize similar levels of stardom and financial rewards.

The promise of mega-paydays naturally appealed to the young Gerry. Davis's contract provided evidence that Jones and Rappaport could deliver on their promises. The numbers vary, as do the particulars, but the Olympic champion was awarded a contract worth roughly $1.5 to $2 million. That is 1970s money. Moreover, the young star was provided ample television time to best connect with sports fans. CBS retained the rights to televise Davis's next fifteen fights and was obligated to pay the pugilist's camp an increased amount as he developed into a more professionally established fighter.

The financial rewards were significant and most impressive. The Davis team was to be paid $40,000 for three six-round fights, $10,000 more for six eight-round contests, and about $185,000 for six ten-round battles. Davis also earned a $50,000 signing bonus, in addition to the television contract worth roughly $1.5 million. Further, Davis was permitted to enjoy whatever live-gate financial rewards were provided by promoters. Once ready for ten-round fights, it was said that fight purses would exceed six figures. Jones and Rappaport retained the right to select Davis's foes, with CBS possessing only a limited power to veto such decisions.

These numbers were astronomical to the young Gerry. To anyone, really. It was difficult to comprehend. But because someone he knew had earned it, the possibility of winning a similar deal became more real. With no trusted mentor to consult, Gerry was left to his own street smarts and youthful logic as his guide. His mother did her best to assist Gerry, but having lost her husband and battling the emotional aftereffects of such an abusive marriage, Mrs. Cooney could offer only so much.

As happens in life, one's higher power often sends help in unexpected forms. By the time Gerry was fielding offers from multiple management teams, he had befriended a bartender at the local bowling alley, Frank Venician. He was also a meat manager who had gone to acting school, where he was taught by actress Kim Stanley. Frank was about ten to fifteen years Gerry's senior, but he had partied and even lived with Gerry for a time. He was armed with life experience and offered the young boxer some advice when it came to his negotiating strategies. He even counseled Gerry on benefits, such as a health and retirement plan.

Frank was blessed with an incredibly sharp mind. Like all, he had his troubles, but Frank routinely provided important insights to his young friend. During the courtship conducted by six to eight serious contenders to land Gerry as a client, Frank provided guidance in the form of what to request or demand. He would take Gerry to see different managers—including Rappaport and Jones—to ask questions and accumulate data.

Frank was a mentor, big brother, and even a father figure, trying to look out for his young friend. It was meaningful for Gerry to have a rock in his life. Frank's mentorship was vital to the young fighter negotiating his way through prosperity that he was not ready to face.

After a few months of negotiating, Gerry signed with the Long Island real estate geniuses/boxing management upstarts. Gerry had secured living expenses, a commitment to train full time, interest-free advances of $200 a week toward future earnings, and a guarantee that he would not have to pay the money back after eight years should he not make it as a professional. It was quite a deal for a teenager in the 1970s. However, the contract was for sixteen years, which, to Gerry's more seasoned mind decades later, was not kosher. Jones has reportedly claimed that Gerry had a lawyer when they signed the contract. Gerry never questioned the length of the contract. To this day, he always encourages others—fighters or professionals of any craft—to ask questions—lots of them—before signing anything.

Still, to a young amateur with big dreams and formidable demons, Gerry felt as though he was just given keys to the world. A different world. His friends were going off to college or in pursuit of whatever dreams they had set for themselves. But college was not in Gerry's cards. Fighting was his outlet and craft, and he wanted to see how far he could go. Rappaport and Jones seemed stable, cohesive, optimistic, and above all, smart. They were likewise from Long Island, and although this wasn't a factor in his decision to sign with them, it provided a level of comfort.

The animosity that would endlessly pit Gerry amid his managers' chaotic relationship was not obvious to him during their early days. It may not have existed at that time, as the duo's formation as boxing managers was still relatively new. At this time, their moniker the "Gold Dust Twins" was employed to convey their business savvy and their expansive financial reserves. In time, their highly creative promotional strategies and the dysfunctional aspects of their partnership would inspire their less complimentary moniker, the "Wacko Twins." Either way, they were successful.

Now a signed professional fighter, Gerry needed a trainer to guide the skills development aspect of his career.

* * *

After adding another young thoroughbred to their stable of fighters, Rappaport and Jones sought out esteemed trainers to harness Gerry's immense talent. Their primary target was Constantine "Cus" D'Amato, the renowned trainer who invented the "peek-a-boo" defense, guided Floyd Patterson to the heavyweight championship, and led Jose Torres to the light heavyweight championship. He would go on to coach Mike Tyson and cultivate the future Hall of Famer's skills during his adolescent years. D'Amato was a unique personality whose battles with the Internal Revenue Service (IRS) led him to focus entirely upon boxing and legacy development. That is, D'Amato shunned making money that would be taken by the IRS, which it claimed the boxing guru owed them.

D'Amato's paramour, Camille Ewald, provided living and training quarters—a fourteen-room Victorian house—for the trainer and his fighters. Jim Jacobs, the entrepreneur with a treasure trove of boxing films, provided finances to make D'Amato's setup a boxing haven for aspiring champions. A space above the Catskill Police Department served as the training grounds for D'Amato and his roster of pugilists.

The pairing of Gerry and the forceful, opinionated D'Amato was not to be. Publicly, failed negotiations were emphasized as the reason why the eccentric boxing genius would not guide Gerry's training. It was reported that D'Amato wanted to both train and manage Gerry. Jones and Rappaport, understandably, would not agree to such terms.

The union likely wouldn't have worked even under ideal management conditions. Gerry's meeting with D'Amato was a lousy experience for the young phenom. The event occurred in New York City. Gerry was more than an hour and a half late due to some train mishaps. The boxing sage was justifiably annoyed by the young man's tardiness but displayed a high degree of arrogance. Gerry was taken aback by D'Amato's incredulity over the lateness, since it was due to factors outside his control.

"You're late to meet me?" was the message that Gerry heard from the old boxing wizard. To Gerry, D'Amato's anger and conceit sounded much like his father.

"Listen, man—I'm late to meet anybody! The train was messed up!" was his response to D'Amato. Gerry sensed similar control issues with D'Amato that his father had displayed. The alliance was unadvisable.

As deferential and people pleasing as Gerry could be, the lion inside was forever waiting to protect him. Always. Something in D'Amato's approach set that lion off. Trainer and prospect just didn't hit it off. Gerry couldn't work with D'Amato and the Twins couldn't agree to terms with the trainer. D'Amato was strange to Gerry, who didn't feel comfortable going to the Catskills with the old sage. Gerry was a young man, and although he perceived D'Amato as dismissive and immodest, he still respected him as an elder and legendary boxing figure.

D'Amato likewise acted professionally toward the Cooney camp. He advised them to consider Victor Valle to train Gerry. D'Amato wasn't alone in this recommendation. Valle had an excellent reputation, had been a successful fighter himself, and had been training fighters for decades.

Gerry's life and career would never be the same.

* * *

Victor Valle is best known for his training accomplishments, but he had authored an impressive professional career in the 1930s. Born in Puerto Rico in 1917, the featherweight earned thirty-six victories, including ten knockouts, and three draws against only two defeats. Two additional fights in 1938, both decision victories, are not included in Valle's professional record due to confirmation difficulties. The eager Puerto Rican native fought when called upon, even when injured. Valle would often break his hands but continue to fight before they were fully healed. Ultimately, the injured hands ended what was an extremely prolific and promising career. He was barely twenty years old but had fought professionally forty-one times in little more than three years.

When his career ended, Valle shifted his focus to training young fighters. His stable of pugilists enjoyed terrific success at the amateur level, including 1978 National Golden Gloves middleweight champion Wilford Scypion. Valle also contributed to the careers of several world champions, such as Alfredo Escalera (World Boxing Council super featherweight champion), Billy Costello (World Boxing Council light welterweight champion), and Samuel Serrano (World Boxing Association super featherweight champion). Perhaps the most historically prominent fighter featured on Valle's long list of trained pugilists is Jose Torres. The Hall of Famer, who won the Olympic silver medal in the light middleweight division in 1956, became the very first Latin American light heavyweight champion of the world.

Valle's training style appealed to the Cooney camp. He was a hands-on mentor who spent a great deal of time in the ring demonstrating the skills he implored his fighters to master. However, Valle wasn't sure if he would train the young man who would soon become like a son to him. Valle, like D'Amato, was considered a boxing genius and was somewhat eccentric himself. He experienced some heartbreak with his junior light-weight champion Escalera, which left Valle considering retiring from the sport that had consumed his life for as long as memory permitted.

Although the emotional angst associated with the fallout was likely the primary reason for Valle's initially hesitation, the trainer cited an overbooked work schedule as the cause. Gerry's size may have also been concerning. Historically, big fighters had not been dominant fighters. It wouldn't be until Lennox Lewis and the Klitschko brothers nearly two decades later that huge men would rule the heavyweight division for an extended period of time. And Valle valued fighters who were defensively oriented. Making foes miss their punches was a valued trait. Gerry's large frame, in contrast, provided opponents with a large target to punish.

Yet Valle agreed to meet with Gerry.

They met at Estoril Sol Restaurant in Manhattan, where Valle outlined his expectations. Like most young people, parts of Gerry rebelled against structure yet also felt safe and comfortable with it. Valle's philosophy emphasized sacrifice, hard work, sexual abstinence for three weeks prior to fights, and discipline. Bodies are like systems, Valle would repeat, and adherence to quality routines was essential. Gerry was immediately on board with most of these standards.

Throughout the meeting, Gerry smiled broadly. Valle couldn't help but like the giant young man. The trainer soon signed with Jones and Rappaport to train the towering—and still growing—young man from Long Island. A day after their meeting, Gerry and Valle began working at Gleason's Gym. Gerry was a block away from Madison Square Garden, his fighting home. Their training foci were diversified and pragmatic. Gerry's long limbs needed adjustment, shortening his punches so that they were more precise. His footwork required coordination. Defense, too, had to be more than increased offensive efforts. Gerry's gentleness, in Valle's view, needed to be ironed out a bit so that the ferocity inside would dominate his mind-set inside the ring.

The future contender now had his guide—one who would come to fulfill the empowering fatherly presence that had been absent from his life.

5

THE FUTURE

An Un-setting Sun

Gerry's professional debut occurred on Valentine's Day weekend, an irony given the holiday's focus on love and the violent nature of the sport. The site of his battle, the Sunnyside Garden, was located in Queens. It was close enough to Gerry's Long Island base to help him feel somewhat at home. He had been used to fighting all over the world as an amateur, but like any transition, the move to the professional ranks carried with it new pressures and concerns. Butterflies fluttered throughout Gerry's insides, but sometimes the echoes of his father's condemnations made the insects flap more vigorously.

Athletes, either directly or otherwise, attempt to simplify their mindsets to focus on the task at hand. One's experience of pressure then becomes virtually nonexistent—after all, if one is centered on the present moment, its consequences (wins, losses) are not considered. This mindset is far easier said than achieved. It is only natural to focus on outcomes such as victories and defeats. However, the more one is able to divorce oneself from results—particularly negative ones—the greater one's adaptability to the moment's demands. In combat sports, where fundamental drives and instincts are accessed frequently in response to unpredictable challenges, the ability to maintain healthy levels of focus is paramount to one's health.

Dealing with pressure, criticism, and his own inner demons was a constant for Gerry. At his best moments he "kept it simple." This is generally a method to shift focus from the possible outcomes to the dynamics over which one has some control. They include effort, focus, and executing the game plan. Gerry was symbolically rising into a new world with this fight, one that could provide him access to his dreams or dispassionately disintegrate all hopes of doing so. The stakes were high, perhaps especially to the team that invested so much time and energy into Gerry's development.

There was no doubt that Gerry's first pro bout had a new feel, distinct from all the amateur fights in which he engaged. Although he had never fought a professional before, Gerry nevertheless understood the process of stepping onto new stages—and the experience of success while doing so. He always found a way. Amid the encouragement of his team and the expert guidance of his master trainer, Gerry lost himself in the moment as he prepared backstage. This was just another fight, he concluded, and the expectations were the same: carry out his game plan.

At six feet, six inches tall, Gerry's imposing presence was almost immediately apparent despite his humble body language. His lean physique belied the explosive power of his left hand, particularly his left hook. The opponent, Billy Jackson, was carefully picked for Gerry's introduction to the pros. At 0–6, with each bout ending in his knockout, Jackson had little hope against the prized Irish heavyweight prospect. Yet he was a big man with George Foreman–like features.

Thousands of fans packed into the Sunnyside Garden Arena. The event was to be one of the last in the historic venue's near fifty-year history. Conflicting forces were raging inside the debuting heavyweight. A part of Gerry was anxious to do combat, another was afraid of failure. Such is the case with all pugilists. Sparring with pros in the gym was one thing, becoming one in front of thousands was quite another.

Even as his nerves raged, Gerry's competitive drive and thrill for competition took over. Although in conflict with Gerry's supportive and nurturing nature, his fighter side—the predatory drive to connect with his foe, figure him out, paralyze him, and see the evidence of impact on his face—also provided Gerry an invigorating outlet for his primal pain and fear. More importantly, fighting was an opportunity to exhibit his skills and prove his worth—just as more traditional jobs can do for others.

The process of fighting was compelling. The tunnel vision associated with sensing an opponent succumbing to his power, on the verge of losing consciousness, activated intoxicating surges of adrenaline. The evidence can be read from a variety of angles: laborious breathing, weakening of the knees, deterioration of the "warrior spirit," differences in how he moves and weaves, backing up, smiling after a precise blow connects, lowering the gloves when they should remain raised. Like a snowball rolling down the hill accumulates momentum, these signs of a weakening foe provide more opportunities to achieve victory, opportunities to land harder and more accurate punches, which could result in a knockout.

Indeed, Gerry's career began with the anticipated knockout.

His youthful vigor fueled the "new-ness" of the experience, thrilling Gerry. Still, a part of his mind centered on what he could have done better and how he could improve. These questions are productive and necessary when meditated upon at a later date. Yet the thrill of combat, of engaging in purposeful activities, fed Gerry's soul and provided a profound sense of meaning. The crowd's cheers were intoxicating and originated an incredible high. Making others happy always produced such feelings for the new professional, and fighting seemed to generate more positive feelings than anything else. His knockout of a professional may have supported great moments for many others, but it was a landmark event in the young man's life.

A legendary career was born.

* * *

Like many young sports superstars, Gerry felt like his career's demise was a lifetime away—he simply couldn't imagine it, no matter how many "old timers" tried to pass along their wisdom.

You'll wake up tomorrow, Gerry, and you'll be thirty-five.

Time goes by really quickly—you won't last forever.

There are only so many more fights left in that big body of yours, Gerry—plan for the future, take better care of yourself.

Their efforts, like those of almost all older adults who desperately try to impart their life wisdom to youth, naturally fell on deaf ears. Youth is often wasted on the young.

Gerry was eager to soar, to continually test his wings. At this stage of his career, Gerry assumed that his camp was guiding him the best way possible. After all, they were professionals and seemed to know what they were doing. Guidance included both what to do and what not to do. So long as Gerry was not being steered in a different direction, he assumed that he was on the right track. This included "blowing off steam" and immersing himself in the spoils of stardom, common activities for people his age anyway.

Guidance, too, included fighting the right people at the right times so that Gerry's skills could be tested, challenged, and nurtured. There is no rulebook for how best to cultivate a fighter's skills, as each pugilist is different based on genetics, motivation, heart, and psyche. A quality rule of thumb is to place younger fighters in combat frequently with manageable opposition that presents predictable—but also some novel—challenges. This approach helps to develop experience and realistic confidence, as well as to present the upstart with good but achievable tests.

In his professional career's earliest stages, fighting frequently was just what Gerry experienced. Time between fights was measured by weeks or a few months, at most. His first ten fights were fought in a shade under twenty months. Discounting a five-month respite between his third and fourth fights, Gerry fought regularly enough to match any quality standards for promising prospects. Moreover, the opponents were particularly manageable for the young phenom, as they featured a combined record of 25–61–6.

All but one of these early fights ended by prompt knockout. The experiences served to hone Gerry's skill sets, bolster his confidence, enhance his destructive finishing capability, and create a sturdy trust in his explosive left hand. Perhaps more important from a business perspective, these fights set the foundation for an impressive overall record. Casual fans—the ones who pay a healthy portion of the fight gate—often make judgments about fighters' records without peering too closely at their list of opponents. Maintaining a zero at the end of one's win-loss record also entitles a fighter to the distinguished claim of being undefeated. Such marketing points were important to anyone's management team.

Mike Jones and Dennis Rappaport, who had entered the boxing world to snickers and amusement from industry stalwarts, had won praise for their quality deals. But, when their creative promotional efforts began to consistently exceed the boundaries of accepted normalcy, more and more fans labeled Jones and Rappaport as "the Wacko Twins" rather than their initial "Gold Dust Twins" moniker. Their financial success continued, however, and so did Gerry's victories.

Gerry was impacted more by team dynamics than public opinion. Rappaport's emphasis on the team—Gerry, Valle, Jones, and himself—working as a family was a powerful message to the contender. This new family featured many dysfunctional traits that were manifesting more as time unfolded. Gerry came from a chaotic household where family members largely acted individually in order to survive his father's abuses. Now he was living this out in his professional family. Its members had specified roles, even though they were not cohesive. Negative dynamics—jealousy, suspicion, resentment—increasingly manifested as the victories accumulated.

Amid it all, spending an untold amount of emotional resources to keep everyone happy was Gerry, the youngest member of the group, whose career actions generated the paychecks.

* * *

The now-professional fighter sometimes moonlighted as a bouncer. Gerry found work at a Long Island nightclub that attracted myriad personalities from the surrounding areas. This included managers from the gym who were surprised to see the young talent perched at the door. Gerry's sincerity connected favorably with older souls—this would be a theme that unfolded frequently throughout his life and inspired a protective instinct in his mentors. The youngster was warned that his professional boxer status made him vulnerable to legal issues should he hurt someone. Gerry's hands could be considered weapons when used against the civilian population. And it wouldn't take much for a schemer to instigate a confrontation and endure an inglorious knockout in order to bank a terrific financial reward. His life was changing, and Gerry had to keep the big picture in mind.

Some components of his changing life were tough. Commuting from his Long Island home to Gleason's Gym was far from ideal. Gerry often wanted to be just a kid, like others his age. Still, he loved training, and found respite from the frustrations of the commute through interacting with others. During his daily travels to Manhattan, Gerry would save a seat on the train for an older gentleman. He always gravitated toward fatherly and grandfatherly figures. The young man, uncommonly for many his age, would genuinely listen to his aged counterpart and even ask many questions about his life. Such interactions generated great energy in the youth.

Gerry authentically loved people. It was only when they were about to become close that the mistrust arose. An emotional wall would materialize, understandably so, given the chaotic environment that was his home. Gerry was a people person and, paradoxically, a loner like many fighters who learn that the world takes from you—usually by those presenting as friends.

Mistrust of others had been ingrained in Gerry's mind since he was first able to decipher his father's words. Secrecy and suspicion of others are common in families parented by an alcoholic. Gerry's experiences also validated a near-instinctive belief that others would eventually betray him. One example occurred in his third professional fight against Jose Rosario, his first battle outside of New York. The pugilists both stayed at the same hotel. Rosario cozied up to Gerry, even requesting "easy treatment" since he had a wife and children. Gerry felt connected to his upcoming opponent. Yet when their battle began, Rosario attempted to steamroll Gerry immediately, surprising the prospect.

Rosario's gamesmanship is not to be criticized. Athletes seek whatever advantages they can. The experience was a teachable one. Gerry learned that a killer instinct was vital for fighters and that every competitor is looking for an edge. Even in training, the sparring partners hired to help prepare him were also out to expand their own careers. All were trying to take Gerry down, and he needed to protect himself and dispose of them. Sometimes, fighters would bring worn gloves to work. Intentionally done or otherwise, gloves with less padding did not protect their hands or their partner's skull adequately, thus increasing damage to foe and self alike. So Gerry's team always ensured that new gloves were utilized. Thus, a tough but fair sparring regimen was promoted by his trainers and was increasingly sharpened as Gerry's early years unfolded.

* * *

Gerry seemed uncomfortable with his growing celebrity at times, almost as though he didn't feel like he deserved it. Yet his love of people, of bringing them joy, and of seeing joy and laughter in the faces of others usually negated any discomfort that he may have felt. Being a member of his entourage or a fellow fighter in his stable felt like surfing a magnificent wave, easily cruising in the wake of an elite battleship, or working alongside the Beatles. There was a strong sense of safety, too. Gerry looked out for everyone and tried to help them reach their goals. And, as gentlemanly as he was, there was always the distinct awareness that the beast inside could emerge to vanquish virtually any foe.

Rappaport and Jones had brought Gerry a steady diet of beatable but durable foes. The frequency and type of fighters was brilliant. The man largely responsible for matchmaking was Johnny Bosdal. Better known as "Johnny Bos," the popular and eccentric Bosdal became a matchmaker for a Tiffany Promotions card on Long Island in 1978. As part of the card, Bos matched Austin Johnson with a young upstart named Gerry Cooney. It was Gerry's ninth professional fight. The Brooklyn-born, six-foot, four-inch matchmaker whose weight fluctuated between 260 and 300 pounds seemed to be a slightly smaller version of the celebrity wrestler who would become Hulk Hogan. The process was established: the Twins provided the finances and Johnny Bos offered the expertise to keep Gerry active, permitting him to accumulate the proper feel for live action against a steady stream of opponents.

Bos seemed to be particularly adept at matching young fighters against competition that balanced both (1) the threat needed to challenge fighters to expand their comfort zone and (2) the need for the fighter to also win and develop confidence in his burgeoning skills. Bos worked more with handshake deals than those secured on paper. Rappaport and Jones trusted Bos with their fighters. Gerry and Howard Davis Jr. were superstars in the making, and they needed optimal matchups. Bos's genius became in high demand. He continued to expand his operations until his clients included Mickey Duff, Main Events, Bill Cayton, and Jim Jacobs. Some of the star fighters whose careers were influenced by Bos include Frank Bruno, Evander Holyfield, Meldrick Taylor, Pernell Whitaker, and Mike Tyson. As with these great fighters, Bos's matchmaking wizardry assisted Gerry's development, each victory magnifying his confidence and capturing more and more of the masses' imagination.

Ten professional wins into his career, Gerry faced his first opponent with a winning record.

* * *

Entering his bout with S. T. Gordon, Gerry's knockouts were occurring quickly and spectacularly. Rappaport and Jones were also doing a fine job promoting Gerry's name through their unconventional methods. Even this early in his career, some began talking about Gerry becoming the first Caucasian heavyweight champion since the brief—one unsuccessful title defense—reign of Ingemar Johansson. Moreover, it had been almost two decades since the Swede won the championship. Despite his discomfort with it, the emerging "Great White Hope" moniker was becoming associated with Gerry with each passing performance.

Gerry's fight with Gordon also exploited other aspects of his roots—it was fought on Saint Patrick's Day weekend. His famed heritage made

Gerry's fighting on or near the holiday a virtual must for marketing purposes. Bobby Cassidy and Sean O'Grady, two boxers of Irish decent, were also on the card. Yet it was more than ethnicity that contributed to the fans' increasing interest in the Long Island giant.

Knowledgeable boxing fans understood that Gerry's superior amateur career helped to solidify the fundamental skills, expose him to pressurized environments, and provide the discipline required for stardom. He was still an emerging fighter, but the physical dimensions, maturing skill sets, and increased punching power suggested that Gerry could make a compelling run in a heavyweight division that had just witnessed the great Ali's defeat to an unheralded Leon Spinks. The loss, avenged seven months later, signified the beginning of the end of the sport's most compelling character and one of its history's greatest champs. Fans needed someone to capture their imagination, and Gerry's one-punch knockout power and increasingly Frazier-esque left hook had great potential.

Although he was fighting beyond New York's borders for only the third time against Gordon, Gerry felt only slightly outside his comfort zone. He had encountered the anxiety of traveling to foreign lands to fight foes as an adolescent amateur. Arising from a chaotic household to defeat more experienced world-class athletes had toughened Gerry's resolve. The internal conflict between fear and confidence sometimes led Gerry to operate on negative, anxious energies, but this transformed to focused, empowering energies as the fight drew near.

At 187 pounds, the 10–2 (9 KOs) Gordon was not a true heavyweight. According to BoxRec.com, experts such as greats Gil Clancy and Dr. Fernando "Ferdie" Pacheco implied that the weight disparity made it a mismatch. Yet history might demonstrate this to be an exaggeration. Gordon's growing talents would one day evolve enough to earn the World Boxing Council (WBC) cruiserweight title. Although undersized against heavyweights, Gordon was a talented fighter. He would go on to accomplish a solid professional career that included the North American Boxing Federation, USBA, USA California State, and WBC cruiserweight titles. The last championship was earned with a technical knockout (TKO) of Carlos De Leon, a fighter who would be stopped only five times in sixty-one fights (two of which were his final fights). Gordon also decisioned future USBA and WBC heavyweight champion Trevor Berbick, perhaps best known for ending an aging Muhammad Ali's career and starting Mike Tyson's championship run with a dramatic TKO loss in the second round. In all, Gordon possessed a strong frame and his athleticism posed a solid challenge at that point in Gerry's career.

The bout took place at the Aladdin Hotel in Las Vegas. Respecting trainer Valle's astute teaching, Gerry intended to aim his punches at Gordon's torso. Pounding the body, after all, tired fighters enough to drop their hands, thus creating more openings to land quality head shots. But it often took too long. It was hard to focus on the body, which generally can withstand more abuse than the head, when one possessed one-punch knockout power. Gordon's holding tactics—inspired by the fatigue instigated by Gerry's attacks—frustrated Gerry, leading the giant to headhunt more than he would if facing a more inspired opponent. The match ended in a disappointing disqualification due to Gordon's frequent holding.

Still, Gerry's professional career now included yet another victory against no defeats.

* * *

After the Gordon fight, Gerry went on to fight into the eighth round in three of his next five fights. The time frame for these bouts was nearly seven months. The frequency of fights and their duration was crucial for young Gerry's development. No amount of sparring can replace live battles. Much of an elite pugilist's success is based on muscle memory, authentic challenge under live combat conditions, and acquiring wisdom from such experiences. The significance of experience is analogous to learning how to swim: a person can read and talk about the action forever, but until the task is tackled, one is never going to truly understand how to perform the activity. It takes direct participation in the activity, enduring and learning from setbacks, and building upon one's successes. Fighting is no different, at least in terms of the learning process.

One important opponent during this era, G. G. Maldonado, nearly took Gerry the eight-round distance. The TKO came with only four seconds left in the fight. The match was twice as long as any that Gerry had ever before fought. Maldonado was coming off a quality win over Nick Wells, the same man who had twice defeated the great Larry Holmes in the amateurs. Being taken to such depths taught Gerry the importance of conserving his energy and adjusting when foes did not quickly succumb to his power.

This time period also produced interesting meetings with other top boxing talents.

* * *

Gerry's first meaningful interaction with Larry Holmes was far more benign than the communications leading up to their eventual fight. But this may have been influenced by premonitions of their eventual clash. The twenty-two-year-old Gerry had just secured his twelfth professional victory, and Holmes—roughly seven years older—had just upset the veteran powerhouse, Earnie Shavers, in a WBC title elimination bout. After years of nurturing his burgeoning abilities with a steady diet of live-action bouts, Holmes was blossoming into the all-time great talent that history remembers today. Gerry, in contrast, was in the early phases of his career, fighting with similar frequency as Holmes had years before.

The undefeated prospect had been training at Gleason's Gym. All of the greatest fighters of the era—and most every era in the epic pugilistic landmark's existence—eventually found their way to Gleason's Gym. Since its 1937 opening, more than 134 world champions trained within its confines. The walls were a tribute to the historic names that had trained in the hallowed domain. It was a place of serious business where boxers honed their craft and pursued excellence if not perfection itself. Holmes was just such a professional. His skills were clearly refined from years of training with Frazier, Ali, Young, and Shavers and then of challenging his talents through frequent fights against manageable but increasingly difficult opponents.

The fellowship among fighters is a powerful one. Few on the planet can understand the experiences that come from life combat. Gerry decided to connect with Holmes and offer his services as a sparring partner. Holmes was courteous and professional if somewhat wary. After all, Shavers—whom Holmes had just conquered—had once employed a young Holmes as his sparring partner. As Shavers grew older and slightly past his prime, Holmes had grown into his own prime. His talents had evolved while Shavers's skills declined. Their sparring experiences together benefited Holmes. He brought new and mostly improved skills to the ring while Shavers brought similar compromised abilities. An intelligent man with expert instincts for his sport, Holmes—consciously or otherwise—may have known that the process could unfold similarly in several years, this time with him as the aging lion and Gerry the young and primed one.

The interaction was not unusual in boxing. Holmes respectfully acknowledged and declined his younger counterpart's offer. It was unlikely that the two would ever work in such a manner for reasons other than possibly planting the seeds of Holmes's own demise. Part of securing sparring partners is to help add dimensions to a fighter's skills as he prepares for a specific opponent. It is often helpful to find fighters of similar build and style as the projected opponent. There were few fighters built like Gerry. On the other hand, a fighter like Gerry would present new challenges and angles to more established fighters, thus a unique option for some elite boxers.

The two would go in different directions for the next half decade or so. But their career paths would collide in a historically meaningful way, changing both their lives and legacies in enduring ways.

6

FIGHTING THROUGH THE HEAVYWEIGHT DIVISION

From his eleventh fight onward, all but one of Gerry's opponents boasted winning records. Journeymen tested the young prodigy, as journeymen do for emerging prospects. Tough, smart, experienced, but perhaps less innately talented warriors often serve as youthful fighters' first real tests in their careers. Such bouts force upon prospects the need to negotiate the frustrations of intelligently timed clinching, crowding, evading punches, and conserving energy. These challenges pressure the burgeoning professional to adjust through suppressing ego and honing boxing skills. Fundamentals, like sticking and moving and parrying and weaving through blows are seen in live action. Journeymen are the barometers of the boxing world, the litmus test to help determine whether a young fighter has the skills, determination, and mind-set to take their career to the next level—thus justifying continued investment from their management teams.

In 1978 and 1979, Gerry fought fifteen times—an excellent work rate. It kept Gerry's existing skills sharp and empowered him to develop new abilities. His team wanted Gerry to develop his right hand and utilize it enough to distract foes from his left hand's devastating power. Gerry's left clearly had historically significant power. Each passing victory validated Gerry's finishing capabilities, encouraging him to trust his skills and power. The victories fueled his killer instinct and promoted additional dimensions to his punching prowess. They emboldened him to charge forward with a seek-and-destroy mind-set.

This "destruction" mentality was working, contributing to Gerry's periodic disregard of his venerable trainer's orders to box more strategically. Gerry respectfully listened and intended to follow through, but the adrenaline produced in battle compelled Gerry to follow his natural instinct to knock his opponent out. It was justified with knockout after knockout. It was hard to showcase the defenses and educated schemes necessary for full development when his foes kept succumbing to his power. Still, Gerry made great progress.

Gerry began to compete against ranked contenders as he became increasingly established. The frequency of his fights decreased as the level of competition improved—and for other reasons including boxing politics and managerial strategies to minimize risks and maximize rewards. Nevertheless, at this point of his career, Gerry was progressing dramatically. His skills were sharpening with well-timed fights. Paralyzing the body to set up flurries to the vulnerable chin was becoming as natural as breathing.

* * *

One foe during this era was Sam McGill. "I didn't know anything about McGill," Gerry recalls. "He could fight, too," he added. Never a contender himself—although he had beaten a top-ten contender, Terry Daniels, in 1971—McGill nevertheless learned under fire from the best. He was a former sparring partner of both Muhammad Ali and Sonny Liston. McGill also boasted a good amateur record, winning the Pittsburgh Golden Gloves in 1968 before turning professional a year later. At thirty-one years old, he enjoyed veteran status in contrast to his twenty-two-year-old foe, was of nearly equal size (six feet, five inches tall), and had won three of his past four fights. The 211-pound McGill was eleven pounds lighter than Gerry. McGill was one of the few to see the final bell against the rising contender, who earned a unanimous decision.

Despite the conflicts and disharmony produced by having a patriarch with severe addiction issues, the Cooney family consistently united to see Gerry fight. However, his mother did not like seeing her son hit, but Gerry's grandmother, Katherine ("Katy"), emerged as an enthusiastic fan of her daughter's son and the sport. "Watch out for the horse cars," she would tell the young Gerry, who soaked up the older woman's caring. The fights often produced so much excitement for her that blood pressure pills were needed in the immediate aftermath.

Gerry's career seemed to rejuvenate Katy, which positively impacted Gerry's moods. He relished making others happy, to see the positive emotions that were largely unavailable to him. His grandmother invested in her passion—painting—as well as socializing and telling jokes. Years later, just days before her death, she participated—at Gerry's request—in an ABC special about the fighter. She told a joke about aging and the memory problems many experience along with it. Their relationship was restorative to Gerry, one that he would cherish throughout his career and decades beyond.

* * *

Although ferocious with his foes, the ring also featured Gerry's compassion at times. Once Gerry mistakenly connected to Valle's chin, drawing blood. The trainer was stunned, and Gerry immediately ceased training and sought to help. The mentor, however, implored Gerry to maintain his focus rather than to express concern over his well-being. A Valle camp was a tough camp. Fighting for survival was essential. Fighting hard was essential, always—even when the elderly Valle caught a punch that would cost more than $6,000 in dental work.

The scene counteracted rumors that would emerge later in Gerry's career. Quoted in a *Sports Illustrated* article many years later, Phil Brown accused Gerry of deliberately hurting him during sparring sessions to boost his ego. Others, like Holmes's trainer Richie Giachetti, stated that Gerry's sparring partners would get fired if they hit back. Rumors and misinformed perspectives were voiced by adversaries or disgruntled fighters alike. A boxer who not only fully feels emotions, but articulates them, as did Gerry, was unusual. Perhaps it created criticism and anger from others or at least set the environment for it to occur.

Even so, while Gerry did not intend to injure his peers, his tenacity toward sparring partners was clearly evident. To him, it was survival. Many did not understand that perception. Criticism that he was too hard on his sparring partners was made throughout the boxing world. Valle wanted Gerry to go after the sparring partners to toughen him up as a fighter. He thought Gerry was too mellow. The camp would fly in fighters from around the country to test Gerry's skills.

The sparring partners would often last one day. Gerry fought hard and damage was a consequence of his efforts. Mitch "Blood" Green—a tough guy who would taunt Gerry—was beaten so badly one day that he never returned—even to get his check. Others were more durable. Roy

Williams, who fought in the great Ali's training camp, was a great sparring partner for years. Their tough sparring sessions contributed mightily to Gerry's development. Larry Alexander, "Big City" Robinson, Walter Santemore, and Greg Johnson were some other great professionals who helped Gerry prepare.

In Gerry's mind, each sparring contest held his future and safety in the balance, as he was operating on the belief that anything positive in his life was going to be taken away from him. This insecurity—common among those whose career windows of opportunities are quite short, such as athletes—was prominent in Gerry's early career and fueled his efforts to a large degree. Moreover, accusations of harsh sparring practices appeared hypocritical, as others suggested that Gerry was too soft or sensitive to be an elite prizefighter. He battled sparring partners with the same ferociousness that armchair boxing experts claimed was nonexistent.

Gerry concluded that the fighters were paid to make him look bad and themselves look impressive, and they had attempted to beat him psychologically. For many, it was an opportunity to display their skills to potential power players who decide to invest resources, such as quality trainers and money. Good performances could help sparring partners to ultimately contend on big stages for bigger paydays. Sports are not unlike other areas of entertainment—there are many talented participants, but one needs opportunities and connections in order to fully explore one's potential. Faring well against big names in sparring is one way that some motivated or desperate fighters gain such a chance (even while risking earning reputations that may prevent them from securing more work as a sparring partner).

Sparring partners are so committed to excelling that they sometimes exceed their job descriptions. Greg Page, a tough perennial contender and former World Boxing Association (WBA) champion, once knocked down Mike Tyson during sparring. This occurred before Tyson's upset loss to James "Buster" Douglas and was unfathomable to most fight fans at the time. "Sugar" Ray Leonard, when discussing the prefight analysis on ESPN's *First Take*, stated that he was almost knocked out by a sparring partner five days before the Marvin Hagler fight. Unlike throwing a baseball or football, it is challenging to "play" boxing without primal survival triggers kicking in. It is only natural for sparring sessions to replicate real fighting more acutely than intended. Still, big name fighters needed to be protected from their own competitive instincts at times.

Sparring was, on myriad levels, Darwin's survival of the fittest in every sense. For every ounce of compassion that the huge heavyweight felt outside the ring, there was a reserve of dark energy consisting mostly of pain and fear that was expressed as rage during combat. Emotions were often experienced at their extremes. This is common for substance abusers and alcoholics. Especially so, it seems, for those nursing unhealed traumatic wounds. As is a theme in Gerry's life, conflicting emotions—and managing them successfully—was a near-constant reality.

* * *

Gerry's career continued at a quality pace. He was fighting nearly every month when he signed to face Eddie "the Animal" Lopez. Preparation was beyond ideal for the insatiable Irish heavyweight. He seemed to own any heavyweight who gravitated to the venerable Gleason's Gym. Superior training was required, as his opponent was a dangerous one. "The Animal" was another young lion boasting an impressive record (12–1). Lopez was coming off a decision win over S. T. Gordon about four months prior. Five months before Lopez-Gordon, Gerry had defeated Gordon by disqualification due to the exhausted Gordon's excessive holding.

Lopez was also a year and a half removed from losing a majority decision to then-prospect "Big" John Tate, whose skill set was polished from an amateur career that included two Memphis Golden Gloves victories, a bronze medal (heavyweight division) at the 1976 Olympics, and wins over future WBA kingpins Michael Dokes and Greg Page. Tate would also win the WBA championship—handing Gerrie Coetzee his first professional loss in the process—en route to authoring a solid career (34–3, 23 KOs). Interestingly, about fourteen months after his bout with Gerry, Lopez would fight another Olympian from perhaps the best collection of amateur fighters produced by the United States—178-pound gold medalist Leon Spinks. The bout occurred a little more than two years after Spinks's historic upset of Ali and ended in a draw.

The durable Lopez would be knocked out only twice in his career. When they fought, Gerry was arguably still in the developmental stages of his meteoric rise, having fought only fifteen bouts and still learning with each passing victory. "Lopez was a rough fighter," Gerry recalled. "Took me the distance." The bout ended in a comfortable eight-round unanimous victory for Gerry. It was only the third time Gerry fought into the eighth round, one ending in a unanimous-decision win (vs. Sam

McGill) and one in a technical knockout (TKO) victory four seconds before the final bell (vs. G. G. Maldonado). The next time Gerry would fight that deeply into a match would occur almost three and half years later against the great Larry Holmes.

* * *

Gerry entered the Felt Forum in New York for the second time in three consecutive fights, this time against Tom Prater. It was the third time in a little more than six months that Gerry competed in the arena. Prater entered the bout with a journeyman record of 19–10–1, but the veteran's experience included some of the sport's future champions. He had gone the distance with a young Larry Holmes and competed against an undefeated Gerrie Coetzee. Prater had also fought Duane Bobick, who had entered their battlefield having won forty-four of his forty-six bouts.

Prater was a quick-moving target who could serve as a good challenge for Gerry's burgeoning skills. Tony Perez, who would go on to referee Gerry's devastating knockout of Ken Norton (ironically on the four-year anniversary of Norton's first-round KO of Bobick) and, later still, Ray Mercer's disturbingly destructive knockout of Tommy Morrison, was in charge of the action.

The bout unfolded as planned. Prater bounced around the ring with energy and as much elusiveness as his skills would permit. The veteran's jab was effective at times. Gerry, having been out six weeks with a broken left hand, appeared slightly off target as he pursued his foe. A mix of head and body punches ultimately debilitated the veteran, leaving him vulnerable to the knockdown. Two vaunted left hooks and a right cross later, Prater fell. Caught up in the moment, Gerry connected with a final left hook as Prater was in the process of falling. Moments later, referee Tony Perez stopped counting as Prater's corner threw in the towel, thus ensuring the safety of their fallen fighter.

Gerry's team—Valle, Jones, and Rappaport—mobbed their young upstart. Gerry wrapped his long arms around the three men, physically uniting the team. Gerry's affection, as always, was primarily centered on the trainer who had become his father figure. He trusted and believed in Valle, sensing the fatherly love that was often hidden behind his tough and disciplined demeanor. As Prater came over to congratulate Gerry, the aspiring champion greeted him happily, as a friend.

As the official announcements transpired, Gerry humbly kept his head down, even while joy radiated through him. He had just earned a great knockout of a durable fighter in front of his hometown. Rappaport held the young man's arm up in victory, smiling widely while doing so. Then Valle, camped out underneath Gerry's elongated arm, looked up and gently cleaned off Gerry's face. The emerging contender fed off the joy emanating from the fans and his beloved trainer.

Gerry was increasingly becoming a name in the heavyweight division.

* * *

The victorious fighter was quickly rising in the rankings. Gerry's popularity soared as he did so. He was capturing the fans' imagination. So popular was the young bruiser that it was rumored that Gerry's managers had already offered the aging Ali—who had remained idle since reacquiring the WBA championship—$2.5 million to fight him at the Garden. Although not yet ranked, Gerry's marketability was clearly exploding beyond even his contemporaries with more extensive boxing résumés. Adjustments were needed and some obstacles had to be overcome as with any sporting career, but Gerry's future seemed limitless—it just needed to be well stewarded.

Soon, Gerry raised his record to 20–0, setting up a bout with John Dino Denis at the vaunted Madison Square Garden. The Massachusetts fighter sported a superb 35–2–1 record. His first loss had come to the legendary George Foreman, who was coming off historic wins over Ron Lyle and Joe Frazier, the latter only four months prior to his battle with Denis. "Big" George had also taken out Scott LeDoux in what became his rampage of knockouts until the legend's first retirement. Denis likewise decisioned Scott LeDoux, who would go on to draw with a young Leon Spinks less than four months before the bronze medal Olympian fought *The Ring* Fight of the Year in conquering the World Boxing Council (WBC) and WBA champion Muhammad Ali. The split-decision victory was a monumental surprise, one *The Ring* magazine also awarded Upset of the Year. No stranger to huge events, Denis fought on the undercard of Ali–Frazier II.

Denis was on a seven-fight win streak after the Foreman loss, and a follow-up decision loss to undefeated Leroy Jones. It was Gerry's fifth professional fight at the world's most prestigious and revered arena. However, it was the "Gentleman's" first co-feature main event at the arena. The two fighters had bad blood leading into the bout. At the weigh-in, a scuffle ensued after Denis poked Gerry in the cheek and relayed some particularly effective insults. Writers had encouraged Denis to poke the young heavyweight. Gerry's response was a fury that was soon equaled by his foe. Even the fighter's seconds were trading verbal jabs prior to the fight.

The battle included Gerry absorbing punishment, taking some quality shots, and fighting successfully through adversity. Gerry's tenacious, balanced attack to the body and head wore his foe down. Denis's nose was bleeding and his lip was cut by the third round's commencement. Moments later, a brilliant left hook earned Gerry a TKO victory (one round earlier than Foreman's stoppage of Denis). George Munch, Gerry's longtime friend and a key member of his training camp for many years, would view this fight as featuring the best left hook Gerry ever threw. The win was Gerry's fifth in what was to become a nine-fight string of conclusive early endings.

A now-familiar scene unfolded—Gerry, in the middle of the ring, joyous over his victory, bear-hugging his team with all the might that his giant frame could muster.

* * *

Gerry closed out the 1970s by TKOing Leroy Boone—a fighter with a good 12–3 record who would go on to fight a top veteran (Earnie Shavers) of the decade and multiple legitimate prospects (Greg Page, Renaldo "Mr." Snipes, Carl "the Truth" Williams, etc.) of the new era. The Virginia native had fought mostly in Virginia Beach, winning his home state's heavyweight championship thirteen months prior. He had never been knocked off his feet—although Boone did have a TKO by six on his resume—and had enough boxing skill and speed to offer Gerry a challenge meaningful enough to teach the emerging star how to deal with frustration.

The event's venue was Atlantic City's Convention Hall. It was the first time Gerry fought in New Jersey. The bout's referee, Larry Hazzard, would go on to more than a two-decade-long tenure as the New Jersey State Athletic Control Board commissioner. The longtime official was inducted into the International Boxing Hall of Fame in 2010. On this particular night, he was the third man in the ring for one of the more competitive fights of Gerry's young career.

Gerry had been up all night fighting with his girlfriend. It was the first time he had allowed relationship issues to impact his preparations. It was not an optimal time for this to occur. Boone was a good challenge at this point in Gerry's career. He also fought to survive, to endure. This makes it hard for an offensive fighter to land his punches and get the knockout. These types of fights were good challenges for Gerry, since it was harder to find openings. He had to figure his way through a veteran's wily survival tactics.

Moments before the fight, Gerry found himself interviewed by legendary sportscaster Len Berman. The emerging contender politely answered Berman's queries in a voice even softer than usual. He denied being nervous while subtly and respectfully attempting to alert Berman that his mind was in preparation mode. Soon thereafter, Berman turned his attention to Rappaport. The manager said that he did not appreciate the "Great White Hope" moniker bestowed upon his charge. He cited that Gerry represented hope for himself, his mother, his girlfriend—and before his sentence could end without hyperbole—for a better tomorrow.

The bout highlighted Gerry's developing skills and ended when a powerful liver shot forced a sixth round TKO. The victory earned Gerry top contender status by multiple boxing organizations. The contest also would represent the end of an important era in Gerry's career. No longer was he being managed to predominantly maximize his skill sets, develop his confidence, and harness his finishing instincts against good journeymen. He would be guided to maximize his marketing potential against riskier, more accomplished fighters. Despite Gerry's unusual youth—he had yet to enter his mid-twenties—he was to be increasingly managed as though he was a pugilist with a limited number of top fights left, as though he needed to be protected to ensure that he attained a title shot with the minimal number of fights possible.

Great experiences were unfolding for the rising contender but his upcoming fights were even greater than his run through the heavyweight ranks and into the division's elite level. The dawn of the 1980s witnessed Gerry fighting three prominent names in heavyweight boxing's golden era of the 1970s. They culminated with future Hall of Famer and famed Muhammad Ali rival, former champion Kenny Norton. This all occurred within the first seventeen months of the new decade, but it marked the beginning of an era that was more complicated than the earlier professional years.

THE WRITING PROCESS

Mom, We're Working with Gerry Cooney

I was lying beside the deathbed of my cancer-stricken mother when I received a text saying that Gerry was willing to work with me. I was beyond excited. I happily rose from the floor—the bedroom did not have enough room for a second mattress—to tell my mother the great news. She was my biggest supporter and believed in me even when I was a poor student who flirted with serious academic consequences. She always thought that I could be a writer. I had turned things around in college quite dramatically, but I never pursued a writing career. Now things were different—I was about to embark on a wondrous journey with a boxing legend.

"Mom, we're going to work with Gerry Cooney! He wants us to write his biography!"

The moment was heartbreaking. It was the first time that my mother couldn't respond to me. The very first time. I pretended not to notice, but the pain was too much—I was careful not to let her hear me, but I cried for most of the next twenty minutes.

Then my mom's head shifted and her eyes opened slightly, and with great effort she shifted her hand to pat my own. Such was the depth of her love for her child. She couldn't find the strength to verbally communicate, but with the last of her strength, she sought to comfort me—even as she entered the final stages of life.

With no ability to help or to ease her transition, I promised her that we would write a great book. I saw a hint of a smile form. It was the last time she was able to acknowledge my words in some way. A healthy sense of urgency was instilled in that moment—a familiar feeling that has been reestablished every time this memory reaches my consciousness.

Part Three

The Top Contender

You take that walk from the dressing room to the ring. That's when the real warrior comes out. Then you climb up those four stairs to the ring. Soon, you can't wait for that bell to ring. Greatest feeling in the world.—Gerry Cooney

7

EVOLVING INTO A TOP CONTENDER

Although there were several important bouts throughout Gerry's early to mid-career, Jimmy Young is the first name that raises the boxing aficionado's eyebrows. Young was a top-rated contender throughout the 1970s, easily the greatest era for elite heavyweight talent. His résumé was impressive by any standard. Young's most important accomplishment was a unanimous decision victory over former champion and all-time great, George Foreman. "Big" George had regained much of the aura of invincibility he had prior to his lone (at that time) defeat by the legendary Muhammad Ali. With five knockout victories since that loss, including his classic brawl with perennial contender Ron Lyle and his second dismantling of the great Joe Frazier, Foreman appeared primed to mount a serious challenge for his lost championship. Young's monumental upset win earned the venerable *The Ring* magazine's Fight of the Year award. It also assured Young's place in the sport's history and ended Foreman's first boxing career.

The victory over Foreman catapulted Young to a number-two ranking. After decisioning Jody Ballard, Young was pitted against number-one contender Ken Norton in a title elimination contest. The nontitle bout was, nevertheless, scheduled for fifteen rounds—the length usually only reserved for championship bouts. Norton had won nine of his previous ten fights, including a knockout victory over the first man (Jose Luis Garcia) to defeat him. The only blemish during this stretch was a controversial loss to the great Muhammad Ali. The high profile, highly competitive fight against Young resulted in a split decision victory for Norton, who was arguably near the peak of his Hall of Fame powers.

This title elimination fight evolved into a championship bout after it concluded. Shortly after the event, Norton was awarded the World Boxing Council (WBC) title because the champion, Leon Spinks, decided to grant Ali a rematch rather than face the new number-one contender. This was the first time that the heavyweight title had been split since Jimmy Ellis and Joe Frazier were recognized as champions in the dawn of the 1970s. Norton would go on to lose the championship in his next contest, a historic confrontation with the legendary Larry Holmes, thus becoming the only heavyweight champion who never won a title fight.

Prior to his conquest of George Foreman and his own narrow defeat by Norton, Young had challenged the great Muhammad Ali for the World Boxing Association (WBA) and WBC championships, only to lose a disputed decision. Young had also twice defeated the tough, longtime contender Ron Lyle. Young was especially durable. In his eleventh pro fight, Young suffered his first of only two career stoppage losses to Earnie Shavers. "The Black Destroyer," regarded by many as boxing's most powerful puncher, had been a winner of forty-three of his first forty-five bouts at that point.

In another example of his durability and resiliency, Young would rematch Shavers to a controversial draw that many felt Young had won. This was no small feat for multiple reasons, including the strong inclination for knockout victims to fall prey to the same result in rematches against their vanquishers—usually the loss occurs in a shorter length of time. Overall, Young authored a quality career that earned him the respect of peer and fan alike. In 1998, ten years after his last bout, Young was recognized as history's thirty-seventh greatest heavyweight by *The Ring*.

* * *

Gerry's career entering the Young bout was less storied than his opponent's pugilistic exploits, which included fights with history's greatest fighters. However, at twenty-three, Gerry had earned the number-one contender ranking by the WBA and number-three contender by the WBC. *The Ring* would have Gerry as the number-two contender by the end of 1980. The six-foot, six-inch giant had knocked out a staggering number of foes en route to a perfect professional record of twenty-two wins with eighteen stoppage victories.

Young had earned the reputation of an especially smart fighter. His famed elusiveness and ability to pick off punches made opponents look foolish, making his somewhat pedestrian 25–9–2 record misleading. Ranked the number-six contender by the WBC, Young had hit a rough patch in his distinguished career, losing four of his previous seven bouts. The skid was perhaps influenced by Young's understandable disappointment in the outcome of his fight with Norton, only one of several important controversial losses. Allegations of poor preparation efforts, as evidenced by his fluctuating weight and underwhelming physical structure, followed Young during this era.

Negative emotions aside, the jaded but experienced Young—perhaps knowing his career as a notable pugilist was in jeopardy—arrived in excellent shape for his fight with Gerry. His physique suggested that Young was highly motivated to resurrect his career. Familiar with fighting the distance, Young had lost almost ten pounds from his career high (237 pounds) eleven months prior. He had also won two consecutive fights, including one against British heavyweight champion John L. Gardner, who boasted a 30–1 record at the time. A master at covering up, avoiding punches, and nullifying his opponents' strengths, Young was still in his physical prime at age thirty-one. According to Gerry's longtime friend and training professional, George Munch, Young was Gerry's toughest fight, given the veteran's motivation to take Gerry's spot in the rankings, his advanced skill set, and incredible experience against some of the best talents in boxing history.

Conversely, Gerry was at a point in which his potential was evident to all who objectively observed his performances, but he was relatively unproven. Even Gerry's most inspired dreams appeared well within reach, but more demanding challenges were necessary to truly assess his talents. Like Young, Gerry had thoroughly prepared. At 224.5 pounds, Gerry's physique was trim, primed, and ready for combat. Fans and experts alike anticipated a competitive bout, one that would prove an immense challenge for the young power-punching prodigy and provide answers to his legitimacy as a top contender.

* * *

The fight's significance, as well as the positive or negative consequences resulting from his performance, weighed tangibly on Gerry's mind. It was a nationally televised fight on CBS. A victory would prove one vital step forward toward a championship shot—but any happiness derived from visualizing this dream was rivaled by the fear of disappointing himself and his supporters. A loss . . . well, that would prove his father's condemnations correct; true to his father's prediction, he would never amount to anything. At least, that is how a loss would be interpreted. This familiar conflict raged in his heart and soul, with self-doubt and diminished self-worth dominating Gerry's mind-set at times.

"Your life always passes before you," Gerry contends, in reference to prefight anxieties. "But once the bell rings, I know I'm in a fight. It's just me and the other guy. There are butterflies, you know, which every athlete has—and has to have. If he doesn't, there's something wrong with him. If he has them and he can control them, he's got a shot."

The hours leading up to the fight with Young were especially challenging to the young contender. Staring out the large window of his third-story dressing room, Gerry kept thinking that his legendary opponent was going to kill him. A part of him wanted to leave, to hide. That part was the same as his childhood self who could not defend himself and keep himself safe. Still, he faced the fear and put himself in position to fight. The process of feeling the fear and fighting anyway was now established. "In the locker room, I just kept thinking—this guy is going to kill me tonight. I thought that I should jump out the window or something. But I had to walk through it."

But the part of Gerry that knew he had the power to knock out any man on the planet, the part that punches back with ferocity once he is hurt, was a much stronger force than his demons. Locker room prayer with Valle often empowered Gerry to view the upcoming battle with balance. The duo would say the Lord's Prayer together in a ritual not unlike those of ancient warriors preparing for battle. The act was cleansing on multiple levels. Most notably, it freed Gerry to fight with vengeance. The battle was for his survival, and he would fight hard and with all his might.

Surviving the unrelenting scolding of his omnipresent demons, which only amplified the normal jitters common to most athletes prior to competition, Gerry climbed the four steps to the venerable field of combat and transformed into the warrior whose inner rage burned so brightly that all remnants of fear dissipated. What was left was the only proven outlet that Gerry's twenty-three-year-old self had for his negative energies: his unfortunate opponent in the advanced chess game that is boxing. He was also pulled forward by the impending thrills of combat—of facing his foe, figuring him out, finding openings, changing the expression on his face, and feeling the wondrous feelings of victory.

The natural instinct to fight often overtook the lessons derived from his training: set the guy up, tire him out, and intelligently employ offense at the most opportune times. Still, the hours of committed training instilled the muscle memory to largely react in these ways, if admittedly not completely. Not yet healthy enough to fully learn, Gerry trusted his inclination to destroy and overwhelm when he sensed that his opponent was hurt. And, why not? His finishing instincts were producing spectacular victories. Moreover, they were gained in near-immediate fashion, which also fed Gerry's impulsive mind, which demanded immediate gratification, ignorant of the long-term benefits.

The event boasted the indescribable but tangible feel of a major heavyweight battle. It would be the second time that Gerry fought at Atlantic City, New Jersey's Convention Center. His previous bout, a technical knockout win over Leroy Boone, had occurred about five months prior. That bout, too, had been a main event. The experience had prepared Gerry well for dealing with the nerves associated with fighting a historically significant pugilist whose experience made him a legitimate challenge for the future top contender.

The tension was akin to a world championship fight. The boxing universe was transfixed by the heavy-handed prodigy's meteoric rise toward the sport's pinnacle. Jimmy Young would help answer many questions about Gerry's legitimacy as a top challenger and provide insights into the actual extent of his vast potential. It was a major event. So much so that Rappaport and Jones bought Johnny Bos—the genius matchmaker and Hulk Hogan doppelgänger so instrumental in Gerry's development—a suit befitting the presence of CBS executives.

This fight was certainly different than any other in Gerry's career thus far.

* * *

The bout was monumental for Gerry's confidence and development. It featured Young landing low blows that escaped the referee's sight or interest in issuing warnings. Gerry demonstrated agitation but maintained his composure and tapped into his frustration—not anger—in a productive manner. "Anger leads a fighter to forget his game plan, to throw it out the window. It got me away from being timid and shy, but it wore me out sometimes, too—took away my focus."

Young was adept at picking off punches and was impossible to figure out. It was hard for anyone to hit Young cleanly on the head with a lead punch, thus necessitating a body attack—something that the still-learning Gerry did not fully appreciate in this fight. During the feeling-out process, Young was catching many jabs and defended well against Gerry's powerful left. But Gerry made adjustments. He mixed up his combinations. Gerry's right hand—something that many said he did not possess—connected meaningfully throughout the bout.

Gerry's controlled aggression eventually competed favorably against Young's savvy and elusiveness. The Irish giant stopped playing chess and made the fight a war. A cut emerged over Young's right eye. A bad one. But Young was able to fend off the youthful aggressor with a mixture of remarkably crafty skills and some low blows. Yet Gerry continued his attack. He was crazed—the sight of blood led him to focus only on the cut and stopping his man with a knockout. The pace was almost relentless. The elevated work rate did not appear to tire the giant, suggesting a mature understanding of how best to inflict maximum damage without punching himself out.

In round four, Young was no longer able to see through the blood. Although the referee—perhaps in deference to Young's incredible durability and resourcefulness—permitted the fight to continue, the doctor immediately stopped the fight between rounds. For only the second time in his respected career, Young was unable to go the distance and succumbed to Gerry's aggressive, educated, and persistent attack.

"It was a big fight for me. Jimmy Young was a big fight for me because no one ever looked good against him. I learned a lot from that fight and Gil Clancy's commentary of that fight. It taught me that I should have kept going to the body after Young was cut, to keep mixing it up. That would have created more openings. I was just headhunting. Amateur mistake."

The Young fight dispelled the myth that Gerry was a one-handed fighter. Throughout the fight, Gerry's patented left hooks, intermittent but explosive left uppercuts, and telephone pole jabs inflicted vast amounts of damage, but they were often set up by various rights to the body. Some rights were meaningful, powerful blows that helped to negate Young's counterpunching skills and consistently hurt him. The increased production was in part due to Gerry having identified his right as being underdeveloped and participating in a weight training program to strengthen his right deltoid. Against Young, Gerry enjoyed immediate results from his preparations.

The dominant victory was a significant boost to Gerry's career. He joined the historically gifted power-punching Earnie Shavers as the only fighters to stop Young before the final bell rang. In his first nationally televised fight, Gerry captivated fans with his ferocity, immense punching power, and imposing size. He affirmed his number-one ranking, which had been criticized by many media personalities. Fifty-one weeks later, a picture of a joyous Gerry celebrating his victory would appear on his first cover of the sports world's most prestigious magazine, *Sports Illustrated.* Gerry would be on the cover two more times in a little over thirteen months. The durable Young rebounded from the loss to earn five straight victories the following year against foes with a combined record of 105–10. This accomplishment won him *The Ring*'s Comeback Fighter of the Year award.

Against Young, Gerry had conquered a very legitimate challenge and emerged as the most-talked-about heavyweight fighter on the planet.

* * *

Gerry's presence was electric, gregarious, and welcoming as he became more of a sports celebrity. He somehow balanced his humility with the transcendent charisma of a rock star. It was what it was—people were simply interested in the heavyweight contender, the real-life Rocky Balboa. Gerry's size was likely a component to his bigger-than-life magic, but it was his genuine interest in others—and ability to communicate it— that was most compelling. This charismatic effect may have been most pronounced at the famed Gleason's Gym, the New York City home of aspiring stars and frequent training grounds of established legends.

Gleason's Gym was run by Sammy Morgan, an older gentleman who became one of Gerry's best friends. His was a grandfatherly presence, an "old fight guy" who lived the sport he loved. He had five Dobermans, each with fighters' names—Jack Dempsey, Gene Tunney, and so on. It was a lesson a day with Sammy Morgan, and often direct in nature: "Fighters are whores and managers are their pimps. Keep winning; the doors are always open. Get in there, make your money, then get out." As the years passed, this colorful conclusion appeared increasingly more accurate to Gerry.

Gleason's Gym boasted the sport's best talents. Through the eyes of one such gifted professional, welterweight Steve Petramale, Gerry's star was brightest. A developing professional at the time, Petramale would ultimately learn from several brilliant boxing minds—Victor Valle, Panama Lewis, Don Turner, and Kevin Rooney. After a brief professional boxing career that ended in the late '80s, Petramale became one of the most successful and respected trainers in combat sports. His expertise nurtured the development of myriad champions, including mixed martial arts (MMA) legends Vitor Belfort, Antonio Rodrigo "Minotauro" Nogeira, Murillo Bustamante, and Dan Henderson. His résumé is an elite one that should land Petramale in the sport's Hall of Fame when the Ultimate Fighting Championship (UFC)/MMA world expands its membership to include trainers.

As established as he is assisting MMA warriors to perfect their striking skills, Petramale maintains his love for the sport that generated his famed expertise. He served as the boxing expert in *National Geographic*'s television special, *Fight Science*. The program featured an experiment to determine which of four combat disciplines—boxing, karate, taekwondo, and kung fu—delivered the most powerful strike. The impact force that Petramale generated was equivalent to that of a sledgehammer. Boxing, not surprisingly, was well represented by Petramale.

In 1980, Petramale was in the early stages of his thirty-plus-year career as a boxing fighter, trainer, and mentor. He was still learning his craft and shared the same trainer as Gerry during a three-year period. Although he would eventually move on to other training camps—alliances in boxing were often fluid and fluctuating—Petramale's time working with Victor Valle empowered him to not only generate the skills essential to a fighter's development, but also to train with the sport's top talents. That included the celebrated heavyweight contender who had just stopped Jimmy Young.

Only a few years younger than the benevolent giant—and, at a fighting weight of 147 pounds, far smaller—Petramale frequently observed Gerry in the way an aspiring contender would view a certified one. It was impossible not to, given the electricity Gerry generated and the attention provided by the ever-present crowds. Petramale often found himself appreciative of Gerry's status, ring generalship, and, most of all, his fierce power-punching prowess. He had never seen, nor would ever see, anyone who punched like Gerry Cooney—an incredible statement from a man who watched the legendary Mike Tyson train. Joe Bugner once noted that Gerry was the most powerful puncher he had ever seen as well. Gerry routinely knocked sparring partners out cold. The power was immense, and he was prospering under Valle's tutelage.

Gerry was treated like a rock star in a sea of legitimate boxing royalty—Roberto Duran, Aaron Pryor, and Billy Costello were just a few of the world champions who frequently graced the storied gym. But it was Gerry's size and immense power that left bystanders in awe. Petramale often thought that watching Gerry hit the pads was like observing Babe Ruth take batting practice—the raw and developing power was simply beyond comprehension. The heavy thud of Gerry's massive fists pounding Valle's pads reverberated throughout the electrified gym. Everyone stopped to watch. Valle was among the pioneers to use pads, giving his fighters scenarios to complete. The boxing sage was animated, shouting as Gerry connected with the pads and signifying the end of the session by punching back.

The young heavyweight was reaching the peak of his powers, a reality that both excited many fans and peers and generated criticism and resentment in others.

* * *

Gil Clancy, who several years earlier marveled at Gerry's potential after watching him win the Golden Gloves, found himself dismayed by how the fighter's career was being managed. Clancy was serving as a matchmaker for Madison Square Garden and, early in Gerry's career, had offered his team manageable fights. Gerry was popular in New York and matching him up with quality opponents was good for business. It was also a necessity for a young fighter to tread methodically but consistently into increasingly difficult challenges. Clancy, the expert trainer, knew that Gerry's victory over Young necessitated a permanent step up in competition. Clancy offered Rappaport and Jones a few fights but was turned down.

Although other factors—including financial compensation and risk-reward analyses—likely influenced Gerry's management team's response, Clancy wondered if the message to their fighter was that he wasn't good enough to overcome the challenges. Such a thought would penetrate Gerry's mind in his private moments regardless of his managers' decisions. The thought would eventually be radically repressed by Gerry's protector side, the highly competitive and ferocious part of his mental makeup. The battle was a persistent one for Gerry. He would fight again in five months and again seven months after that—too much time considering these battles' brevity but not an excessive amount of time for a rising contender.

Yet.

8

COMBATING THE VETERAN WARRIOR

Talk of a Holmes bout began not long after the Young victory. Gerry was undeniably a legitimate top-five contender—and the top contender in many insiders' opinions—with an undefeated record that boasted nineteen knockouts in twenty-three fights. He had that one-punch knockout power that captivated fans with only a passing interest in boxing. At six feet, six inches tall, the 225-pound Gerry had matured into a physical specimen. And, as a reflection of just how far our nation had yet to progress, Gerry's skin tone also made him an instant attraction.

The press, as it naturally does with any Caucasian heavyweight with contender-level skills, increasingly labeled Gerry the "Great White Hope." This practice had been consistent since 1908, when the great Jack Johnson became heavyweight champion of the world. Although boxing, like every institution of our country, took far too long to incorporate diversified talent into its operations, the sport eventually became dominated by nonwhites. In fact, after the legendary Rocky Marciano retired in 1956, only one white champion was crowned—the Swede Ingemar Johansson in 1959—and he lost his only title defense. Gerry consistently distanced himself from the label that plagued more recent contenders like Jerry Quarry and Duane Bobick.

Before competing against the great Holmes, the rising contender needed more quality fight experiences. Ideally, such fights would provide him with challenges that were manageable yet difficult enough to take Gerry out of his comfort zone, where evolution occurs. That is the intricate balance faced by all fight managers—or at least those who are fortunate enough to guide the careers of potential authentic contenders. It is art mixed with science. From the business side of the equation, securing a fighter with name recognition was also a necessity.

Another 1970s legend would suffice.

* * *

Five months after his inspiring conquest of Jimmy Young, Gerry faced another respected and perpetual 1970s contender. However, rather than encountering a skilled boxing technician like Young, Gerry's foe would be the power-punching brawler Ron Lyle. The established warrior was a fan favorite in part due to his exciting fighting style and unique background. A matchup with the increasingly popular Gerry, who by this time was transcending the sport and legitimately appealing to the general population, was sure to generate quality ratings and terrific box office numbers.

Lyle's professional resume was outstanding. Beginning at the advanced age of thirty, Lyle would earn several important victories—including a second-round knockout of Buster Mathis, who retired after the defeat—en route to a perfect 19–0 (17 KOs) record. Lyle's achievements earned him the status of a top-five contender before his upset loss to the experienced Jerry Quarry. Lyle persevered and rebounded from his first professional setback. Another solid run produced eleven more wins and one draw. During this time, Lyle defeated former champ Jimmy Ellis and the tough, charismatic contender, the "Argentine Strong-Boy" Oscar Bonavena. Lyle's streak elevated his record to an impressive 30–1–1 (20 KOs) and earned him a shot at fellow contender Jimmy Young.

The Young fight began one of the modern era's most unusual and impressive fight series. In the incredibly short span of eleven months, Lyle competed against four of the decade's best fighters—Young, George Foreman, Earnie Shavers, and Muhammad Ali. Foreman and Ali are recognized by most legitimate historians as two all-time great fighters, while experts regard Shavers as boxing's most powerful fighter ever due to his knockout proficiency. Young, though not as esteemed as the other three, was nevertheless an incredibly gifted pugilist who achieved a distinctive professional career. In fact, Lyle lost the first of these battles—to Young—in the stretch's least inspiring performance: a fairly one-sided decision loss. A close and inspired technical knockout (TKO) loss to Ali followed, then a TKO victory over Shavers, and finally a knockout loss to Foreman in what was *The Ring*'s Fight of the Year in 1976.

* * *

Life outside the ring became even more exciting for the top contender. The Young conquest catapulted Gerry's standings in the boxing world. He was now experiencing dream events on a near-daily basis. Among the most surreal moments of all was a call from Muhammed Ali—Gerry's hero—to Gerry's mother to convey that he was "going to be OK" against Lyle. It was almost as if it was happening to somebody else. The validation from the media and fans more than kept Gerry afloat amid even his most challenging moments—it fueled his faith that he could prove his father wrong and become somebody, someday.

For Gerry, to be "somebody" was to be the champion of the world—the greatest title in sports.

* * *

Educated, fair analyses of pugilistic contests invariably consider the prefight perceptions of the public and experts. Otherwise, the results skew history's objectivity, particularly when the outcomes are overwhelmingly decisive. This is often the case when boxing historians consider the value of Lyle as an opponent at this stage of his career.

Critics may reasonably consider that the thirty-nine-year-old Lyle, who entered the ring with an impressive record of 39–7 (27 KOs), was largely compromised by his advanced age. He was clearly heading toward the end of a historically significant career and had enjoyed moderate success in the nearly five years since his phenomenal brawl with Foreman, fighting ten times with eight victories. Moreover, Lyle's relatively slow hands, average footwork, and tendency to drop his left hand after throwing jabs all combined to suggest that Gerry would be able to connect with his foe. If Gerry meaningfully connected, he would most certainly inflict immense damage, something a fighter in his late thirties with a long history of ring wars would be unlikely to survive.

Even so, although he was three fights removed from a surprising and disappointing knockout loss to unheralded Lynn Ball, Lyle remained a proud, confident, and dangerous fighter capable of muscling his way to an upset victory of a young phenom. Lyle likely possessed the best knockout power of any of Gerry's previous opponents, and many were uncertain whether Gerry could handle the knockout capabilities of the veteran. In addition, Lyle's age may have been misleading, since his career's late start likely saved him much of the "ring wear" experienced by most top boxers—enough, perhaps, to offset some of the damage incurred from his legendary brawls.

Lyle remained a physically impressive specimen. At six feet, three inches tall, Lyle boasted a respectable seventy-six-inch reach (although television statistics indicated that it was eighty inches) and an authentic toughness that few possess. Though not as large as Gerry, whose six-foot, six-inch frame produced an eighty-one-inch reach, Lyle's physical dimensions, ability to perform favorably in severe brawls, and fearsome power made many boxing enthusiasts anticipate a quality, competitive matchup. Lyle could still box, commanded formidable power, and boasted a quality chin. His physical conditioning that evening suggested that not only did he maintain his enviable stamina, but that he was highly motivated to recapture past glory.

The old warhorse was confident going into the fight. Lyle told Gerry that, if he had to, he would crawl across the ring and bite Gerry on the leg if that's what it took to win. Lyle claimed before the fight that he was in the best shape anyone could be, citing his blood pressure as being a product of his health (stating to Larry Merchant that his blood pressure was 171 over 20—the reporter, answering Lyle's question as to what he thought of it, simply stated that he was not a blood pressure expert). The fight was billed as the Coliseum Collision, a play on the fight's location, the Nassau Coliseum.

The atmosphere, like that of Gerry's fight with Jimmy Young, had the intense feeling associated with major heavyweight championship fights. This was likely due to multiple factors. One primary determinant was that the bout took place at the Nassau Coliseum, located in Uniondale, New York, making Gerry the favorite "local boy." Even though Gerry's dominating performances captured the imagination of boxing fans around the country, those residing in his native Long Island were especially enamored by Gerry's growing superstar qualities. And in Lyle, Gerry would be facing a man who repeatedly fought legends, had a history of awe-producing battles, and possessed the skills, doggedness, and experience necessary to truly test whether Gerry was a top contender. Boxing had two of its biggest names—Marv Albert and "Sugar" Ray Leonard—commentating the fight.

It was Fight Night.

* * *

The two warriors couldn't have displayed more contrasting prefight rituals. Lyle was restless and somewhat animated as the ring announcer began his requisite communications. He paced around the ring, gestured toward the crowd, and bounced off the ropes until he was introduced. Gerry, in contrast, appeared stoic with downcast eyes as he stood dutifully in his corner. Head bowed as he received a neck massage from his beloved trainer, Victor Valle, Gerry's quiet intensity and sharpening focus was clearly evident throughout the prefight events.

The public address announcer, Jimmy Lennon, told the audience that the winner of the featured bout would likely fight for the championship against the winner of the Gerrie Coetzee–Mike Weaver WBA title fight. Oddly, Lennon asked the crowd to sit down in order for the bout to begin, stating that it couldn't commence otherwise. Lyle was then introduced to boos and some respectful cheers. This was to be expected given the location. As Gerry's introduction began, the joyous crowd erupted in cheers. Gerry, perhaps striving to maintain a quality sweat or working off any remaining nervous energy, threw combinations and bounced up and down as he` was announced.

The fighters were soon called to the ring's center. Future Hall of Fame referee Arthur Mercante relayed his instructions, the fighters squared up for the traditional prefight face-off. The veteran Lyle stared hard at Gerry, no doubt trying to instill fear in his young adversary's heart. Gerry, as was his tradition, stared calmly but meaningfully at his opponent's core. It was a way of communicating his intention to destroy the body. After a brief touching of the gloves, the fighters returned to their respective corners, with Gerry kneeling briefly in prayer before rising to engage in battle.

Lyle, wearing red trunks with blue stripes, appeared fit, trim, and ready for a slugfest. His career exploits no doubt encouraged him to trust his heart and toughness. Being in shape could only amplify such validated confidence. Additionally, much like Jimmy Young prior to his fight with Gerry, Lyle likely sensed that his career absolutely depended on a superior performance. Lyle's preparations appeared disciplined and comprehensive as he entered the bout at 211 pounds, his lightest weight in more than four years.

Gerry, clad in his familiar white trunks with green stripes, marched to the ring's center to meet the strongest puncher of his burgeoning career. Boxing analysts, like "Sugar" Ray Leonard, believed Lyle would be aggressive and attack Gerry early in the bout. No doubt the veteran wished to apply intense pressure on his heralded foe and to quickly and harshly test Gerry's ability to absorb his power. Indeed, although the best name on Gerry's resume—Jimmy Young—was a marvelous and deceptive boxer, he was not a feared and aggressive puncher. Lyle was. He wanted to take Gerry to as-yet unknown depths of pressure and adversity. And, as boxing enthusiasts profess, power is the last attribute to diminish in aging knockout artists. Even if some of the critics' barbs were fair, Lyle's massive fists could still steal consciousness from his victims.

Lyle had the tools to impose his game plan.

* * *

The early moments featured an energetic Lyle, bobbing and weaving, trying to land his destructive blows. The veteran, paradoxically, also appeared cautious. This may have been due in part to an early, quick jab that seemed to briefly snap Lyle's head back. As the seconds ticked away and amid the crowd's chants of his last name, Gerry increasingly landed effective combinations. He paced the fight with intelligent, thudding jabs to both the body and head. Such blows not only damage the body, but also distract the recipient's focus, manifesting doubt to surreptitiously plague his mind. Like a patient predator systematically tiring and priming his prey, Gerry's long jab and ferocious left hook to the body consistently landed. Numerous connections appeared to tangibly hurt his famed opponent. Gerry's right was vital to setting up the utterly devastating destructive power displayed in his left-handed punches.

Years of combating some of history's greatest fighters naturally blessed Lyle with the caginess of an informed survivor. Finding that Gerry's punches could generate significant damage, Lyle tried different tactics to both protect himself and to place him in position to hurt Gerry. Lyle alternated attempts to stay outside Gerry's extended reach, as well as to take the fight inside. Both failed. Gerry efficiently—and with a developed instinct honed by years of intense training and actual fighting—adapted to Lyle's attacks.

The dismantling process progressed. Brilliantly executed combinations to the body slowed Lyle, strategically creating openings for ruinous blows to the proven warrior's head. The struggling Lyle soon found himself against the ropes. Alarmingly powerful left uppercuts to Lyle's body could almost be felt by spectators fifteen rows back. The crowd, acutely sensing a spectacular and quick ending, became increasingly frenetic as the round's shrinking time limit threatened to save the ailing Lyle from falling. A final, calamitous left hook to the ribs forced Lyle to crumble down and through the second and third ropes to the outside canvas. The collapse was as comprehensive as it was unique. An official tried to help Lyle back in the ring, but Valle pushed him away, yelling that the fighter needed to do that on his own. Lyle lay on the canvas, clearly dazed, gasping for air, and pushing out his mouthpiece as the referee counted him out. The crowd erupted in deafening support of their hero's latest monumental victory.

In the moments after the final blow, Gerry felt compassion for Lyle. He was such a warrior all of his life. But as bedlam ensued, Gerry was able to feel the thrills of his victory. An exhilarated Gerry raised his long arms to the crowd. The appreciative fighter repeatedly blew kisses to his adoring fans. He was soon mobbed by his team, who joined with Gerry to embrace the undefinable feelings associated with being the subject of a mass assembly's joy and admiration. It was the seventh first-round knockout of Gerry's career, against the hardest puncher he had yet faced.

Gerry would soon reach out into the crowd to connect directly with his fans. Earlier in the day, Gerry's great friend Frank Venician advised Gerry to reach out to the crowd after he knocked out Lyle. The words did not make sense at the time, but when the knockout occurred, Venician guided Gerry to do just that. Gerry now understood. It was a most powerful moment. Gerry felt connected, as if he were one with the masses. These moments were among the most magical of Gerry's life.

Gerry took the microphone and, with a little girl smiling as the gentle giant held her, expressed his love to the crowd. No collection of words can articulate the power of such a moment, which are experienced by a precious few. All who do describe it as the greatest high, one that overwhelms any artificial means of reaching altered states of consciousness. Gerry, his fists pumping, soaked in the fans' adulation of him, his performance, and what appeared to be his destiny: status as an all-time great heavyweight champion.

The postfight interview displayed the twenty-four-year-old Gerry's maturity and humility. With Valle camped caringly under his long left arm, the rising contender deflected every hint of success to his trainer and noted that his managers made the fight happen. He expressed readiness to fight for the championship but deferred the matchmaking to his managers. Mike Jones soon declared Gerry ready for any of the champions.

"Sugar" Ray Leonard stated that Gerry would hold his own against either Holmes or Weaver. He expressed near-awe for Gerry's punching power and size, even though he felt that Holmes's experience, size, and quickness would be too much for Gerry at this stage of his career. Another fight might provide the experience that Gerry needed to take his development to the next level.

Mike Weaver was seen as a more appropriate matchup. Larry Merchant outlined the optimal game plan for Gerry, one that he theorized was the best strategy since the announcement of the next possible matchup occurred prior to the Lyle bout (an unusual practice): fight the Weaver-Coetzee winner, which would be a more manageable fight, and set up a champion-versus-champion bout with Holmes that would be more marketable and command a higher percentage of the purse. Gerry had proven that he could fight foes without being awed by their reputations. In fact, he imposed his will on them. At the same time, Merchant questioned the Twins' management of other fighters: their strategy of guiding their charges with extreme caution to championship fights did not prepare the fighters to win.

At this stage of his career, Gerry was actively pursuing his potential and becoming a fighter capable of transcending his sport.

* * *

The beating guided Lyle into a much-deserved retirement. Lyle would return to the ring almost fifteen years later when, at age fifty-four, he would fight—and win—four more professional contests. When he was unable to secure a rematch with his former adversary, George Foreman, Lyle put the gloves down for good and would ultimately devote most of his time to training young athletes.

The extraordinary performance added perceived authenticity to Gerry's skills and top-contender status. "Sugar" Ray Leonard clarified that Gerry had two hands—just that the left one was stronger. The giant was becoming respected as a uniquely destructive finisher, but questions remained regarding his stamina. Further, although Lyle was the hardest puncher Gerry faced, he did not connect enough to test Gerry's chin. Consequently, Gerry's capacity to absorb powerful blows and his ability to persevere through legitimate adversity was still questioned by some. In many ways, Gerry was penalized for his dominance, as many scribes would focus more on harshly criticizing his opponents' records rather than objectively assessing the skill sets Gerry displayed in the contests.

Gerry's next bout would catapult his career and popularity to uncommon heights of prosperity, promise, and hope while at the same time plant the insidious seeds of his championship dream's demise.

9

IT'S (ALMOST) TIME

Harold Smith—the major force behind Muhammad Ali Professional Sports, Inc. (MAPS), whose influence skyrocketed in an unfathomably short period of time—invited Gerry to his home for Thanksgiving. Gerry absorbed the news that he would fight the great Ken Norton. The veteran warrior came out of retirement after fifteen months to deliver the young Tex Cobb—three months removed from a technical knockout (TKO) of the the powerful (if also compromised from a recent retina surgery) Earnie Shavers—his first loss. This fight was called "the Battle of the Jawbreakers," since Cobb had broken Shavers's jaw and Norton famously did the same to Muhammad Ali in 1973. Cobb had sixteen knockouts in seventeen fights entering that contest. The fight was a competitive and compelling slugfest that featured immense heart from both fatigued warriors. Norton was proud, confident, and ready for a final championship run. Meanwhile, Gerry's vanquishing of Lyle was compelling for the distinct lack of competitiveness and full demonstration of destructive power.

Norton's performance suggested that the veteran warrior's body simply needed some time to rest. And perhaps more importantly, his mind required a reprieve to fully accept the loss of his beloved adviser and friend, Bob Biron. The eternally optimistic Norton had been deflated. He had been going through the motions where passion once thrived. Two underwhelming performances—against Shavers and LeDoux—led to his brief retirement, but Norton was empowered by the Cobb battle. The victory, the latest in a long list of accomplishments that would one day lead him to the Hall of Fame, put Norton back in the championship picture. Norton had defeated one undefeated, tough young contender and was ready to combat another rising star. Norton felt that he was a better fighter than he was four years prior.

And Cooney-Norton was worth $80 million, or so promised Smith.

* * *

Smith's influence was reason enough to have strong faith in his words. He had been paying fighters beyond what was considered fair and naturally became popular among the most important population in the sport—the warriors whose courage and effort consumers pay to see. The man formerly known as the clean-shaven Ross Fields still wore the casual clothes more often seen in informal settings and remained a "regular guy," but now he sported a wild beard and carried bags filled with hundreds of dollars on a regular basis.

The euphoria that accompanied discussion of the Norton fight was amplified in the aftermath of Gerry's victory over the esteemed contender, Ron Lyle. Lyle had even stated that Gerry was among the hardest hitters he had ever faced in a career that included battles against George Foreman (83.95 career KO percentage) and Earnie Shavers (76.4 career KO percentage). Yet accepting praise and swimming in the natural joys of personal victory was sometimes a struggle for the contender. Gerry's brain was used to living in search of threats and absorbing emotional abuse, even when it came from his own internal self-talk. It was a way of life—familiar and strangely "normal." He didn't feel safe without being vigilant. It left Gerry open for pain and disappointment, so he permitted himself only so much joy and emotional closeness with others.

Yet Gerry felt comfortable with Smith. He appreciated his straight talk, blue collar, the respectful ways in which he communicated with people of any background. Smith was normally an energetic personality. There was good reason for Smith to be happy. It was virtually impossible for young promoters to steal thunder from Don King's imperialistic grasp on the heavyweight division's best fighters, but he was doing it one fighter at a time. A few years prior, Smith was a single Earnie Shavers power right hand away from snatching the heavyweight title from Don King before the resilient champion Holmes—whose career was governed by King like most other top fighters—recovered to stop Smith's valiant contender. Now, with Gerry willing to headline his card against a name like Norton, Smith had a shot to compete for the headlines—and future fighters.

* * *

The Cooney-Norton rivalry may have begun three months prior to Norton's battle against Cobb. Norton was part of the broadcast team, along with Don Dunphy, for the Cobb-Shavers fight. Gerry appeared, as well, offering his views on the fight and answering questions regarding his boxing prowess. More specifically, Gerry was asked about his right hand, which was not respected by some in the media. Gerry politely stated that he was training to improve it.

Norton had complimented Gerry by saying that he was a better fighter than Cobb, who Norton later implied was a limited fighter. Gerry and Norton seemed to verbally spar regarding Shavers's health, Gerry stating that the legendary puncher's surgery and treatment was successful, while Norton insisted that the aging "Black Destroyer" was greatly compromised. Norton appeared to have much energy, joking about race while also ensuring that Dunphy spoke appropriately regarding race references. This contrasted to Gerry's polite and deferential demeanor. Little did Norton know that the fatigued fighter battling Norton's own conqueror from less than a year and a half earlier, Shavers, would give Norton hell in three months, while the unassuming contender and his co-announcer would end Norton's career less than nine months later.

Ironically, it was Gerry who was originally scheduled to face off against Shavers. Cobb had replaced Gerry on short notice due to a muscle tear in Gerry's back. He had been fighting in Nassau Coliseum and was examined by the New York Islanders' physician, who advised Gerry not to fight. Gerry had hoped that the fight would be postponed—a battle against Shavers would have been explosive. Cobb's limited training time may have somewhat compensated for Shavers's retina issues. Both men fought through exhaustion and sloppily many times. Cobb's dissolution was likely due to inadequate preparation and Shavers's to the natural consequences of accumulated damage from an untold number of fights and training camps.

Whatever the case may have been, the evening's two announcers eventually would find themselves opposing one another in the ring.

* * *

The makings of the Norton fight would become more complicated not long after the world was introduced to the 1980s. The former entrepreneurial force behind MAPS was being investigated for fraud and embezzlement, among other offenses. In 1981, the FBI caught up with Harold Smith, whose reputation for generously paying fighters was well deserved—but apparently funded by stolen money. He, along with two accomplices, would be convicted a year later of robbing Wells Fargo Bank of an astounding $21.3 million. The investigation thwarted any hope of Smith completing the Norton fight as the pressure mounted from the Feds.

The news was disturbing to Gerry. He genuinely liked and cared for the beleaguered promoter. The man paid fighters what they were worth. Known for offering fighters bags of cash, Smith didn't seem to spend the money on himself. He wasn't even a homeowner—he mostly traveled in a pickup truck and preferred sweat suits over designer suits. But he did love to party—he really, really loved to party—and owned a racehorse or two. Still, the man enjoyed life and appeared to relish seeing others happy, too. This was a life approach that Gerry gravitated toward and found himself continually cultivating.

As the months unfolded, more of Smith's story was revealed. He was signing champions and staging fights but consistently losing money. Still, Smith maintained that the "This Is It" card, featuring Gerry against the former champ Norton, would provide him the resources to pay off his debts and return the money to Wells Fargo, with enough left over for himself and those he loved.

Whatever his intention, Smith would not be in a position to carry out his proposed plan. He would eventually be sent to federal prison for more than five years before gaining his freedom on Halloween 1988. He soon returned to the boxing scene, trading in his relaxed clothing for business suits. Ironically, Smith's best success came in advising an aging Larry Holmes, who no longer had use for managers, with his finances during the latter stages of Holmes's illustrious career. This would include signing the biggest fights in Holmes's later career, including Ray Mercer and a championship shot at Evander Holyfield. Smith would also pursue Mike Tyson and had some connections to Tommy Hearns. The former promoter proudly wore his new title of "consultant," something Smith proclaimed he originated.

The unfolding events were detrimental for Gerry, too, as the Norton negotiations needed to be restarted. Another delay. It was more idle time for a youthful athlete struggling to maintain focus. Without a target to concentrate upon, without the impending threat of another warrior centering efforts on destroying him, Gerry couldn't engineer the healthy sense of urgency to meaningfully train. Perhaps this has to do with the activation of the fight, flight, or freeze stimulus. Once one knows the difference between maintenance training and cultivating a fighter's body under the pressures of forthcoming combat, it is difficult to manifest intense motivation during idle months. Such workouts seemed like treading water—at least, that was how it felt to the youthful power-punching pugilist.

Far from a significant factor at this stage in Gerry's career, delayed fights would become a primary one in the future.

* * *

The initial date for the Norton battle—February 23, 1981—was canceled due to Harold Smith's troubles and the dissolution of MAPS. Gerry took the delay in good spirits, despite having peaked during his training at the Catskill's Concord Hotel. He had retired nine sparring partners while breaking one's eye bone and referred to the card cancellation as being "laid off." He likened the setback to those he experienced as a construction worker during his teen years, which included working on the Yankee Stadium renovation.

On the date that he should have been fighting the boxing legend, Gerry had commenced training at Gleason's Gym, owned by Bruce Silverglade and Ira Becker, on West 30th Street. Meanwhile, the fight was rescheduled by the fighters' management teams. Gerry was confident that the fight would occur at this point in his career. He had little reason to believe otherwise. His team was getting him fights regularly. Further, he was likely to earn a million-dollar payday. For now, he would continue at the gym until returning to the Concord, which he viewed as his primary training camp environment. The location was selected in part to minimize temptations to overly engage in the city nightlife, a key consideration for almost anyone in their mid-twenties but particularly so for celebrities like Gerry.

The twenty-four-year-old was living the dream coveted by all the boxers in what was a well-established gym. All were hungry, focused, and unaffected by the gym's deterioration. Gerry was at his peak mentally, as well—concentrating on the task at hand, trusting and listening to his trainer, and shifting focus to effectively utilize his anger and fears as offensive attacks in the ring. The talk about whether he could take a punch or go the distance didn't seem to truly enter into Gerry's mind-set. He used humor to deflect such questions. More importantly, he anticipated having one or both of those questions answered against Norton—and he rose to those challenges. The conquest of Jimmy Young, Ron Lyle, and every other opponent had infused Gerry with a belief in his skill sets that empowered his progress. But it was Gerry's faith in Valle that was most inspiring—Cooney trusted the diminutive five-foot-seven boxing sage without question. Most young fighters are not privileged to have such a powerful resource, and Gerry appreciated his trainer.

The young contender was coachable and affable. These two qualities enabled him to take the disappointment of the delay in stride. Valle's optimistic view deeply influenced Gerry's perspective. He was fond of saying, "when it rains, there is a reason," and that life's events have a way of working out for the best (even if we do not know it at the time). At the same time, Valle respected how disappointing it is to have a fight canceled, particularly after a quality training camp.

The fight was soon rescheduled. The new date called for a nearly seven-month layoff. It was the longest of Gerry's career thus far, though not unusual for upper tier contenders.

* * *

The picturesque setting surrounding the world-famous Concord Hotel greeted Gerry as he stepped outside the massive building's front doors. Training camp in the Catskills was always a welcome reprieve from the normal routine of Long Island life. Having a solid purpose, Gerry was able to optimize his concentration during workouts. He remained disciplined outside the gym. Norton was the biggest fight of his life—and Gerry's best chance to prove his father wrong, to prove that he, Gerry, was somebody. He, Gerry, was good. He, Gerry, would not only amount to something but was already something special.

Tourists of all backgrounds, hailing from many countries and nearly every state, converged at the Concord throughout the year. It seemed like every one of them eventually came to see the giant heavyweight spar. Valle's direction and energy were a central force in the gym. "We gotta think when we fight, Gerry!" Valle's voice rose above the persistent tumult of the collective training noises, the spectators' conversations, and Bruce Springsteen's gravelly voice bellowing from a tape player. "Jabs, hooks, crosses, footwork. Set up your punches, set up your defense. Defense, Gerry—keep your hands up!"

Gerry's punches were crisp and efficient, his foot movement increasingly natural, his focus sharp. He was on his third or fourth sparring partner, a muscular fellow that Gerry didn't remember seeing before. At this point, it didn't matter. He simply was trying to survive the onslaught of sparring partners, each watching the others to identify a flaw that they could exploit. The hunter was certainly the hunted. This realization fueled Gerry's competitive spirit and paradoxically made him the predator—an apex predator.

Gerry's body seemed to move on its own honed intuition, particularly in response to his foes' offenses. He didn't need to think too much; his body was just responding. When he did think, Gerry centered on the basics that Valle had instilled in him. He was using his size to cut off the ring. Those knowledgeable in boxing observed Gerry with great appreciation. The fighter was peaking at just the right time. Training was as much an intuitive art as it was a science, with so many variables that it was hard to quantify. Both Valle and his fighter had communicated well with one another. Their training performances were better than ever.

Onlookers with a less extensive appreciation of the unfolding dynamics watched with eager anticipation. Such was the case with power punchers. In baseball, some hitters simply command everyone's attention—each pitch is focused upon because a tremendous display of home run power could unfold at any moment. The same was true for fighters like Gerry, Foreman, and Liston. The force of their destruction was bred from a combination of innate strength, leverage, quickness, timing, and flexibility. Tightness decreased one's power, whereas relaxed muscles maximized the magnitude of impact. Myriad dynamics were occurring every second to produce exceptional athletic performances.

Gerry was setting up his punches and setting down his aggressors with an unusual degree of prowess. Like a finely tuned watch, the movements flowed perfectly according to the moment's demands. His hands were incredibly quick for such a long-armed fighter, and Gerry knew how to place them. Cutting off the ring to trap his adversary, Gerry worked the body in a manner that herded the fighter against the ropes. Adrenaline flowing, lost in the moment, Gerry connected time and again, pausing appropriately to land the telling blows.

The headgear clung to his perspiring head as Gerry avoided the latest fist that came his way. Defense was not his primary focus—finding opportunities to land his punishing blows always seemed like the best option—but Valle had been on his case about it. Quite a bit, actually. The experienced trainer was aware that his giant charge needed to be aware of all aspects of fighting. Strategizing methods of developing and nurturing Gerry's potential—and consistently implementing them—was his primary purpose.

"That's it, Gerry. That's right. You got to move that head, pick those punches off with your gloves—that's right, Gerry. Least movement possible, that's what we need. Move that head, pick off those punches! That's it, Gerry!"

Several punches landed to Gerry's torso and then one connected with his unprotected nose. Pain radiated from the center of his face, spreading out beyond his eyes. As the physical hurt expanded in range and intensity, immediate rage overcame Gerry's consciousness. Mindful application of his game plan simultaneously evaporated, replaced by an irrepressible need to inflict damage on the man in front of him.

"Don't get mad, use your skills, use your mind—get even," Valle would preach to Gerry. Anger leads one to fight emotionally. This could fuel punches and provide the intense energy needed to finish fights, but it also can rob one of focus. Incredible Hulk–like rage and destruction is compelling, but it uses up energy and must be used judiciously. Outside the throes of combat, the strategy of using one's skills made sense. It was something with which Gerry identified; however, it simply wasn't something he could always sustain while in battle. Youthful impatience was one factor, and his success with simply marching forward seeking to destroy was another. Additionally, physical pain activated the monstrous demons within, the ones that had resided in his heart since childhood. But it was the lure of being in control of his destiny that was most compelling. Not like his childhood, when inflicted pain could not be avenged.

But Gerry, no longer a boy, could fight back now—and he did so every moment in the ring.

* * *

The night before the fight, Gerry ran into fellow heavyweight Jerry Quarry at Gallaghers Steakhouse. Quarry encouraged Gerry to "take Norton out" because, when Norton was preparing to fight Quarry years prior, Norton taunted him by coming on to his wife. Quarry paraphrased Norton as saying that if his wife wanted a real man, she should visit him. Gerry liked Quarry. He couldn't promise him anything, but one thing was certain: Gerry felt as though he could beat anyone in the world at that moment, including Norton.

* * *

Rappaport and Jones's "Gold Dust Twins" moniker historically was used to describe two people working together toward a common objective. Here, the perception was that the boxing newcomers were nurturing their prizefighter's career in a joint quest for the world championship. Heading into the Norton event, it appeared as if the Cooney camp was harmonious and focused on developing the fighter into the greatest pugilist permitted by his potential.

Yet, symbolic of his relationship with the two business partners, Gerry was pictured one week before his bout with Ken Norton between Rappaport and Jones, his giant hands jokingly covering both of their mouths. The young heavyweight was often in the middle of the two savvy businessmen. But instead of closing their mouths, Gerry would do the opposite and open his ears and attempt to ease tensions and encourage harmony. Such was his instinct, honed by years of attempting to defuse his chaotic and dangerous home environment. Gerry also worked with one while watching the other, which helped to ensure that he was treated fairly.

Regardless of any friction that unfolded in the camp, Gerry's concentration remained sharp as camp progressed. Gerry trusted his instincts and zeroed in on his sparring partner's ribs. Kill the body, and the head will fall. That was an old boxing axiom that had been ingrained in his head since his earliest days in the gym. He felt solid. His punches were crisp, even if they weren't always thrown exactly as Valle demanded. His breathing was steady and in rhythm with his offensive onslaught. His stamina was sound, permitting him to spar hard for longer than ever against a great cadre of professionals. In fact, Gerry likely had the best sparring partners of his entire career: Walter Santemore, Jiff Sims, Tim Witherspoon—all had been a part of the camp at some point.

The contender was ready to become a boxing legend.

THE WRITING PROCESS
Healing through Giving

The day was not unlike most others for Gerry. A routine trip to the boxing gym, where at-risk kids made their regular journey to work with the former number-one contender. But it was anything but routine for the guy in Gerry's passenger seat.

The ride was a surreal one for me—traveling with a boxing legend and having regular and inspiring communications with him was in itself an incredible reality. I often felt unworthy of the opportunity to do so and also of working on this book. This awareness allowed me to better understand Gerry's own emotional struggles in his early life and young adulthood. At this point of our book-writing journey, I had yet to shed the impostor syndrome, fully welcome the great fortune that had been placed before me, and thus be in the best position to help others.

We discussed myriad topics—life, recovery, heartache, redemption, and experiences shared with other boxing legends. I felt honored and privileged to learn about how some of my heroes acted behind the scenes in the company of peers. I experienced the unfolding events as though I was floating outside my body, observing someone else's incredible expedition toward realizing his dream. It was hard to act as if this was normal, but I tried.

Ironically, the day was a unique one for many people: pockets of New Jersey experienced an earthquake. This was the first such occurrence that I could recall in more than four decades of living in the state. The news came from Gerry's beloved wife, Jennifer, via a cell phone call. Gerry and I happened to have driven out of the area by the time the ground started to shift in Gerry's hometown.

We eventually arrived at our destination. The gentlemen managing, maintaining, and supervising the gym were all of similar spiritual quality as the celebrity boxer arriving to their community-centered training grounds. I felt comfortable, right at home, and inspired.

The gym's old-school atmosphere boasted quality equipment. Pictures of the greats, such as Ali, Tyson, Holyfield, and the gym's own legend, Gerry Cooney, adorned the walls. Equally motivating were the quality connections Gerry had with all of its inhabitants: trainers, managers, and, especially, the children and adolescents.

As an experienced counselor, I had become attuned to pain in others on significant levels, and I quickly noticed that the adolescents' hard looks represented internal agony rather than anything malevolent. With "Eye of the Tiger" and similarly energetic songs playing in the background, Gerry happily trained the kids. He was turning back time as he did so, providing the same love and encouragement that he had needed at that age. His residing pain was alleviated even as it inherently empowered Gerry to connect with the youth. Such is one of the consequences of trauma, depression, and other such adversities—it provides survivors with a certain *knowing*, an understanding of torment that is naturally sensed by others who have endured the same emotions, even though each person's experiences are unique.

As Gerry emphasized defense and attacking the body (something that contemporary trainers seem to largely disregard), he also centered on taking healthy risks, trusting oneself enough to risk setbacks, and creating options in combat. Just like life. Gerry was teaching chess in the ring— methods to place oneself in optimal position to land punches, to deflect or avoid counterblows, to create and maximize opportunities. To confront, embrace, and manage emotions. Anger can be controlled and directed intelligently, but it also can be destructive. Like fire, anger must be managed in the ring and outside of it.

All of the students were serious, focused, and working hard. Yet fun was manifested throughout the sessions. Gerry's focus was nearly tangible. Each moment was spent purely with his trainee. The positive energy was sparked by the smiles—infrequent on the faces of the hardened children—that erupted whenever Gerry loudly huffed when their punches connected with his mitts. The power of authentic caring was akin to the impact water has on a starving plant: it was instantly soaked up. Before long, spirits rose significantly. The students enjoyed the drinks, wraps, and other boxing equipment Gerry brought from his own storage supply. They readily absorbed his corrective but encouraging feedback regarding techniques.

At one point, Gerry paused a few moments to ingest some water. Some businessmen approached him about a potential endorsement of their product, one that would also include Gerry's former foe and current great friend, Larry Holmes. Gerry interacted with them with the same gregariousness and humor that he employs with all whom he encounters. Some preliminary details were relayed as Gerry prepared to get back to work, his shirt drenched with sweat. Refueling with water and other liquids, Gerry joked that he would agree to listen more if the gentlemen would face him in the ring. Only one—a somewhat portly, middle-aged, bespectacled fellow who didn't appear to have ever stepped upon an elliptical much less into a boxing ring—didn't understand that Gerry was joking.

Just then, Gerry's attention shifted to a young man who approached. I happened to be watching the scene unfold. The businessman became ghost white, slowly began rolling up his sleeves and cautiously asked his colleague to hold his glasses. I found myself saddened that I was the only one watching this funny scene unfold as the man mechanically walked up the ring stairs. His facial expressions broadcast extreme anxiety—enough to almost paralyze him, which may have explained his methodical progress up the stairs. I could be wrong, but I recall witnessing his knees buckle a time or two as he scaled those steps.

I couldn't hear them well, but it appeared as though the businessman's colleagues were encouraging him and laughing, neither of which empowered the clearly frightened man. A few heartbeats later, Gerry turned to see his would-be sparring partner unsuccessfully attempt to negotiate the ropes and step into the ring. The struggle was real. Gerry clearly saw the man's distress, assured him that he was joking, and laughed only when relief and humor replaced the man's extreme concern.

I likely would have had the same reaction to a proposed sparring session with the imposing giant—perhaps this is why I found the event so funny—even more so now despite the passing of several years.

The afternoon ended with the children and adolescents working together to straighten up the gym. They worked with cohesion and purpose.
At some point, each young person connected with Gerry. Every moment
was a profound one for the children—but also for the boxing legend. "I
love making the kids laugh," he said as we began our journey back home.
"They're in pain, I was in pain. Boxing allows us to connect. They're
fighters, in the ring and out of it. Everyone can connect on that level, the
fight for life. So we heal together. I need it; it keeps me alive." Through
giving his time and perspectives to young minds, Gerry assigned meaning
to his own emotional pains—the insights derived from his agony can
benefit others.

Being mindful of the process, especially as it occurs, is a healing gift
beyond description.

Part Four

The Legend

Boxing is an art. It's an art of self-defense. I knock people out as soon as I can to get them out of there.—Gerry Cooney

10

THE PRODIGY PREPARES FOR BATTLE

The thunderous smack of Gerry's gloves on the practice pads resonated throughout the large dressing room. A light but steady sweat shone on Gerry's torso as he dodged a couple of jabs from Valle. The venerable trainer expertly alternated between methodical attacks to prepare Gerry's defensive reflexes and setting up the pads for Gerry's offensive responses. He created situations for Gerry to identify. He had to adapt quickly. Just like in a real fight. Gerry's muscle memory was being warmed up so he could react immediately to the demands that Norton could force upon him—in less than a half hour or so.

The preparation ritual also helped the rising contender to manage his emotions. Action always seemed to do that, particularly when it was specialized and compellingly focused: boxing was straightforward, his antagonist clear, and he could answer offenses against him. With his cherished guide in his familiar position of holding gloves for Gerry to pound, the Irishman felt connected. No longer alone. Boxing had a way of easing that sense of isolation, even though he was always the only one going into the ring, the only one going into harm's way. No one to help him. Yet the one who could help was clear: Gerry himself. It was a welcomed reality after threats to his safety in childhood. Now he had full control of his destiny.

Active combat was Gerry's most productive coping mechanism for the enormous emotions welling inside. So, too, was direct preparation for it. Meaningful training compelled his attention. A lot was occurring; he had to focus. Even though his mentor's words were direct, his tone harsh, the sounds were familiar and comforting, given the context of the moment. "Keep your chin down, Gerry! You got to keep that chin down."

Gerry dodged another elaborate right cross from his trainer before dutifully responding with a crisp left hand. "Yeah," he managed between controlled breaths. A straight left was deftly picked off by Gerry's glove. The fighter was centered on the task at hand, which was to avoid or catch Valle's punches and to counter with sharp blows and combinations. Gerry's body was intelligently responding to familiar patterns through educated muscle memory and without obstruction from unnecessary thinking. The surroundings seemed to fade into nothingness—the people walking in and out of the room, the cheers and words of encouragement that seemed to follow each movement. Nothing existed except he and Valle.

The actions performed in this simulated fight were slow-motion previews of the upcoming battle. Tailored to counter Norton's strengths and to accentuate Gerry's own, the game plan was cemented in the contender's mind and body—the product of focused repetition of discussion and training movements. Gerry's body was conditioned, after countless rounds of sparring with similarly styled fighters, to respond immediately to the expected in-ring adversities. Through countless repetitions, Gerry's body established a muscle memory that can recognize in-ring patterns, thus educating his boxing intuition. Live action would solidify the lessons, but Valle's camp had re-created true battle conditions as best as could be expected. The same process was the standard of almost any elite athlete's training. For warriors like boxers, however, disciplined workouts not only engineer the difference between victory and defeat, but also health and serious injury—even survival and death.

Another precisely performed combination seemed to manifest on its own, though paradoxically, Gerry felt completely in control. His mind seemed immune to the echoes of his father's condemnations. That part of him that was intent on protecting Gerry, to prove that he was worth something, had fueled Gerry's power of concentration. His focus was on the moment—this simplicity compounded his power and effectiveness.

Gerry snapped two powerful jabs at Valle's pads and felt them give way as the power flung the trainer's arm backward. The fighter heard further instructions, but the words were simply sounds at this point. Action was his sole focus, his only reality. Imposing his will and carrying out his game plan was the targeted outcome, but it would be accomplished through the realization of myriad miniscule actions employed in equally myriad miniscule moments. Gerry responded even quicker than his thoughts manifested.

"All right, Gerry—it's almost time," Valle stated as he stood up straight.

* * *

It wasn't until a moment later, when Valle began taking off his pads, that Gerry fully absorbed the words. *It was almost time.* The door opened and a professional said, "Cooney, you're up." Fear began formulating in his belly, threatening to rise up into his heart and mind. This is normal for all fighters. Such fear is vital in order to realize peak performance. Moderate levels of anxiety help people be alert, an obvious key attribute to anyone entering combat. Optimal levels of stress can excite the fight response of the brain, whereas too much can lead to "frozen" or flight behaviors. This wasn't an option for fighters. Still, Gerry's demons constantly sought energies that would set his fear free and sabotage him, and the contender needed to be in control. Action was his antidote. Action and focus.

Firing off several shadowboxing combinations, Gerry effectively cooled the rising nerves. The process was something of a paradox. Energy was released but also amplified. Nerves were cooled, but excitement was fueled. Shadowboxing, losing himself in the moment's actions, eliminated negative thoughts before they could take root and plague his mind. Gerry took a deep breath as someone—he wasn't quite sure who—helped him put on his robe. He was immersed in his fight plans. Gerry knew that ne needed to get Norton to feel his power.

The world's number-two ranked heavyweight according to the revered *The Ring* magazine was ready to fight the former champ who had reestablished himself as a formidable number-ten contender. Moreover, boxing's heads of state Don King, Jim Jacobs, and Bob Arum were undecided when asked to predict a winner. Some still viewed Gerry as a prospect, even though he had earned elite contender status. Fighting Norton would prove to be a landmark event in his young career. In a few moments, he would walk toward the ring and into the greatest moments of his career.

* * *

"Future champion of the world!"
"Go after him, Gerry!"
"Let's go, Champ!"

The arena was loud, the energy palpable. The encouraging shouts came from all around him, but Gerry's focus was centered upon coordinating his legs as they maneuvered him to his battleground. It was an odd sensation—he was almost observing, rather than commanding, his legs to perform the simple task of walking. It seemed, too, that Gerry was floating high above the ground, somehow detached from his body. Paradoxically, Gerry's senses were sharpening dramatically—each crack in the floor, the rhythmic pounding of his heart, and the soft cloth of his robe against his skin seemed to take on the magnificent detail.

The contender's senses were sharpening in preparation for battle.

Gerry's body instinctively called upon the adrenal glands to participate in its most primal survival system—the fight-or-flight mechanism. The adrenaline was beginning to flow throughout his body, preparing its organs and putting him in position to either do battle or flee. The latter wasn't an option, even though the fearful child in him remained. Somewhere. If Gerry couldn't be seen, he couldn't be hurt—but that wasn't a realistic strategy like it was when he was a child avoiding his father's physical and psychological abuse. Even so, as Gerry felt the emotions from his scarred child-self, circumstances commanded that his fighter-self remain in complete control. The actuality of the impending fight activates the fighter aspect of Gerry's psyche, protecting him.

All fighters know this process.

Seemingly a half second later, Gerry was a few feet away from the ring steps. Four steps. Climbing them was like transitioning from one world to another more violent—and more honest—one. The Madison Square Garden crowd cheered their support as their hometown fighter acclimated to the ring's confines. Everyone in the famed sports arena, it seemed, was Irish at the moment.

Gerry quickly navigated the wooden stairs. The process was akin to a powerlifter removing most of the weight from an eight-hundred-pound barbell. The energy in the arena seemed palpable as he rose to the top step. Standing on the ring apron, towering over all the spectators, Gerry felt his focus sharpen to an even greater degree. He was tapping into something not quite describable—even while a healthy sense of caution remained. Gerry slipped through the ropes and stood upright, firing off combinations before settling into a steady pace.

Gerry peaked mentally, spiritually, and emotionally—a welcomed perfect storm of positive energies.

* * *

Norton had been the first to approach the battleground. An argument can be made that the veteran appeared focused—or concerned. Frequently, the two occur alternatingly. If concern dominated Norton's mind, it was likely influenced in part by his battles against two legendary punchers, Earnie Shavers and George Foreman, both of which ended early for Norton. Gerry boasted similar degrees of power, suggesting that this might be a bad matchup for the former champion.

If high levels of anxiety existed, they were in direct contrast to Norton's public remarks regarding Gerry's accomplishments not impressing him. Norton also made a compelling argument that he was motivated and a better fighter—more intelligent, stronger, and quicker than before. He had appeared quite confident and seemingly prepared to replicate his handling of Duane Bobick. Bobick was another undefeated Caucasian heavyweight who was coached by Norton's old trainer, the legendary Eddie Futch, and managed by heavyweight legend Joe Frazier. Bobick had boasted thirty-eight wins and lots of knockouts on his résumé, thirty-two in all. That fight had occurred precisely four years to the day before the Cooney-Norton fight, was also at Madison Square Garden, and resulted in a fifty-eight second technical knockout Norton victory on national television.

Ironically, this bout would end in a near-identical time frame but in an even more devastating fashion, and with Norton on the receiving end of a definitive loss.

* * *

Both warriors had immense pressure to win, resulting in a heightened sense of urgency to impose their will. Norton, a veteran of myriad extended fights on some of boxing's biggest stages, sought to take his foe to deep waters and to drown him. After all, Gerry had only eighty-six professional rounds leading into the bout, ten of his knockouts occurred within two rounds, and he averaged roughly three-and-a-half rounds per fight. Stamina was something of an unknown for the popular young contender. He had gone the distance before but not into the championship rounds. Norton would want to test Gerry's ability to do just that. Whatever the method of securing a positive outcome, both men needed a victory.

Despite his Hall of Fame résumé, Norton's status as a top contender depended upon a quality performance and a win. A victory would catapult him into contention for a rematch with the champion, Holmes. Adding to what was already a more successful career than Norton had ever imagined, stepping onto the championship stage again would be quite lucrative. Gerry, with his expansive popularity and the unwanted status as the latest "Great White Hope," needed a convincing win over one of the biggest names in heavyweight boxing history if his streamlined journey to a title shot maintained its momentum.

Still, in the moments before the fight, consequences of outcomes naturally faded as the sharpening reality of impending combat became all consuming.

* * *

The monotone voice of the ring announcer Jack Lee, clad in an early '80s version of chic garb, sprang clearly through MSG's sound system. A yellow and black, jagged-designed sign hung above the announcer's dual microphones. It simply featured the classic "MSG" acronym, but it was enough to alert anyone to the fight's location.

As the obligatory announcements of the vital but unknown professionals associated with the bout were made, the main event combatants paced like caged animals. It was important to remain loose, to nurture the pre-fight sweat that was essential to beginning the bout in optimal condition. Tight fighters are more prone to being caught. Knocked out. This is particularly true for heavyweights, whose punches are generally more powerful and destructive than smaller fighters, although the threshold of consciousness remains largely similar. The margin separating absorbing blows and losing consciousness generally decreases as the fighters' sizes—and punching power—increase.

As he was being introduced, Norton kept his head low and his heavily muscled back toward the announcer. He was announced as weighing 225 pounds, a quarter pound less than Gerry and tied for the heaviest of his career. Still, the warrior's physique was astonishingly magnificent, one that wouldn't be out of place alongside Mr. Universe contestants. In fact, *The Ring*'s Randy Gordon stated not only that Norton may have been in the best shape of his illustrious career, but also that he would likely beat any heavyweight other than Gerry. Norton's body had simply evolved as the years progressed.

Norton was no longer the svelte 205 and 210 pounder who battled Ali so incredibly in their first two fights. The fighter who began boxing in the marine corps relied a bit more on his power these days, as his reflexes and speed naturally diminished with age and ring wear. Against Gerry, Norton appeared bulkier while maintaining a body fat percentage that would be the envy of any athlete.

The sixth-ranked World Boxing Council (WBC) contender remained active as the announcements unfolded. All fighters manage prefight stressors in their own way. Some celebrate the enormity of the moment and drink in the crowd's energy, while many simply wish to be alone as they focus on setting their minds right. Norton faced his corner, his back to the announcer at the ring's center. He briefly turned after his name was broadcast to the masses, barely acknowledging the respectful cheers mixed with some jeers from those faithful to the hometown hero. Soon after, as Gerry's introductions began, Norton again turned in the direction of the ring's center and Gerry's corner.

As the moments unfolded, Gerry was becoming more eager to fight. He wanted the bell to ring. Gerry was the number-one contender for both the World Boxing Association and WBC titles (and the number-two contender according to *The Ring*'s annual ratings in 1980). Gerry was also a 4–1 favorite to win the bout—in fact, for many, there was an expectation that Gerry should be dominant, a reality that can either bolster a young fighter's confidence or place immense pressure upon him.

Yet somewhere the scared child still resided inside. The boy was unsure of his ability to endure—and frightened of any form of physical conflict. This was inevitable. After all, the child version of Gerry was never able to fight back against his abusive father, who was so monstrously bigger to Gerry's child eyes that he appeared to be domineeringly unstoppable. It was this part of Gerry that viewed Norton as just that: menacingly bigger than life and undeniably capable of destroying Gerry at will.

This guy's gonna kill me!

What the hell am I doing here?

The passing moments were long, surreal. Seconds unfolded like minutes, minutes like hours. Gerry's eyes were directed to the ground, observing his massive boxing boots on the canvas. Senses high and alert, Gerry's body was preparing for combat with a healthy sense of urgency that suggested peaked preparation and optimal focus. Suddenly, like a fallen fighter belatedly picking up the referee's count, the ring announcer's words resonated with Gerry. The young contender was outside his mind and into his senses, almost fully in the moment.

As his record was announced, he lifted his eyes to gaze at his opponent across the ring. Norton was pacing, as boxers do, lost in his own prefight thoughts and rituals. Gerry stood stoically still. Then, after Gerry's name was announced, his stillness suddenly manifested into action as he unloaded a quick combination. The crowd cheered wildly in response, which resonated with the young man. The twenty-four-year-old, less than a decade into his boxing career, was poised to headline a major professional card at Madison Square Garden against a future Hall of Famer.

And he was absolutely primed, prepared, and intensely focused for battle.

11

A HERCULEAN DESTRUCTION OF A LEGEND

The prefight standoff occurred as referee Tony Perez relayed his final instructions. It was similar to most of Gerry's previous fights. Even Perez's presence had become something of a fixture in the young contender's fights, as he had refereed Gerry's battles with Young, Denis, and Prater. The popular "Gentleman" Gerry briefly glanced at Norton's face, which featured downcast eyes, before staring directly at Norton's chiseled midsection. This wordless act communicated Gerry's intention: to relentlessly attack and ultimately destroy his opponent's body.

The increasingly lost art of body punching was even more unique among those with one-punch knockout power. The allure of generating highlight-reel knockout blows was too seductive for most. Although far from the disciplined fighter that was within his potential to realize, Gerry maintained his dedication to this strategy. He did so as much as one could expect from a young contender still honing his skills and discipline. The body-punching strategy was sound: when the body is compromised, the arms drop, and openings to connect with an opponent's head become more plentiful.

Valle stood beside his giant charge, a Q-tip resting in his mouth like a cigarette. The respected trainer rubbed Gerry's chest vigorously to ease the natural tension developing in his fighter's ultra-prepared body, his right hand open and circling counter-clockwise as his left massaged Gerry's neck. Gerry was in the best shape of his entire life. But as the mind affects the body so, too, does the body affect the mind. Valle's actions expressed reassurance to a young man once more graduating to a new, bigger stage. His was the fatherly support that Gerry naturally had gravitated toward in early adulthood to fill the void left throughout his first two decades on earth.

The seemingly omnipresent Rappaport flanked Gerry's left side. Some in the boxing industry wondered if the controversial co-manager was capable of forgoing an opportunity to be seen by the cameras. Yet Rappaport and Jones were guiding his career quite well to this point. Gerry's maturing bank account and expanding popularity was evidence of their business and marketing savvy. Gerry fought frequently enough and against increasingly more challenging fighters against whom he could display his skills. This optimally expanded Gerry's professional development, preparing him for his most important fight to date.

Preparing him for Norton.

* * *

Norton was beyond ripped. A true Hercules. Yet any concern regarding Gerry's ability to inflict damage was extinguished. The intense attention to the moment prepared Gerry's brain to attack the body, to fight, to change his foe's facial expression. There was no time or energy remaining for investment in any negative beliefs about himself, including his father's words.

Gerry's steady glare clarified this intention to his foe. This couldn't be done enough. Mind games in sports are commonplace, but they take on a more significant importance in combat sports. On such stages, the consequences not only affect the sporting outcomes, but can also affect one's health or even survival. Gerry, as a child of an abusive alcoholic, was well versed with hiding his emotions and displaying those that were appropriate for survival. In the ring, this meant a heart devoid of fear and replete with bad intentions, even while nerves might exist below the surface.

As Perez completed his instructions, the fighters briefly touched gloves. The time for battle was seconds away. Norton, the future Hall of Famer, only three years removed from his historic battle against Larry Holmes, was the obstacle in Gerry's path to riches, increased fame, a chance to realize his quest to earn the greatest title in sports—and to an even more precious goal—to prove his father wrong, to prove that Gerry was worth something. This was a persistent goal that was frequently satisfied, though only for a finite amount of time. Each fight provided another opportunity to overcome Gerry's unhealed emotional wounds, to overcome his father's condemnations. Each win could not quite eradicate those harsh words, so long ago spoken but so alive in the darkest recesses of Gerry's mind.

The internal battle was not fully stifled. The shifts between peace and chaos can be instantaneous. The magnitude of the moment, considering the potential outcomes, led to sabotaging thoughts in Gerry's mind—and competing confident ones:

Look at the size of this guy! Former marine, trained to kill—this guy's too good, way too good!

I'm going to take him out—destroy him!

You're worthless, Gerry. How can you compete with this guy? He broke Ali's jaw!

Gerry re-centered on the moment. He walked to his corner, reached out to the ropes and briefly squatted as low as his limbs would permit. Gerry sprang up as Valle met him and kissed Gerry's cheek before exiting the ring. Gerry soon would be alone to face his celebrated opponent. Gerry had support from—and connections with—others, but he had to fight alone. Everyone exists alongside numerous others, establishing meaningful connections with many of them, but we ultimately live out our life journey alone. This takes courage similar to the courage required of those entering combat sports—which are essentially microcosms of life, with lessons, growth, and outcomes fast-forwarded within the confines of the fight's duration.

Bouncing up and down to keep his body loose, Gerry awaited the start of the battle. Across the ring, Norton—age thirty-five according to Madison Square Garden's "tale of the tape" but estimated by BoxRec.com to be thirty-seven at the time—shuffled his legs back and forth to maintain his prefight sweat and looseness. He twitched his shoulders periodically, perhaps an unconscious effort to rid himself of any excessive nervous energy that could affect his own concentration. Norton was, after all, just as human as Gerry and every other courageous athlete donning boxing gloves.

The combatants raced to the ring's center upon the bell's chime. A surge of optimism overwhelmed Gerry's consciousness as he sized up his foe. He was directly confronting the adversity that, at times, had empowered his inner worlds' negative beliefs. No longer was Norton the monster depicted by Gerry's demons. He was a mere man, mortal, and able to bleed and falter just like Gerry himself. Not only that, Gerry sensed that he could take this legend—no, this man—out.

Hey, this guy ain't so big!

That positive realization empowered Gerry to fully utilize his emotional strength and, by extension, his punching power. The latter put Gerry on course to generate a historically brief and brutal conquest.

Excitement, bred from realistic hope, surged through Gerry's veins.

* * *

Exhilaration fueled Gerry's entire being as he observed that Norton, while formidable, was a man who could be defeated—not a monster who would absolutely destroy Gerry. The confidence bred from his legitimate skills and abilities now resided without opposition in Gerry's mind and heart. He was realistic, not overconfident, and focused. Gerry centered his attention on the task at hand. Gerry allowed himself to trust the process of solving his foe's equation and knocking him out.

Incredibly eager as he was to impose his will, Gerry's disciplined training kept him at an educated pace. His eyes were trained on Norton's supremely sculpted abdominals—the body, as boxing experts say, was Gerry's prime target. Destroying the body would lead to a more tired foe. A broken rib would hasten the process. A patient, strategic power puncher is the most dangerous one. On this night, Gerry was determined to follow Valle's directions literally and carry them out with single-minded focus.

Gerry cautiously inched forward before the fighters exchanged jabs. Gerry quickly fired a couple more before eating a Norton left. It landed on his forehead, the preferred landing mark for the recipient if a fighter gets hit in the skull. This area is among the hardest areas of the body, and one reason why trainers encourage their fighters to keep their chin—among the most vulnerable areas to knockout—tucked in. Doing so exposes the durable forehead while protecting the chin.

Gerry found himself swimming with the rhythms of the fight's flow—each movement transpired naturally, every response to Norton's aggressions was spontaneous and seemingly innate, all punches thrown with purpose and precision. The contender was simply allowing his performance to manifest. He was purely in the moment. Gerry didn't consider the past and didn't know what was coming, but he truly felt right, in control—safe, even. There were no thoughts, only action. Natural, pure action.

Gerry's efforts forced the future Hall of Famer to back up. Like many fighters, Norton was at his strongest when moving forward. He was used to imposing his will through his advanced physical strength. The two bigger power punchers who dominated Norton—Foreman and Shavers—backed Norton up, too, preventing him from getting his shots off.

The persistently active Norton kept moving his arms, changing levels, and firing off punches to feel out and confuse his young opponent. Gerry stalked his foe like an apex predator facing an equally dangerous counterpart for territorial control, leading with quick jabs as he sought to land a meaningful blow. Then, quite suddenly, Gerry landed a right hand—something his detractors claimed he didn't have—that buckled Norton's knees. The hurt fighter began implementing a bobbing defense similar to what was made famous by Joe Frazier rather than his honed crab and peek-a-boo style.

The legend was already in survival mode.

* * *

Gerry somehow tempered his aggressive instincts to headhunt and destroy his opponent and attacked the body briefly before targeting Norton's head when appropriate. Norton became more defensive, raising his arms in a style reminiscent of Archie Moore's cross-armed defense. He also bobbed his torso dramatically to present a harder-to-hit bull's-eye for his audacious opponent. However, Norton was being herded into the corner. With limited space to move, Norton became an increasingly stable target. Always a strong finisher, Gerry sensed an opportunity to end the fight. It was a near-predatory instinct. The finish line was suddenly in sight.

Power punchers are at their best when their foe is backed up against the ropes or corner, where they are as stationary a target as possible, so as not to negate the punches' impact by moving and creating angles. Gerry strategically leveled his adversary with his powerful offense. Gerry angled his body to generate as much power as possible in his blows. He took an educated risk by throwing more elaborate power punches rather than shorter, simpler ones. Doing so exposes a fighter to his foe, creating windows to be hit himself or to get caught by an unseen strike. These were the ones that usually knocked fighters out. Yet the risk was worth the reward, as Norton was clearly impacted by nearly every succeeding punch.

Unlike many power-punching young fighters who exclusively head-hunt when opponents are hurt, Gerry focused on mixing his blows between Norton's body and skull. Norton, his back to the ropes, somehow managed to reverse positions with Gerry. Such is the ability of veterans who have fought some of the greatest pugilists in boxing history. The body and brain may lose processing speed, but acquired wisdom helps compensate for much of the loss. At times when a fighter is rocked, the body wisdom becomes an enormous benefit, as it responds effectively to the ever-changing ring conditions. Norton had taken himself out of a dangerous position and into one that allowed him to press the attack or to move away from further punishment, allowing himself some time to recover.

The former champ engaged the young contender. Gerry and Norton commenced to fight hard at close quarters before a left hand wobbled Norton again. The former champ once more found himself in the corner—only this time, he was completely trapped. Gerry missed two uppercuts designed to immediately remove Norton from consciousness but landed a left uppercut that simply stopped Norton's defensive efforts. Another right followed almost instantly. A right uppercut and short left hook sent Norton slowly slumping to his knees, suddenly defeated, his back pressed against the corner. The speed of the punches made it difficult to identify which blow generated the knockout.

Norton was almost completely out, but his position against the ropes would not allow him to crumble to the ground. Gerry, as all fighters are instructed to do, kept fighting until the referee stopped the bout. His jaw was clenched as he instinctively pounded the former marine with every ounce of power that he could muster. The overriding emotional mind-set at such moments is primitive—kill or be killed—although that is not the rational intention, which is simply victory. The reality demonstrates the differences between our primitive and more advanced brain regions. This separation explains how fighters, lost in the throes of combat one moment, can embrace their former targets as friends only moments later.

Gerry briefly looked at Tony Perez, but the referee was not stopping the fight, so Gerry kept fighting. It wasn't long before left hooks and right crosses forced Norton to a deeper, scary level of unconsciousness. Gerry was landing brutal, undeflected blows. Perez was slow to intervene after Norton lost consciousness, which occurred several eternal moments before the official end of the bout—a mere fifty-four seconds into the first round.

Gerry had knocked Norton out more definitively than what may have been George Foreman at his best. Most would call it one of the most destructive knockouts in boxing history. Many at ringside were worried that Norton was seriously hurt from the uncommon devastation. Unfortunately, Perez, who remained a top official for some time, would also oversee another historically brutal knockout when Ray Mercer demolished Tommy Morrison in 1991.

On this May night at the Garden, a decade before the Mercer-Morrison clash, the former champion stared blankly as Perez helped him into a more natural seated position. The agony of a historically harsh knockout defeat couldn't even register in Norton's dazed mind. That wouldn't come until later, if at all. The veteran fighter was a known proponent of positive thinking, greatly influenced by the legendary Napoleon Hill, and wasn't known to dwell on setbacks. Norton had much to reflect positively upon. After all, he had accomplished an all-time-great career, one that would earn him induction into the World Boxing Hall of Fame in 1989 and the International Boxing Hall of Fame three years later. But against Gerry, the former protégé of the legendary trainer Eddie Futch had suffered as devastatingly decisive a knockout loss as ever in the history of big-time fights.

It would be the last bout of Norton's esteemed professional career.

* * *

Gerry, in contrast to Norton's severely compromised condition in the immediate aftermath of the bout, was in the ring's center, immersed in the glories of manufacturing an exhilarating victory. The young man's mind had been conditioned to largely minimize, deflect, or divert any positive emotions regarding himself, but the precious moments after victory erased all evidence of his father's abuses. He had earned the twenty-fifth victory of his then-flawless career.

Hugging all those within his elongated arm's length, Gerry smiled broadly and laughed loudly in the ring's center. Standing tall amid the now-crowded ring, Gerry raised his arms and happily answered the cheers of the crowd. He was meaningfully connecting to the masses and fully in the moment. There was no future nor past—just the moment, and the bliss it contained.

* * *

As organized chaos ensued in the arena, Norton remained laid out in his corner, his back resting against the lowest padded turnbuckle. Packs of professionals, including the ringside physician and concerned cornermen, attended to the fallen legend. Gerry soon made his way to Norton, peering through those hovering over his defeated foe. All fighters know the dangers of combat, and although each must fight with the distinct intention to inflict harm in order to secure victory, none wishes to permanently disable a foe, no matter what the prefight tough words indicate. There is a fundamental and unifying respect that most fighters possess for one another. This was particularly true in the aftermath of fights. Unable to verify Norton's condition but confident in the assistance he was receiving, Gerry walked to the other side of the ring where he was greeted by myriad supporters, all of whom were celebrating the contender's ninth consecutive knockout.

But it was Gerry's interaction with Victor Valle that was the most significant. Stooping his six-feet, six-inch frame dramatically to come face to face with his trainer, Gerry playfully knocked foreheads with his five-feet, seven-inch trainer and surrogate father before lifting him off the ground. Soon after, the famed ring commentator Larry Merchant interviewed Gerry for the television audience. All fighters sought this interaction, for when the fighter was the first to be interviewed by Merchant, it usually signified victory. Rappaport, ever the promoter, was right by Gerry's side as the cameras rolled.

Merchant and Gerry briefly discussed the fight's happenings. In a bout lasting fifty-four seconds, any reflection needed to be succinct. Valle stood proudly beside his fighter, Q-tip in his mouth, seemingly continually prepared to administer healing arts to deep cuts. Merchant inquired about Gerry's feelings regarding how others would perceive the bout. Gerry distanced himself from caring about those who chose to view him negatively. Instead, he reveled in those who were supporting him. This was a magnificent feat for an adult child of an alcoholic. Such individuals frequently crave people's approval, feel especially vulnerable without it, and are uncomfortable with interpersonal conflict or disapproval. But on this night, which featured the most impressive victory of his professional career, Gerry had reached the pinnacle of mind and body. And it showed in his responses.

When asked about his future, Gerry expressed trust in his manager's expertise and decisions. Each member of his team had a role. In the euphoria of victory, Gerry experienced a superior sense of cohesion with those close to him. Gerry felt like a member of what seemed to be a stable family, if only for the most temporary of proverbial heartbeats. He felt safe, secure, and hopeful. Gerry was experiencing a peaceful and sturdy faith in himself and his future. This was bolstered by the comfort he felt with those around him, protecting and guiding him in a way that his child self never experienced.

The victor didn't care if he fought Mike Weaver or Larry Holmes—his management would decide that, and Gerry would simply fight who was in front of him. The format had been working brilliantly. Holmes was the recognized champion, but Gerry knew they'd eventually fight. Heck, by beating Weaver for his World Boxing Association championship, Gerry would likely generate more money by fighting Holmes in a title unification bout. Valle estimated a 25 percent improvement in Gerry's physical and mental strength with a fight against Weaver, making him a more formidable rival for Holmes. Whatever the case would be, Gerry was fighting regularly and winning in spectacular fashion. His dominant victory had emphatically solidified his place as the world's top challenger to the most prestigious individual title in sports—the heavyweight championship of the world.

Shortly after Merchant's last question to Gerry, Rappaport began campaigning against Don King and Larry Holmes, stating that each refused to sign a contract, despite publicly declaring a willingness to do so. Rappaport concluded by promoting his fighter's potential for greatness. The manager, ever the salesperson, nevertheless believed in Gerry a great deal. It was hard not to have faith in the giant athlete, particularly after the Norton destruction. The young man had yet to be seriously challenged in the ring. Ardent boxing fans were captivated by his power even while uncertain about whether Gerry had a chin and championship heart. But from a marketing standpoint that included mainstream sports fans, Gerry possessed astounding power, definitively knocking opponents out, and an appealing and compelling personality.

However, the upcoming months would prove to be among the most confusing, frustrating, and challenging of Gerry's existence. The quest to generate the largest purse possible divided a nation, strained race relations, and ultimately contributed mightily to derailing what seemed to be a surefire Hall of Fame career.

Yet on this particular night, Gerry was at the pinnacle of his sporting career and lost in the hopes of an even greater future.

* * *

At the same time, as he stood tall amid adoring fans, eager sycophants, and true allies, Gerry was only moments away from unknowingly sowing the seeds of profound sabotage. His dreams of championship glory, of establishing his place among the pantheon of heavyweight greats, were about to be undermined by Gerry's own actions. Actions strongly influenced by an insidious union of biology, trauma, and unhealed emotional wounds. Alcohol would increasingly become a key part of Gerry's life, perhaps due to his imposter syndrome and not knowing how to fully feel his fears and joys. The heights achieved by this victory would lead to severe alcohol abuse.

On this night, Gerry could have defeated anyone in the world, but it would also essentially be the end of Gerry's career.

* * *

The locker room was a joyous one. Norton was not just an established legend, but he was also ranked number ten by *The Ring* and number six by the World Boxing Council. It was a great victory. Thirty-five years later, Larry Holmes acknowledged to RingTV.com that he thought Norton was going to beat Gerry. Norton was a contender, and Gerry completely dominated him.

The event was hard for his brain to fully compute. Gerry's broad smile and consistent laughter was authentic but bred largely from his observation of others' enjoyment. He wouldn't fully allow himself to feel the natural happiness that accompanies achievement. Trauma survivors frequently have such thought strategies. Feeling safe actually can be a trigger for feelings of fear, as the survivor's brain connects letting one's guard down with being hurt.

As powerful and persistent as the negative thoughts could be, external stimuli can serve as a life preserver at times. An unusual sight pulled Gerry from his thoughts. Victor Valle was composing his variation of Al Jolson's famous 1928 hit, "Sonny Boy." Gerry's diminutive, gray-haired trainer and mentor belted out each lyric with a visceral tone that could touch the toughest of souls. The effort swelled Gerry's heart with the sense of acceptance and love that he had yet to experience. Valle had become the supportive—if also tough and sometimes flawed—father figure that Gerry never knew, a reality that was underscored by the rendition's final modified line, "You're my son, Gerry boy."

Gerry saw the happiness of those surrounding him, most of whom he loved like family, and experienced great strength and satisfaction from observing their happiness. He had reached the pinnacle of his capabilities, had eradicated his trauma-fueled fears enough to truly listen to his intuition, both from his body and mind. But although he should have been enjoying the moment, his upbringing seemed to take on a new power—he was hit very hard. As high as he felt in the ring, Gerry didn't really know how to accept success. He had done so up until this point, but something about the Norton victory proved to be too much. The emotions highlighted a hole in Gerry's life.

But the alcohol was filling it.

* * *

As the night unfolded and his entourage came to include an old flame, substances were introduced. Alcohol, Gerry's preferred chemical, was as plentiful as can be expected. But something else, something incredibly sinister, was introduced: cocaine. Gerry would later joke that he never liked cocaine; he just thought it smelled good. It took him away from the moment, away from the pain and confusion, made highs far higher, and allowed him to party longer.

As people turn to substances not only to deal with negative emotions but also to prolong and heighten positive ones, they develop tolerance. This leads to increased use to get the same high, which only works for a while. In time, substances are required simply to feel "normal" and, later, to avoid the horrors of physical withdrawal. Tonight, hours after his greatest and most spectacular victory, one that occurred years before his physical prime, one that should have been the platform for even greater heights, Gerry's career essentially came to an end as his alcoholism became incredibly empowered.

This deterioration process would unfold over nearly a decade, with each year consisting of myriad strange happenings in the oft-insane world that is the sport of boxing.

12

AFTERMATH

Gerry's destruction of the great Norton would be the last heavyweight headliner at Madison Square Garden for more than a half decade, until another young phenom named Mike Tyson took on his rival, Mitch "Blood" Green. The young contender was atop the world. At the postfight press conference, Gerry felt compassion for Norton as the latter was asked how hard Gerry punched. That wasn't necessary. The next day, Gerry was on *Good Morning America* and a slew of other morning shows. All this after an unusually active night of getting wasted. It had been the first time that Gerry stayed up the entire evening due to partying.

His life was changing and alcohol was becoming more and more important.

* * *

The aftermath of Gerry's destruction of Norton was a blur for the young contender. The doors were opening up so widely that the unguided Gerry couldn't help but to vigorously investigate them. He was on the front page of seemingly every newspaper in the nation. The scariness of his knockout victory suggested that Gerry's power had already attained all-time-great status. The media, starved for a personality in the post-Ali sports world, gravitated to Gerry's compelling persona with great excitement. To many, he was the world's undisputed heavyweight contender, even though he still needed a few fights to more fully realize his potential.

Meanwhile, boxing politics and complications related to signing for fights prevented Gerry's team from securing fights in a reasonable time frame. Mike Weaver, the World Boxing Association (WBA) kingpin, was the preferred target for Gerry's next match. It made perfect sense. A victory would strap a belt around Gerry's waist and create even greater interest in a Holmes battle. Weaver was also a more manageable foe than the great Holmes. Yet Holmes was a much bigger payday. It was a great challenge to face, since Gerry was the number-one rival for both titles, and the Twins explored both avenues, even while disagreeing as to which path to take.

As a result of these continuous debates, along with the difficulties of negotiating big-money fights, properly protecting and nurturing Gerry's burgeoning talent no longer seemed to be a priority. The fighter's ability to produce large paydays became profound once Gerry catapulted to the near-unanimous status of number-one contender. Additionally, efforts to secure good fights simply were thwarted by boxing political pressures. For example, the WBA nixed the tentative October 22, 1981, bout with Weaver, who had to fight James "Quick" Tillis first, despite Gerry being ranked number one and Tillis number three. A technicality forced this matchup; Tillis had been the highest ranked contender at the time Weaver was due for a mandatory defense.

Meanwhile, Gerry awaited his chance on the championship stage, his finely honed fighting skills and instincts becoming duller with each passing week of inactivity.

* * *

Idleness is dangerous for alcoholics. Boredom can promote the desire to get drunk or high, a state of being that becomes increasingly important to the sufferer. Addiction is an insatiable beast that feeds until it destroys its host or is effectively addressed. As his fame expanded along with the time between meaningful training camps, Gerry's partying opportunities grew exponentially. His codependent-influenced desire to be liked by others naturally magnified his natural inclination to make others laugh and feel good about themselves. Seeing others experience joy always produced a sense of peace and purpose in Gerry. But during lonely moments or those in the company of substance-dependent friends, Gerry's addictions took over. As his body developed tolerances to alcohol and other substances, it forced his brain to seek other avenues to produce highs. Uncontrollable urges are typical of those authentically addicted to substances.

Cocaine's introduction into Gerry's life was devastating on myriad levels, and its use would last five important years of his career. It produced a euphoria that immediately pushed away the traumatic memories, the emotions they produced, and more contemporary worries. His brain's reward system unloaded all it had to offer when Gerry ingested these substances, far more than any natural actions (such as meaningful connection to others, food, sex, etc.) could entice it to produce. However, as his use increased, his body's ability to realize the same high decreased. There was a ceiling to the good feelings that could be produced, and they kept dropping. Eventually, use could not produce even normal levels of good feelings, and depression symptoms invariably followed (after all, whatever effect a substance has upon ingestion has the opposite effect as it wears off).

The partying increased to incredible levels. Gerry would take a limo to Studio 54, and despite lines around the block, he would be invited inside and led to the most happening rooms of the club. Cocaine bowls would be passed around, alcohol would be flowing, and people would offer mostly anything to the fighter. Gerry indulged but stopped at heroin. That wasn't an option. Yet he would take impromptu trips across the country and across the world on the whims of an alcohol-induced euphoria. The drugs and alcohol filled a hole in his soul produced by his childhood traumas. He liked being away from his pain. Awkwardness, shyness, feelings of not belonging—they all went away. He felt normal. This was the curse, because it was a lie. Substances were becoming an essential component in Gerry's life. Every night, there was a place to go. Gerry was partying heavily, but he seemed to be managing.

The manageability of Gerry's life was an illusion. Life was great, but the boxer's lifestyle had many unfolding negative consequences that wouldn't be noticed until the clarity of sobriety was achieved. The primary result was that the contender who destroyed Norton, certainly the very best version of Gerry, and perhaps among the very best in heavyweight history, was no more. By every measure and standard, alcohol and recreational substance use was the most devastating and enduring opponent Gerry ever faced.

* * *

With no fight scheduled in the aftermath of the Norton win, Gerry's sense of purpose was diminished. Alcohol distracted the fighter from this important gap. Training without a clear foe was akin to a ship sailing with no destination. It is difficult to invest the same energies to honing skills and challenging the body when a fighter has no identified opponent. It was like treading water. So Gerry filled the time enjoying himself— sailing, traveling, and partying.

Even while appreciating and engaging in joys reserved for a small percentage of the population, Gerry longed for simpler times when the best fighters were matched up with their elite counterparts. The current era's susceptibility to political issues was a nightmare. This, combined with two shrewd, disciplined businessmen who creatively pursued their goals of minimizing risks while maximizing profits were the main factors that kept Gerry inactive for prolonged stretches of his prime. Without anyone trustworthy to discuss these issues, Gerry was forced to rely on each manager watching the other. Even when it was clear that he wasn't getting the fights he needed, Gerry reluctantly accepted his managers' explanations, which were based on the real problems of boxing politics and of securing fights without signing with the sports' most notorious— and successful—promoter, Don King.

Don King's promotional success is not debatable, and he was nearing the pinnacle of his powers in the 1980s. He promoted more than five hundred championship fights during his career, including some of the sport's most historically significant events, and he has been an International Boxing Hall of Famer since 1997. The *New York Times* even listed King as among the one hundred African Americans who helped to shape U.S. history during the twentieth century. King's business mind is brilliant. It can also be described as ruthless at times.

There are myriad numbers of quotes describing King's bottom-line efficiency. Randall "Tex" Cobb, however, may have summed it up best when, according to the May 6, 1983, edition of the *Glasgow Herald*, he described to *The Ring* his frustrations with Don King, who reportedly lightened Cobb's purse by $700,000 for not properly promoting his championship fight against Larry Holmes. In response, "Tex" stated the following: "Don King is one of the great humanitarians of our time. He has risen above the great term 'prejudice.' He has screwed everybody he has ever been around. Hog, dog, or frog, it don't matter to Don. If you got a quarter, he wants the first twenty-six cents."

King's negative influence on Gerry's career would prove to be dramatic.

* * *

As Gerry awaited a solid contender—or the champ, Larry Holmes himself—to combat, his formerly burgeoning skills increasingly atrophied. His managers were shrewdly seeking the biggest payday possible, one that ultimately would result in historic distributions of money, but their fighter's development was sacrificed in the process. One may argue that Gerry's abilities were being severely compromised—after all, he had fought less than two active rounds in more than a year at this point. This unhealthy streak would extend to twenty months before Gerry's shot at a prime version of Holmes. As compelling as Gerry's destruction of Lyle and Norton were to the masses, the lack of ring time after these fights actually contributed to Gerry's relatively poor preparation for realizing his treasured championship dreams.

Creative options to maintain Gerry's skills may have been developed and entertained, but they certainly were not acted upon. Fighting overseas or in Canada, where King's influence was not as absolute, were options for keeping the young contender busy. Doing so, however, could have eliminated a chance at mega-millions. This is not an uncommon occurrence in heavyweight boxing, where almost all fighters have some degree of a "puncher's chance."

Tommy Morrison, a contender in the 1990s whose power-punching style, massive left hook, and skin tone led many to anoint him the "Great White Hope" of his era, lost out on millions for a proposed title unification fight against World Boxing Council (WBC) champ Lennox Lewis after he was defeated by unheralded Michael Bentt. Morrison—who had recently bested George Foreman for the vacant World Boxing Organization (WBO) title and defended it eleven weeks later—would eventually fight Lewis two years and eight fights later (the bout had been for Morrison's lightly regarded International Boxing Council heavyweight title), but the stage (and earnings) was far smaller than it would have been had Morrison not lost his "stay busy" fight.

Life and career management is subject to countless interpretations and strategies. None works for all, and some work for many. Tommy Morrison's management team elected to keep their fighter busy—even after his potentially flatlining loss to Michael Bentt, who had a superb amateur career (148–8, four-time New York Golden Gloves champ) but had fought professionally only eleven times (while already having a blemish on his record) and would go on to lose his WBO heavyweight title in his next fight. Like Gerry, Morrison was in his mid-twenties and still developing. The consistent work was enough to land him a shot at the great Lennox Lewis. After one more victory, an HIV diagnosis led Morrison to an early retirement. He would fight two more professional bouts more than a decade later.

Like Morrison, it can be argued that Gerry had the potential to survive even a disappointing upset loss before fighting Holmes. He had plenty of time. The prospect of two undefeated warriors doing battle may be far more compelling, and some fighters are not capable of overcoming knockout losses; however, Gerry's development was worth the risk. From a marketing perspective, Gerry's power would have again captured the public's imagination after a few spectacular knockout wins—much like Morrison's comeback after his first defeat to Ray Mercer—something the young contender was a virtual lock to produce.

Few fighters remain undefeated throughout their careers, a reality that the Twins knew was both a rarity and a precious commodity to protect. However, such records are not necessary to generate huge paydays, particularly when the fighter is a heavy-handed knockout artist. Mike Tyson, George Foreman, and Lennox Lewis are but three of the fighters whose legends and bank accounts grew significantly even after upset and definitive knockout losses. As a fighter in his mid-twenties, Gerry's development required opportunities to expand his skills—and to negotiate setbacks, if they were to occur.

The alternative was to remain idle enough to atrophy his established skills and obstruct the development of new abilities.

THE WRITING PROCESS

A Fan Hangs with Gerry

The Westfield, New Jersey, Starbucks was operating at its usual frenetic pace. The downtown suburban establishment was almost always packed to capacity, but several small tables were available near the store's back entrance. I calculated the odds of them remaining that way would be about another twelve seconds or so.

As we waited in line, I wondered how comical the scene would be—Gerry, at six feet, six inches tall, and I, at six feet and an expansive 285 pounds, hovering over a table just large enough to comfortably house a *People* magazine.

"Hey, Gerry—how's it going?" asked the youthful, bright-eyed man behind the register.

"How's it going, big man? Everything good?" Gerry responded, handing the young man his well-used coffee thermos as he did so.

"Not bad; you know how it is—always crazy here. Be right with you, Gerry." There was no need for the former contender to voice his choice of beverage.

"Thanks, bro," Gerry replied before turning to me. "We have some good stuff so far, don't you think?"

"Of course!" I responded. "We're going to have another good day today, too. Like I said—let's look at today like we're doing a book only on the fight with Mr. Norton. Take it one step at a time, you know? As much detail as possible."

"Sure, sure. What do you want?"

"Well," I began. I was a little taken aback, as I viewed our conversations as best when they were free flowing. Plus, my notes were in my tarnished black "professional" bag. "I talk with a lot of fellow boxing fans. They seem to be interested in certain types of info. Behind-the-scenes type info that—"

"Bro, I meant what do you want to drink. Come on, everyone's waitin' for ya!" Gerry's beaming face expressed joy and humor. Despite his efforts always to put me at ease, I suspect I still came across as rather stiff many times. Customers and workers alike were staring at me, waiting for my big decision.

"Oh, ah—extra-large iced coffee, please. I got this, Gerry—please."

"Get the hell out of here—get it next time."

Normally, I would argue adamantly, but something told me just to thank the boxing legend for his generosity. "I appreciate it, Gerry."

"No problem. So, *what do you want?*" He voiced, poking fun at my earlier confusion.

I laughed in response as the liquid gold was delivered. A simple man, I never put anything in my coffee and waited as Gerry created his preferred concoction. Not long after, we were at one of those comically small—for us—tables.

We began discussing the Norton fight. Gerry's account provided so much information, which he dispensed matter-of-factly. Immediately, I found myself battling imposter syndrome—the belief that I didn't deserve to be talking to the man, to be working on his biography. It was the same battle, I would come to find, that Gerry himself struggled with periodically for some years.

"Well, you gotta understand that—Hey, what's your name, big guy?" Gerry asked a little boy just being seated to his left. Startled at first, the preschooler smiled widely as he craned his neck as far back as it could go. "How old are you?" Gerry asked happily.

Giggling noticeably, Gerry's new friend proudly held up three fingers.

"Three?" Gerry expressed, theatrically feigning great surprise. "I thought you were four!"

The boy giggled hilariously at Gerry's facial expressions and delivery. The interplay continued for several more moments, with the boy's parents joining in on the fun. It was doubtful that they knew that they were talking to one of the most visible athletes of the early 1980s—the young couple likely had been born in that decade—but they were enjoying their time with the friendly giant.

As was I. The whole experience of getting to know Gerry had been an informal one. Despite my stiff demeanor at times—including this day— our talks quickly were evolving into a great friendship. This was evidenced in many ways, including the absence of any formal writing agreement. Years into the project, neither one of us had brought up finances or any other issue that traditional businesspeople would have long discussed. Both of us trusted one another, despite the risks of doing so. For Gerry, he was divulging a terrific amount of personal information. For me, the untold number of hours could be for nothing if Gerry decided to write with another author.

Indeed, there was a great deal of unspoken trust established between us two Irish guys. Perhaps it was due to many of our shared challenges: people-pleasing tendencies, a fundamental fear that we weren't worthy of our good fortune, and struggles maintaining a healthy relationship with food. Likewise, our developing bond was also strengthened by a fervent desire to help others, a strong spiritual faith that God is guiding our lives, and a dedication to humbly fulfilling our respective destinies while doing as much good as possible.

As the interview continued, I found my internal monologue including a prayer in which I recited: "I can help make this book—one that would obviously, if done well, be inspiring to others—not only a reality, but a great success."

"You know, this thing is really going to be something. You know what I mean?" Gerry's words pulled my attention back to the moment. I had been focusing on consequences, both positive and negative, instead of the task at hand. The mind is like a wild horse many times, and mine still needed to be trained. "I talk to people all the time. I know this stuff can help a bunch of people. We all go through stuff, you know what I mean? We all have skills and talents, too. I can't do what you do, with that school stuff and all, and you can't do what I can do in the ring. We gotta find what we can do, do it, and enjoy the ride. That's the type of stuff we need to get in there—that book."

"I hear you, Gerry—we'll get there, one step at a time. Just be patient, okay?"

"I'm in your corner, bro, all the way. But I'm going to get you in the ring soon enough, so you better start getting in the gym. You're looking like you're putting on some pounds, bro!"

After an hour or so of discussion, our talk was coming to an end. The material could generate an endless number of pages, I knew, which added to the enormity of the project. A wave of anxiety overcame me, but then I reminded myself to keep it simple. Plan and strategize, but focus on executing one step at a time.

"You got it, Gerry!" I managed between hearty laughs. Incredibly, I found my resolve to complete the project expand exponentially. A sturdy handshake and hug later, Gerry excused himself from the table, secured a refill from his Starbucks friends, and vacated the establishment. The room seemed to mourn the loss of his presence, losing quite a bit of its positive energy.

Now, it was time to transfer Gerry's insights and stories onto the computer screen—and, God willing, into the interested hands of publishers.

Author John Grady, photographer Joe DiMaggio, and author and former boxer Gerry Cooney.

Gerry's mother, Eileen.

The Cooney family: Eileen, Michael, Stevie, Gerry, Eileen, Madeleine, and Katherine (Grandma).

Gerry with brothers Michael, Stevie, and Tom.

Victor Valle issuing instructions to his charge.

Gerry connecting with the crowd in celebration.

Gerry with Richie Barathy and George Munch.

Eyes of the tiger.

Relaxing on Long Island Sound.

Gerry with his managers Mike Jones and Dennis Rappaport.

Gerry landing a punch against the legendary Larry Holmes.

Winter running with Hilton Cohen, Mike Bintonti, Bob Folks, and George Munch.

Gerry with Gleason's Gym owner Sammy Morgan.

Victor Valle guiding his charge between rounds.

Roadwork with George Munch.

Gerry spending time with the youth group kids.

Addressing the press with John Condon and Victor Valle.

Gerry meeting the press alongside Victor Valle and his team.

Meeting with two legends, Larry Holmes and Howard Cosell.

Gerry fighting Larry Holmes.

Victory!

From adversaries to best friends: Gerry embracing Larry Holmes.

Former boxer and author Gerry Cooney.

Part Five

Journeying toward Destiny

My road hasn't always been paved well, you know what I mean? Everyone knows what that's like. Everyone goes through tough times. I have that, too. I think that's why I connect with others.—Gerry Cooney

13

FIGHTING FAME, EGOS, BUT NOT THE CHAMP

The athletic environment can be a perfect reprieve from the demands and pressures of the outside world. Work has similar effects for nonboxers—the occupational tasks may differ, but the process is the same. Other times, performances are impacted by external forces. Some fighters have more difficulty compartmentalizing and focusing on drills, sparring, and fully consuming the wisdom derived from the opponents' videotaped fights. They are impacted by environmental factors—sometimes they are exceptionally motivated to succeed and therefore become more disciplined; other times their focus is fractured, leading to less-than-optimal preparations.

Still others view the sports field as the battleground where great triumphs of social progress are realized. Jack Johnson's heroics, which included defending his championship amid the realistic possibility of being lynched sometime after the battle, have been largely unappreciated by history. Meanwhile, legends such as Jackie Robinson, Joe Louis, and tennis great Althea Gibson are renowned for their contributions to knocking down racial barricades that prevented superior earlier African American athletes from competing on their sports' most elite stages.

During the 1980s and for many decades before, perhaps the sports world's most elite stage was the heavyweight championship bout—and Gerry was now in line for his shot, but it would come amid much racial discord.

* * *

Racial dynamics and discussions can generate powerful emotions in most human beings. In addition to the persistent spotlighting of race topics, champion Larry Holmes seemed deeply affected by numerous realities preceding the proposed bout with Gerry. As negotiations progressed and regressed, Don King's divisive words magnified Holmes's inner resentments and provided explosive fuel for his charge's inner fire. Multiple external happenings appeared to amplify Holmes's anger and sharpen his resolve to win. The demands made by Gerry's management team generated personal animosity in the champion, sometimes bringing out the worst of the inherently classy, generous Holmes.

Perhaps the most vivid example of Holmes succumbing to his resentments occurred after his decisive third-round technical knockout victory over former World Boxing Association champion and Olympic gold medalist Leon Spinks. Climbing out of the ring to sit alongside Howard Cosell, Holmes displayed ease. Clad in his white and red robe and with an arm lovingly draped around his wife, Holmes wished his daughter a happy birthday, expressed kind words to his children and friends, smiled, and joked.

Centering Holmes's focus on the recent battle, Cosell asked the champion to analyze the fight and how his anger led to improved performance. Holmes dutifully responded, but soon discussed his compassion for Spinks. Why, wondered Holmes, was the fight not stopped earlier? Holmes's concern for his foe was a continual theme throughout his career. He had asked the same question in his earlier fights with Ali, Scott LeDoux, and Earnie Shavers. He had implored the referee to call the fight so the beating would cease. It appalled Holmes that Shavers's eye was so compromised early in the fight. He wanted Shavers to quit or have the fight stopped—Holmes didn't want to unnecessarily hurt the powerful fighter. Later, Holmes famously was knocked down by an epic blow only to miraculously rise, alerting all to his championship heart and resiliency. Holmes knew he couldn't keep giving his foes such compassion. Yet in fights against Spinks and Renaldo Snipes, Holmes would hold back so as not to damage his adversary unnecessarily. His compassion almost cost him the title against Snipes and was a lesson that he would not repeat against his next challenger—Gerry.

The Spinks postfight interview continued. The gracious victor complimented Spinks as a "helluva athlete." But the conversation's tone dramatically changed a few heartbeats later. Holmes's demeanor altered instantly once Gerry's name was invoked by Cosell. The proposed challenger, guided by an ABC aide, was making his way to the venerable announcer when he caught the champion's eye. "Howard," Holmes coldly began. "I'm going to slap his face if you bring him over here, and I don't even want to talk about it. Cooney, he can't put his name on a contract!" The anger was clear and present and likely a reaction to the public, which refused to embrace Holmes's proven—and well-earned—greatness, yet fell in love with Gerry, whose compelling personality and prodigious power captured the imagination of the masses. Many thought Gerry's skin tone also influenced his popularity. Holmes, who had two Caucasian sisters-in-law and several biracial nieces and nephews, was not a bigot— he was simply a hurt person who was lashing out.

Cosell's invitation for Gerry to join them may have been viewed as insulting and disrespectful. This was Holmes's moment. He just had been victorious over a former world champion. There were no plans to do a joint interview. Circumstances encouraged Gerry to once again take time, adulation, and (indirectly) money from Holmes. Perhaps that was how the champion interpreted the situation: Gerry was privileged and favored because of his race and other factors, while Holmes had paid his dues each arduous step to the top.

Holmes's perspective may have been influenced by the public's luke-warm response to his genius skill sets and perfect record: they simply did not love him at the time. The immense shadow of the legendary Ali would have prevented any fighter—even an all-time-great talent like Holmes—from being fully embraced. The fact that the public loved Gerry was understandably infuriating. The reality is that the general public is captivated by one-punch-knockout power and views masterful boxing skills in a secondary or even tertiary light.

Decades later, Wladimir Klitschko would dominate the heavyweight division in a manner similar to Holmes—knocking his foes out after a methodical and often unspectacular offense—and, likewise, he was not embraced readily by the American public. Although intellectual and en-gaging, neither legend possessed a dynamic personality. Gerry and Ali did, and they connected favorably with the masses.

The champ's emotions became more intense as his angry thoughts fueled the developing inferno. A few heartbeats later, Holmes declared to Gerry, who was now within earshot: "We gonna fight right now if you come over here! Right now!" With little warning, Holmes backed up his words by lunging at Gerry. Meticulously dressed in a suit and tie, the contender sported a perplexed but ready look that soon evolved into a bemused one. All the while, the esteemed boxing expert Bert Randolph Sugar had kept a steady hand on Gerry's torso to keep the fighter from pursuing Holmes.

Gerry had felt threatened by Holmes's tirade, his senses becoming alert as adrenaline coursed through his veins. Gerry noticed that he was instinctively preparing to defend himself. He was simultaneously astonished as he observed the melee that unfolded. Because he harbored no personal ill will toward Holmes, Gerry did not have the powerful negative emotions required to duplicate Holmes's actions. He was distinctly and emotionally removed from the chaos as Holmes was restrained and guided back to the dressing room.

Gerry had to immediately overcome numerous factors in order to maintain a stately manner. Pride, no doubt a key component of many upper tier athletes, was threatened, and some might feel the need to save face in response to such an overt challenge—especially when it occurs in front of television cameras. Competitiveness, too, could be a factor as the intimidation/mind game is particularly important in combat sports. Gerry also had to thwart his developing anger at Holmes's insults. All of this, combined with the compromised restraint that comes from youthful vigor, would make it difficult for most people to maintain their composure. Ironically in this altercation, it was the older, more experienced professional who had been directed by his emotions.

Holmes was on edge, gathering steam for the showdown with his power-punching future challenger, and perhaps trying to get into Gerry's head a bit. The contender was a young man who had never stepped onto the championship stage and may have been susceptible to such mind games. Everyone wanted to see Holmes fight Gerry. The fight was a compelling one that would put Holmes on the brightest stage of his illustrious career. The fighters were on a collision course and Holmes's actions may have been intended to plant some disruptive seeds in Gerry's mind.

The event's aftermath featured a gradual ease of shock and concern for most, and Gerry found himself quickly overcoming the intense emotions it generated. There were some moments that he thought that he would hit Holmes to defend himself, but the champ never got close enough. Confusion began to dominate Gerry's mind-set. How could a champion—*the champion*—behave in such an intense, unprofessional manner? The area was secured after a few moments. Gerry and Cosell sorted through the uprooted ringside furniture in their interview space. The legendary announcer accidently had been elbowed by Holmes, resulting in a small cut on his lower lip.

As Gerry unfolded a nearby chair to sit down, Cosell recalled a story about Dan Rather being "pushed around, and he said, 'All in a day's work.'" Cosell paused as he was provided a long, white towel, which the commentator used to wipe his mouth. Gerry briefly used the other end on his own face. Then Cosell continued, "So that's all in a day's work." The celebrated announcer then called for a commercial break so that he could tend to his bleeding lip. "This is not as easy a business as it looks," he quipped.

The young Gerry appeared affable as Cosell observed that the boxer had "a smile across his face for the whole human race." It is uncertain whether Cosell chose this phrase as a subtle message that Gerry wasn't feeding into the developing racial strife. Whatever the case, Gerry's expression grew more serious when he was asked his feelings about Holmes's actions. He condemned the champion's behavior as "silly" because it "put harm on people." Obviously, he was referring to the slightly injured sixty-three-year-old Cosell.

Gerry also opined that the episode was "orchestrated from him [Holmes] and Don King." Gerry, who was a little more than a month removed from the Norton victory, described King's $5 million offer to fight Holmes, clarifying that the offer occurred after he had "signed to fight Mike Weaver in October." Gerry then provided a brief fight analysis implying that Spinks could have continued against Holmes, in contrast to Holmes's position that the fight was stopped too late. Gerry relayed that Spinks was hurt, but his "eyes were clear, and [he] was just trying to survive." Spinks, according to Gerry, may not have been as injured as his corner believed. When advised that it was the referee who stopped the fight and not Spinks's corner, Gerry calmly and diplomatically acknowledged that the referee has the best point of view to make such decisions.

When asked if Holmes's antics made Gerry "want him more than ever," the contender displayed class. He didn't feed into the alluring fires of negativity. Instead, Gerry expressed his focus on his next scheduled opponent, his love for his vocation, his pride in being an American, his desire to do his best, and a need to keep fighting and learning as he quested for the heavyweight championship of the world.

Refusing to focus on resentment and hate and viewing situations in the context that human behaviors have explanations (which differ from excuses) empowers a person to greater peace of mind. Outside of the ring, Gerry was naturally inclined to be reasonable and affable, and growing up in a chaotic environment led him to develop skills that suppress tension rather than excite it.

Cosell appreciated Gerry's interpersonal approach. He congratulated Gerry on his classy, humble behavior and literally patted him on the back as he did so. The sports journalist had always been a kind and encouraging influence in Gerry's life. The interview ended with Cosell joking that although he was happy that Gerry attended the postfight interview, he wished it was Gerry's lip that was busted instead of his own.

The psychology behind Holmes's behavior was most likely based on the chronic underappreciation he experienced. He certainly was never a racist. That his condemning comments regarding Gerry's status of number-one contender being the result of his being white were voiced by others was debatable—and Gerry's ranking was legitimately based on his achievements compared with those of other top contenders. But hurt people hurt (other) people. Holmes did not connect with the media and the fans in the manner that Gerry did, much the same way that Marvin Hagler waited a long time before he would be marketable enough to generate the massive paychecks enjoyed by his archrival "Sugar" Ray Leonard. In his quiet moments, Holmes saw Gerry as another fighter trying to take his head off, and he was preparing to defend himself by honing his already masterful skills—including, at times, those related to gamesmanship.

* * *

Once it was accepted that Weaver would fight Tillis, negotiations began for postfight happenings. Promoters, managers, fighting organizations, the fighters themselves—there are so many players, decision makers, and political alliances producing ever-unfolding dynamics that it is almost unfathomable that any fight actually occurs. Even so, it wasn't long before it appeared that the championship defense schedule was organized.

Famed promoter Bob Arum announced that the Weaver-Tillis winner would fight Gerry within four months (i.e., the following February) at Caesars Palace in Las Vegas. Gerry reportedly was set to fight on the undercard against an as-yet-unnamed top opponent. Arum was to promote the card, with Tiffany Promotions president Sam Glass—a Long Island attorney and a friend and business associate of Rappaport's—set to promote the Cooney-Weaver fight (if Weaver got by Tillis). Representatives of all three fighters had met at Weaver's home to finalize the deal. Rappaport publicly stated that the agreement was signed by everyone except the New York–based Cooney, but the fighter was to sign shortly. The arrangement also called for compromises necessary to drop multiple lawsuits involving Arum, Rappaport, Jones, Tillis, and Glass. The arrangement was intended to eliminate the barriers to making the fights happen.

The positive news, however, soon evaporated.

* * *

Understandably, Gerry's managers would never permit their prizefighter to compete on an undercard. He was now far too marketable—the most marketable fighter in the heavyweight division. Yet Gerry simply wanted to fight, something meaningful to train for, undercard or not. The good news was that Gerry would fight shortly before that card against an undetermined contender on an unspecified date and at an as-yet-unknown site, thus enabling the winners to still fight on the championship stage.

Matters soon became more complicated. Holmes publicly stated that he wanted to fight the winner of the Weaver-Tillis match, which would unify two major titles. But this may have been a negotiation ploy. To confuse the scenario even further, Rappaport and Jones were also exploring their options with the dominant World Boxing Council champion. Holmes was frustrated with how the negotiations were progressing and publicly denounced the Cooney camp's financial conditions. Holmes said that Gerry should fight Greg Page, the undefeated prospect whose celebrated amateur career featured a December 1976 three-round exhibition session with a thirty-five-year-old Muhammad Ali in front of twelve hundred people in Trinity High School's gym. Ali's compliments about Page's power led reporters to proclaim the young man a boxing prodigy and "the next Ali." The fight with Gerry would never materialize.

King pulled out all the stops to leverage more money for his fighter—or himself, depending upon one's point of view. According to Holmes's biography, *Against All Odds*, Rappaport claimed that King tugged on his counterpart's passion for civil rights by including the Reverend Jesse Jackson in discussions. Jackson professed that parity of purse, which

Gerry's management demanded, could set back the civil rights movement by decades.

Rappaport's business sense overrode his respect for equality. He cited market value of the fighters based on the money they could generate regardless of race. The color that was important was green—the money—not black or white. King seemingly harbored a similar mentality, but his shrewdness was beyond compare—as was his ability to dominate the heavyweight division to the point of near monopoly. It was difficult getting key fights because King demanded a piece of the fighters he promoted, and Gerry's team refused.

Yet, when there are mega-millions to be made, compromises are made.

* * *

The Holmes-Cooney fight needed to happen. The argument for financial parity was a fair one based on the fighters' ability to generate ticket sales. Holmes was the champion, but he was not compelling to the masses. Gerry was the attraction, much like Muhammad Ali or "Sugar" Ray Leonard had been. But the thought of evenly sharing the riches was understandably difficult for the champion. People have difficulty comprehending elite, multi-millionaire athletes' fixation on deriving every cent possible. Yet the egos that empower their upper echelon sports capabilities also conclude that compensation validates their success. Money is seen as a measure of success and status. The same is true for the managers and promoters who negotiate the finances. Money becomes a way of keeping score, and all players—athlete and manager alike—want to win.

Ultimately, Gerry's camp moved on to negotiate a historic deal with Holmes, one that would become the richest fight in history and that guaranteed $10 million to each fighter. The contender would secure the same purse as the champion—possibly the first time a challenger enjoyed complete financial parity with the defending champion. This factor offended some boxing purists. Holmes was the blue-collar champion who worked from the bottom floor of heavyweight obscurity to the epic heights of the championship realm. He was a proven warrior who had thrived in competitive title fights and had many title defenses. Gerry hadn't experienced similar levels of adversity due to his destructive and overwhelming power. Some felt that his skin tone and marketability unfairly secured a larger portion of the purse. Yet Gerry possessed the best claim to top-contender status, he had efficiently eliminated all of his opponents, and he was a proven marketable commodity. It was a good deal for all parties.

The event would unfold at Caesars Palace in Las Vegas and be televised on both pay-per-view and closed-circuit television. It was originally scheduled for March 15, 1982, but would be postponed until June 11 after Gerry tore muscle fibers in his left rotator cuff. The fight would be viewed by fans throughout the world. Additionally, the cable giant HBO would rebroadcast the battle a week later, a format that seems to have become a tradition. Sometime after HBO aired the fight, it would be available to even more viewers on ABC.

The drama related to the proposed Weaver-Cooney title fight, however, continued even after the Holmes-Cooney fight was finalized. Weaver reportedly obtained a temporary restraining order to cease ticket sales for the bout. Weaver's argument was that he was contractually obligated to fight Gerry if he defeated Tillis (which occurred). It was a $5 million contract. As with one's view of history, the reality was subject to interpretation. Gerry's camp alleged that it was Weaver who had breached their contract, thus permitting Gerry to find a fight elsewhere.

* * *

Gerry's Irish roots connected him to some of boxing's most historic figures, including Jack Dempsey, James J. Braddock, and John L. Sullivan, widely recognized as the first modern world heavyweight champion. Rather than centering discussions on pride in Gerry's heritage, the media focused on race. The "Great White Hope" fever, as was the case during Jack Johnson's reign, captured the boxing world's attention.

Sadly, the "Great White Hope" focus also connected to the core dynamics that fuel societal racial divides, thus providing fertile ground for the promoters to exploit tensions and generate the public's interest. A small minority of Gerry's zealous supporters, those who made Gerry a champion of the white race against his will, used the fight against Holmes as a battleground for their distorted belief systems. Gerry, whose sole investment in the outcome was the realization of his championship dreams, was uncomfortable with this aspect of the bout. Not only was the media centered on the issue, but Gerry started receiving mail from the Ku Klux Klan.

Vigorously discarding race-centered communications without consideration, Gerry found the clarity of mind necessary to properly prepare for his championship shot. He was surrounding himself with friends, training hard and playing hard, traveling, eating, joking, and fully living his life. Gerry had fans with dire health conditions, and he would entertain them. He grew up in pain his whole life, and he loved helping others forget theirs, if only for the day. These interactions fed him, kept Gerry alive.

The race talk surrounding the fight was never a part of his focus. Gerry just wanted to live and fight to make his dream a reality.

14

THE DREAM BECOMES REALITY

For the first time in the post–Muhammad Ali era, the boxing world enjoyed the indescribable buzz that is generated from an authentic mega-fight. So it was that the thirty-two-year-old Holmes (39–0, 29 KOs) was scheduled to step into the ring against Cooney (25–0, 20 KOs), roughly seven years his junior. The event's official announcement occurred short-ly after the classic battle between "Sugar" Ray Leonard and Thomas "Hitman" Hearns. The Don King–orchestrated event commenced a mere forty-five minutes after the thrilling bout's postfight press conference, in the very same room where the two exhausted combatants had respectfully discussed the new World Boxing Council (WBC) and World Boxing Association (WBA) champion's incredible technical knockout of the pre-viously undefeated Hearns in the fourteenth round.

The Holmes-Cooney fight's promotion was consistently centered upon Gerry's attempt to become the first Caucasian heavyweight cham-pion in more than two decades. Or, at least, that is largely how King presented his views, as did his charge, Larry Holmes. Although certainly not a racist, the champion frequently brought up the issue, often quite harshly and directly. Dubbing Gerry the "Great White Hope," or, when attempting to be particularly divisive, the "Great White Dope," Holmes was using the race issue to capture the attention of the general public. Boxing fans were most assuredly buying the fight, but the average sports aficionado required some convincing to do so. Sensationalizing the fight-ers' skin tones was one method of generating extensive interest. Gerry's management team—in particular, Dennis Rappaport—was also accused of inciting the offensive flames of racism to instigate greater monetary figures.

The promotional tour also generated great memories for Gerry. Distancing himself from the incessant questions regarding the fight's racial overtones, Gerry kept company with some of the entertainment industry's brightest stars. Sylvester Stallone, Frank Sinatra, Chevy Chase, Rodney Dangerfield, and Billy Joel are a few who spent time with the "Gentleman." All were supportive and accepting of Gerry, who authentically appreciated their kindness. Elton John, for example, once sent Gerry's mother flowers when she was convalescing in the hospital. Such efforts were readily embraced by Gerry, who was gaining acceptance from some of the biggest celebrities on the planet.

It was a remarkable experience for a young man who never secured acceptance from his father and was persistently seeking validation.

* * *

Gerry's training camps typically began six to eight weeks before the fight. As with most elite fighters, Gerry's camp was filled with established professionals with decades of experience. He kept it simple: each person did his job. The managers feuded regularly, but Gerry concluded that each would be on guard against the other and identify any malpractice. It was a dysfunctional scenario, akin to harmful family dynamics. Like a successful assembly line approach to manufacturing superior products, Gerry centered on his job and expected his hired support to do theirs: he did the fighting, and they did their thing, whatever that might be to each particular individual.

Gerry's use of substances was becoming more of an issue than at any time in his career. Valle never confronted Gerry head-on regarding his excessive partying, perhaps because Gerry hid the extent of it. Alcoholics are quite skilled at minimizing or masking their use. Yet Valle may well have sensed the issue and acted upon it. The harder Gerry ingested substances, the more difficult his training. Valle may have been trying to compensate for Gerry's self-destructive decisions while allowing the young man to blow off steam. Valle was acting in the best interests of Gerry the fighter—and Gerry the young man, who became like a son to him.

* * *

The result of the incredible training schedule would be Gerry weighing in at nearly the same weight as his previous three fights. This would be a positive sign were it not for the horrifically hot weather. Gerry's body would lose enough water weight to fill a small lake, and he didn't have much excess to provide. Ideally, Gerry should have weighed in at about 240 pounds so that he could more readily lose fluids without consequence. The effects of dehydration can range from lack of energy to headaches, low blood pressure, dizziness, and more. Uncomfortable outcomes in any situation, but particularly dreadful in combat situations in which every factor can be a determining one.

The extra weight Gerry had piled on through his drinking had been worked off in the gym. The toll severely taxed Gerry's body. He fell short of the optimal eating and rest patterns necessary to amplify his training's effects, to prevent hunger and eating binges, and to provide constant energy during his waking hours. This included consistent meals to promote quality energy and healing from the wear and tear of training. Dependable sleep patterns, so vital to physiological and psychological health, were also compromised with excessive drinking episodes. Although alcohol tends to induce sleep, the quality of sleep cycles is negatively impacted by the chemical.

All this, and Gerry was to fight Larry Holmes, one of the greatest heavyweights of all time.

* * *

Gerry's will to win, despite his self-sabotaging efforts, was far from extinguished. It dominated his consciousness whenever family dynamics and substance use were outside his focus. There was also a part of Gerry that derailed himself, so if he lost, there was an excuse. Largely inspired by his father's condemning words, this part operated outside of his awareness and warred with the champion inside that promoted quality preparation efforts. Most times, the contender listened intently to his beloved trainer, even though Gerry often employed the combinations that felt most natural to him at the time. He ate according to his instructions—fresh fruit and vegetables, whole grain breads, and appropriate levels of protein—and kept himself hydrated during his training. He even stopped drinking excessively a few weeks prior to the fight, quite a feat for an alcoholic (though far from an optimal effort).

Gerry sometimes experienced dry mouth and excessive thirst throughout this time period. When a person feels thirsty, he or she is already dehydrated. This is of particular concern for fighters. Dehydration can compromise the body's ability to regulate its temperature, carry nutrients to necessary regions, remove wastes, lubricate joints, and protect tissue and organs. Such shortcomings often lead to muscle cramps, decreased strength and power, and elevated heart rates.

The stress of preparing for such a massive fight was also a factor. Certain levels of stress can lead to optimal performance by creating a healthy sense of urgency to complete tasks. Too little stress leads to boredom and even can contribute to depression symptoms. Too much stress can lead to anxiety or even a complete meltdown. This can occur with an excessive focus on outcome, such as a win or a loss. Sparring and training distracted Gerry from such thoughts. His sense of honor and desire to please his loved ones and fans often alleviated his stress levels. Gerry couldn't feel for himself; he lived life through other's lives. It was great to see loved ones happy. He wanted to win for himself, but also for all of his supporters.

Gerry's response to stressors was working hard in the training room—and even harder while partying.

* * *

Alcohol's heightened influence contributed to Gerry's demons becoming more and more powerful. His father's condemnations had evolved into firm belief systems. They led to rational levels of concern, such as not preparing optimally, and accelerated pessimism. Gerry's ability to go the distance with Holmes increasingly became a concern. He questioned if he would be able to fight fifteen rounds if needed, and although this thought often motivated Gerry to train harder, it also brought up low self-esteem dynamics. People typically manifest what they center their attention on—even when that attention is focused on avoiding something. This, combined with Gerry's innate programming to devalue himself, was enough to impact his preparation and performance.

Addiction and unhealed emotional wounds considered, Gerry's career and life activities were akin to a runner competing in a marathon with a two-hundred-pound backpack. Gerry had risen to become the top heavyweight contender on the planet and was preparing for the shot to dethrone a gifted world champion.

* * *

From a purely boxing perspective shielded from promotional consid-
erations that so often prevent the most compelling fights from taking
place, the Larry Holmes—Gerry Cooney fight was a 1980s fight fan's
dream come true. As with most eras—save for the previous decade,
which ultimately produced several Hall of Famers—the heavyweight division was suffering from a dearth of exceptional talent. This battle, in
contrast, provided compelling dynamics that produced inspired debate
among boxing enthusiasts. It featured two undefeated warriors—one an
established and dominant champion nearing the end of his physical
prime, the other a legitimate number-one contender whose youth suggested that his potential was still unrealized. The former was battle-
tested, immensely skilled, and highly motivated to secure his status as
one of boxing's all-time-great champions. The latter had destroyed every
challenge set before him with a Herculean left hook that forced compari-
sons to the legendary Joe Frazier.

Gerry's rise to the championship bout captured the boxing world's
attention. Since his 1977 professional debut, Gerry had consistently
pounded all but four of his opponents into submission. His victories included knockouts or technical knockouts of the durable Jimmy Young,
future Hall of Famer Ken Norton, and power-punching Ron Lyle. Critics
would contend that each of these fighters was aged by the time they
succumbed to Gerry's prodigious onslaughts. The degree of dominance in
Gerry's performances largely negated this perspective, earning him status
as the world's top contender for the heavyweight championship. Still,
there were many who used Gerry's success as evidence that he was not
necessarily qualified to face the mature, supremely talented Holmes. Boxing scribes like to know how a fighter handles severe adversity—the true
test of one's championship heart—and Gerry had yet to be challenged to
such a degree.

Meanwhile, Holmes's physical and mental attributes were already
well documented. Owner of perhaps the most effective jab in history, the
champion boasted remarkable recovery powers, quality defense, good
power, and impressive reflexes. He was incredibly versatile in his ability
to beat people. Right crosses, overhand rights, and left jabs were all used
as weapons to secure victory.

Holmes's development may have been among the most strategically
advanced in history. His burgeoning skills were honed under fire from
some of the greatest names to ever contend in the heavyweight division.

Holmes dutifully served as a sparring partner for greats like Ali, Frazier, Shavers, and Young—while each was in, or close to, his prime. At a time when his ability to learn was most elevated, Holmes experienced lessons taught by some of the greatest talents the division ever produced.

Apprenticeships with Muhammad Ali and Joe Frazier during Holmes's formative professional years provided a powerful foundation on which to build his legendary career. These invaluable lessons began in 1973 when Holmes sparred with Frazier. It was perhaps the most motivated version of "Smokin'" Joe, who was training for perhaps the most anticipated rematch in boxing history—his second fight against Muhammad Ali.

Holmes routinely felt the power of Frazier's historic left hook. As a result, he endured and overcame many physical consequences. Most prominently, Holmes once suffered three broken ribs. Still, he kept the injury to himself; sparring with the legendary Frazier was too fantastic an opportunity for the future champion to forego. Moreover, Frazier was uncommonly kind and supportive of his sparring partner, housing him in the best local hotel, picking him up to run each morning, and paying him a quality (at the time) salary of $375 per week. Holmes, affectionately called "Rover" by his mentor for his in-ring movement, presented Frazier with a quality imitation of the magnificent Ali, while Frazier offered his young sparring partner an untold number of lessons—each of which would contribute to Holmes's eventual all-time-great status among history's greatest champions.

By beating Hall of Famer Ken Norton in a classic, utterly grueling fifteen-round split decision, "the Easton Assassin" Larry Holmes had earned the coveted WBC world heavyweight championship. Since that 1978 contest, the champion had repelled the challenges of eleven contenders. His emerging legacy was no doubt compromised by the immortal Muhammad Ali's shadow—Holmes had struggled most of his career to secure the proper recognition of his accomplishments. Although supremely skilled with stupendous levels of courage and resilience, Holmes simply couldn't connect with the public as could his mentor, Ali.

In terms of entertaining through personality and words, Holmes was akin to a baseball player who hits for average attempting to hit home runs. It just wasn't his game. Convincingly defeating Gerry, a fully qualified contender whose imposing six-feet, six-inch frame immediately commanded respect among foes and friends alike, would bolster Holmes's hunt for recognition.

Fully motivated in the heart of his superb career and the prime of his WBC heavyweight championship tenure, a determined Larry Holmes prepared to utterly vanquish his giant adversary.

* * *

Gerry, although the number-one contender for some time, required more experience to be adequately equipped for the primed Holmes. He was still learning to fight. Three or four more fights would have properly prepared the young heavyweight to take on the world's best. Unfortunately, the combination of King making fights difficult to assemble and Gerry's management team understandably wanting to secure the highest reward fights, led to Gerry taking on Holmes earlier than was optimal.

The contender was also developing his coping mechanisms. He was learning how to safely and productively experience feelings. Emotionally attuned to others, Gerry often assumed the pain of those surrounding him. His compassion was genuine and expansive. Surviving authentic depression symptoms can empower one to be more empathetic and aware of how others suffer their own life plights and challenges. For the codependent person, these positive attributes can become exhausting. Compassion fatigue is often prevalent. With all that surrounded him and with few coping mechanisms to utilize, Gerry found himself giving without regenerating, depleting his physical, emotional, and spiritual energies.

All the while, the warrior inside awaited its outlet—the structured war zone that is the squared circle. It was always a reprieve from addressing difficult relationship dynamics, emotions, and everything in between. But Gerry's generous heart was not yet controlled, leaving him vulnerable to spirit-sapping dysfunctional relationships and unable to fully feel joy for himself. The fighter was also a protector of others, and sometimes this was a disservice to his development.

The fight within was far more daunting than anything the great Holmes—or anyone on the planet—could offer.

15

TRAINING FOR THE CHAMP

The days were flying by. They contained incredible experiences, meaningful interactions, superb training sessions, and excessive partying. At times, it was difficult to fully embrace. Despite years of validation as a fighter and person, a part of Gerry still heard his father's demeaning words. It formed a wall in Gerry's emotional life, one that prevented him from fully experiencing the good times. The wall prevented Gerry from fully feeling emotions because he was afraid of losing the good moments. Such defense mechanisms and beliefs are frequently formed during the childhood years and, without intervention and effort, can remain throughout a person's life. One's beliefs regarding self can lead to self-fulfilling prophesies. People tend to manifest what they focus upon or believe, even when both are outside one's awareness.

The mind sees what it expects, generally.

At the same time, there was plenty of evidence that Gerry was worthy of his accomplishments. His charisma and personality often transcended racial divides. The great Ali, Holmes's former mentor who had employed a young Holmes as a sparring partner, connected favorably with Gerry. The legend once stated that Gerry could punch Holmes so hard that the champ's ancestors would feel the pain. He produced cherished memories that the challenger would long remember.

One such event occurred at a Caesars Palace gala to honor champion and challenger. Everyone Gerry ever had wanted to meet was present. Boxing greats like Ali were in attendance. So, too, were other prominent sports stars like Kareem Abdul-Jabbar and Magic Johnson. Even Rocky himself, Sylvester Stallone, joined the star-studded affair. These elite names were present to honor Gerry's upcoming clash with the champion—and to celebrate the young contender himself. The event was a magical one for the young man—each moment was better than the last.

* * *

By 1982, the public was starved for a legitimate threat to Holmes's heavyweight title. Some questioned Gerry's credentials to be that threat. He was certainly the legitimate number-one contender—it was hard to argue otherwise—but this was due, so said his detractors, to the dearth of talent in the heavyweight division. They argued that since the quality of Gerry's opposition was suspect, it was unclear whether he could take a serious punch, and no one knew if he could go the distance. Sometimes, such analyses frustrated Gerry, who recalled that prior to bouts with his big-name conquests (e.g., Lyle, Young, and Norton), some predicted that he would lose. But because Gerry disposed of them in dynamic fashion, the victories were somehow cheapened in the eyes of critics.

The press sometimes criticized both champion and contender.

Fighting in the wake—and incredibly long shadow—of Muhammad Ali, the most charismatic and arguably the most legendary champion of all time, Holmes had difficulty connecting to the public. Any frustration that Holmes may have felt was justified, but his accomplishments were clearly not appreciated fully by the masses. He was amid the second-longest reign in heavyweight history, he had methodically conquered his era's top contenders, and he had clearly demonstrated championship levels of skill, heart, and determination. Such factors generally lead to extreme levels of respect, if not adulation, but Holmes was left feeling the need to convince the public of his greatness.

This was enough to generate profound levels of human emotions in Holmes. Witnessing his less-established foe receiving the public's love and attention must have amplified his angst dramatically. Holmes fed into the promoters' racial exploitation of the fight, verbally antagonizing Gerry publicly and condemning his credentials as number-one contender. Although it is true that the most anticipated event in recent sports history was partly due to the unfortunate—if financially successful—magnification of racial tension between the fighters, the truth was that Gerry was a clear number-one challenger.

The fighters handled public criticism differently. Gerry mostly smiled and expressed optimism—"I have a feeling that things will be all right"—

suppressing any irritation or activation of his demons. The champion's own nerves would be touched mostly when his foe was complimented. Holmes would respond with harsh character assassinations of Gerry, labeling him the "Great White Dope." Such attacks fanned the flames of racial tension. Other verbal punches were crude and beyond offensive. According to a 1982 *People* magazine article, Holmes surmised that Gerry could be one of the retarded children with whom the champion once worked. Such quotes were symptoms of a good man's frustrations directing his thoughts and words. If the comment was designed to upset his younger challenger, it succeeded in generating anger normally reserved for in-ring battles.

What most fans did not realize was that the challenger had several relatives with African American blood. It is estimated that Gerry is more than 9 percent African American himself, as his great-grandmother was African American. Although the champion's positive familial relationship with Caucasians was known but not acknowledged, save for Jerry Izenberg's, "Holmes-Cooney: A Matter of Pride" television special, Gerry's background would not be known until 2016.

* * *

Gerry's drinking opportunities expanded along with his increasing fame. Many unwittingly enabled his addiction rather than intervening. Valle may have known of Gerry's developing problems but responded by being tougher on his charge. Gerry's body was young and resilient but not indestructible; it was susceptible to excessive training. Overtraining, to the layperson, might be interpreted to mean over-prepared. The term might signify that a fighter is exceedingly ready for combat. However, its effects may be as detrimental as not preparing enough. Muscle fiber can break down into the blood. Without rest, the body and mind have no time to heal and build up what the intense training broke down. Consistent sleep is vital. So, too, are intelligently planned days off. Fighters generally train for two months before their events, with their nutrition and rest closely monitored by expert professionals. It is up to the fighters and their teams to do their jobs.

Gerry's increasing addiction behaviors did not permit his body the rest it required. His drinking episodes were sometimes fueled with cocaine, thus depriving himself of restorative rest. Perhaps equally destructive, Gerry's binges left him vulnerable to a near-persistent state of dehydration. Alcohol interferes with the body's ability to regulate fluid levels and can prove destructive to an elite athlete's performance.

The cycle of excessive productive stress—that is, the breaking down and arduous work necessary to create muscle memory and bolster ring intuition—and destructive abuse (i.e., addictive behaviors) was consistent by this time in Gerry's career. Gerry's episodes of "blowing off steam" were followed by more rigorous training sessions. Valle made him train harder. And harder. This increased the need for optimal nutrition and rest, which was not permitted by Gerry's demons.

And so the injuries mounted as Gerry simultaneously trained his body for war while sabotaging his efforts to do so.

* * *

Athletes, like those in any other profession, can benefit from healthy levels of anxiety. It alerts them to potential dangers and pitfalls. This insight can then be applied in positive, productive ways, such as generating solutions and game plans. If a person is then able to become immersed in the here and now while focusing on the task at hand—to trust that his or her preparations will produce the body wisdom necessary for sharp responses to adversities, to trust one's battle plan while maintaining flexibility to the moment's demands—then he or she travels the path of peak performance. Against the great Holmes, Gerry possessed diligent appreciation that his endurance would be tested like never before—he wasn't so enamored with his power, unlike many boxing fans, to believe with certainty that the champ assuredly would fall in the early rounds.

Still, the sabotaging nature of addiction and unhealed emotional wounds negated some of Gerry's preparations. At some points during training camp, Gerry centered more on what he didn't want—that is, to get tired—rather than on the solution to preventing exhaustion—increasing his endurance. This despite having fought fifteen rounds in sparring three times and feeling good about doing so. Still, concerns remained due in large part to the echoes of his father's assurances that Gerry would never amount to anything.

The result was a slight but consistent tension that combined with other stressors to compromise Gerry's preparations. The concern disabled Gerry from being as aggressive as optimal during his fight. Thinking sometimes got in the way of reacting naturally to training conditions, delaying the body's development of the wisdom needed to optimally respond—to react and respond naturally, without the impositions of extended thought, so that it can immediately protect itself amid the adversary's fists.

This is a relatively common occurrence that plagues athletic performances and regular, everyday life efforts as well. Typically, human beings manifest what they center their awareness on, even if it is negative. It is far better to be pulled by our hopes and goals and guided by our intuition than pushed by fears and regrets. By detaching from outcomes, a person can dedicate more energy and focus on the here and now, thus improving the quality of the actions—as well as the likelihood of valued results.

Gerry was still developing these skills through intuition, as no one was guiding him through these psychological minefields.

* * *

Three weeks into 1982, an injury sidelined Gerry only a few days before his Friday-night four-round exhibition against Joe Bugner (in addition to two additional three-round exhibitions with sparring partners). Gerry was devastated, Jones reportedly said, and did not want to talk with anyone. He acknowledged that Gerry wanted to fight, but he and Rappaport could not risk it. Four weeks from his first title shot, Gerry found that his body was not responding to treatment. He had partially torn some muscle fibers in the back of his left shoulder, severely compromising his punching power. A physical exam and related tests would provide answers as to whether Gerry could resume his training regimen, but an athlete knows his body better than anyone. The shoulder injury was serious enough to postpone the scheduled March 15 battle.

Worse, if news reports were accurate, it also threatened to cancel the bout. The frustrated champion stated that he was searching for an alternative opponent, although it is unclear just how willing Holmes was to risk a $10 million payday by fighting another contender. Anything could happen, as Holmes's scare against Snipes suggested. Gerry avoided thoughts about the financial happenings and politics—his management team was there to handle those matters—he just wanted to fight, to have something meaningful for which to train. Gerry hadn't even watched the Holmes-Snipes fight; he was focused on his own maturation, trying to minimize the damage of ring rust and, of course, having fun outside of training.

Some wondered if Gerry was playing games, avoiding the fight, or something in between. A few boxing enthusiasts suggested that Gerry was replicating Rocky Graziano's alleged faking of an injury to sidestep a battle with longtime friend Jake LaMotta. Even though Gerry was diag-nosed with a torn rotator cuff, Holmes himself suggested that Gerry wasn't handling normal aches and pains that fighters simply persevere through. The words were another product of Holmes's frustration, which was fueled by his own decisions at times. One example was when Holmes refused to pose for *Sports Illustrated*, because Gerry was going to get the cover while Holmes would get the inside flap. After Gerry's famous *Time* magazine cover with Sylvester Stallone, Holmes had difficulty participat-ing in any photo shoot with Gerry.

That was part of the psychological chess game played between ath-letes—the fighters were trying to make each other crazy, each trying to get the upper hand in a fight that could be determined by even a slight factor. Every effort counted.

* * *

As with any big event, rumors clouded the actual happenings. HBO—the cable juggernaut negotiating to provide the fight's first taped replay—quickly announced that the fight was called off and rescheduled for April or May (the fight would ultimately be fought on June 11). The time frame was also confirmed by Loren Cassina, who was involved with the organ-ization of the closed-circuit and pay-per-view television outlets.

The champion ultimately remained intent on fighting Gerry—he once stated that the only way the challenger wouldn't fight him would be if he died—but he possessed the option of fighting someone during the inter-im. The resurgent Jimmy Young was viewed as a viable contender. It is only pragmatic to secure multiple options should one unexpectedly falter. Young had won five fights in 1981, which accounted for all of his fights since his loss to Gerry. Young's success had earned him *The Ring*'s Comeback Fighter of the Year award and top-ten contender status in all the major organizations. Holmes was understandably confident in his ability to conquer Young without endangering his mega-fight with Gerry. The veteran heavyweight had been in Vancouver working with Gordon Racette, who was challenging Trevor Berbick for the Commonwealth (British Empire)/Canadian heavyweight title.

The fluidity of the unfolding drama was astounding. Millions of dol-lars and massive egos naturally produce conflict and compelling interpre-tations of reality. The Cooney camp insisted that neither fighter could fight in the interim unless the fight was postponed more than sixty days from the original date. According to Young, years earlier Holmes and

Young promised each other that if either became champ, the other would get a shot. Holmes was fulfilling that promise. Young had maintained his weight and was only ten pounds removed from his ideal condition.

There were a great deal of mixed reports. Holmes publicly remained unfazed with the uncertain future of the Cooney bout. He contended that he could return home and maintain his fight-ready shape. The champion also insinuated that he would use that trim body to defend his title against somebody, even if it wasn't the giant contender.

Tex Cobb was depicted as a worthwhile challenger who could generate interest (Cobb would eventually fight Holmes five months after Gerry's championship bid against Holmes). Cobb had rebounded with three wins after enduring two blemishes to his record with back-to-back losses to former champ Ken Norton (SD 10) and unbeaten upstart Michael Dokes. Nevertheless, Cobb was ultimately unavailable: according to Joe Gramby, Cobb's manager, the fighter had to turn down a tentative $400,000 payday to fight the champion because Cobb only recently returned to training. Cobb reportedly had broken his right wrist a few months earlier in a street fight in which the fighter was supporting a local sportswriter.

Gerry's injury had been a sustained one. He had been enduring elevated levels of pain as late as mid-February. He woke up with his left shoulder stiff enough to be nearly immobile. Little power was generated by his vaunted left hook as he attempted to work through the pain at his Kiamesha Lake, New York, training grounds at the Concord Hotel. To complicate matters, Don King and copromoter Sam Glass had concrete obligations to Caesar's Palace. A thirty-two-thousand-seat temporary outdoor arena was in the process of being constructed for the event, and other outlets were also dependent on the fight occurring: closed circuit locations and television networks all had serious interest in the fight unfolding on schedule. An increasingly alarmed King campaigned for a team of doctors to confer about how best to assess Gerry's condition. The implication was that Gerry's current doctors were not competently treating their client. Bob Halloran, head of Caesar's Palace sports promotions, likewise harbored a sense of urgency, demanding that the contender be treated at the Mayo Clinic.

The public was likewise becoming more anxious for the title fight. Those who were invested in the concept of a white heavyweight champion were hopeful that Gerry could achieve against Holmes what Jerry

Quarry and others could not in the previous two decades: becoming a dominant Caucasian heavyweight champion. This unfortunate focus was shared by too many in American culture. To such people, Gerry had a legitimate shot at becoming the first long-tenured white heavyweight champion since Rocky Marciano ruled the division in the 1950s. A perfect middle-class gentleman who could paradoxically dominate a primal combat sport was compelling to many—almost an incarnation of the light and dark sides of humanity.

But first, Gerry needed his shoulder healed enough to be capable of fighting fifteen rounds against the undefeated champion.

* * *

Eventually, the battle was rescheduled for mid-June, and Gerry resumed his arduous workouts as he maintained his social connectedness. His fame had led him to meet celebrities from myriad fields. More importantly, fame provided Gerry opportunities to be validated by terrific people. Gerry's interactions with Bob Hope were particularly healing and soothing to the young heavyweight. The comedian exuded warmth, and his humor and acceptance radically empowered Gerry, who instinctively longed for approval from paternal figures. The atmosphere around Hope was enjoyable. When Hope assured the young man, "You're one of my guys, Gerry," the historically gifted entertainer created a memory that will endure for as long as Gerry lives. Experiences such as those with Hope were life preservers that prevented the rising star from drowning.

In fact, one of the more meaningful events of this era came during the filming of "Bob Hope's All-Star Birthday Party" in Annapolis, which aired about two weeks before the big fight on May 25, 1982, on NBC. The special was aired in the 8:00 pm slot on Sunday and featured a host of celebrities. Both Gerry and Holmes were part of funny scenes with the comedy wizard. Hope challenged both fighters at separate rings, with Hope using comically huge gloves as he sparred with first Gerry and then the champion. Each fighter was equipped with funny lines and multiple stars served various roles in each "fight," including Leslie Nielsen, Charlton Heston, Sammy Davis Jr., and Robert Goulet. Don King was also introduced as the matchmaker.

Years prior, Bob Hope had been an amateur fighter going by the name Packy East. According to BoxRec.com, Hope made a finals appearance in an Ohio novice championship. The experience added some authenticity to his comic contest with Gerry. During their fight, Gerry feinted (a boxing move to divert attention) and Hope responded like an experienced fighter would. The two laughed. Gerry had heard that Hope had fought before and in that moment felt incredibly connected with him. Such moments—of connecting authentically with others—were the ones that made the fighter feel most alive.

The overall event was a fantastic one that showed the fighters' fun sides. Given the racial tensions generated by those promoting it, the Bob Hope special was a welcome break from the emotional strife. In most ways, the process was a healing one for Gerry. Such was the impact of Bob Hope. Gerry felt accepted by a friendly, nurturing mentor.

The event also harbored some stressful dynamics. During a particular skit, one of Hope's friends played Gerry's trainer. Victor Valle was un-comfortable with anyone else being portrayed as Gerry's trainer. The fiery boxing sage's frustration confused and hurt the contender. Conflict in his heart ensued—Gerry appreciated the unfolding moments of filming scenes with the legendary comedian, but a part of him felt guilty that Valle felt hurt. As with all his loved ones, Gerry felt responsible for their feelings, even though his influence did not extend that far. No one can be responsible for another's feelings, but many adult children of alcoholics struggle with fully accepting this reality. Overall, Valle's frustrations did not ruin the event for the boxer, but it did modify the enjoyment a bit.

* * *

The training camp for the Holmes event featured some challenging days. At least, challenging when compared to the camp preparing for Norton, which was ideal. Gerry's muscles often felt weak after long training sessions and extensive nights on the town. Gym intensity was excessive at times. Sparring partners were seeking to take Gerry's head—each watching the other's sessions in the hopes of dropping the world's top contender. Most had their own trainers present and consulted with them as other fighters tested Gerry's skills. Gerry fought them with the same intensity as he fought live fights.

Gerry, many times, appeared as emotionally compromised as his body was exhausted. His desire to fight seemed to wane at times. This was concerning to insiders because Gerry always had been an enthusiastic gym fighter. The lethargy was, perhaps, most pronounced three days prior to his championship quest. Gerry produced such lackluster efforts against his sparring partner Walter Santemore that he quipped to the assembled fans, "I looked like his sparring partner today." Gerry was overtrained, and his body was alerting him to it.

Throughout the course of training, however, Gerry's youth and passion for combat were ultimately enough to compensate for physical and emotional fatigue. The fighter's recuperative abilities were at their peak. His heart pulled him to the championship fight. It was exhilarating to be in combat. Fighting for the championship inserted a productive sense of urgency to the healthy portion of Gerry's psyche.

Still, his body could take only so much.

* * *

The days leading up to the big fight were predictable. The press would set up camp in preparation for those who would soon follow, the myriad professionals associated with the combatants: trainers, cornermen, promoters, managers, and all who constitute the pugilists' entourages. The activities were routine, too. Public workouts often were held or at least were open to sportswriters. A new community of boxing insiders would congregate in the immediate grounds surrounding the field of combat. Though often competing for stories and information that would set them apart from their peers, columnists and reporters would mingle and bond in the shared joys and struggles associated with their occupation.

Fans and celebrities would arrive to occupy the remaining rooms of the nearby hotels. When fight night arrived, they would be sure to make it to their seats in time for the main event, though not much earlier. Boxing legends, as well as current stars hoping one day to earn that title, would flock to the general combat area to secure some media time and to connect with their peers. After all, only a minute fraction of the population understood the rigors and glories of combat sports, and theirs was an innate fellowship that comes with such experiences. One needs to be enthusiastic—and, perhaps, slightly out of one's rational mind—to be a fighter, and the love of fighting was intrinsic if not always immediately felt among active and former pros alike. Thus, big fights attracted most of those with the unique experience of having professionally competed.

The boxing authorities provided their predictions to the eager public. Carmen Basilio forecast a Cooney knockout within six rounds, but many other greats displayed conflicting or contradictory beliefs regarding the outcome. Sometime after the destruction of Lyle, Emanuel Steward—one of the greatest boxing minds in history—had predicted that Gerry would win the title in two years. Steward would, in the buildup to the title fight, predict a win for Holmes due to Gerry's infrequent fighting schedule. Vito Antuofermo thought that either Gerry would win early or Holmes would win late. Rocky Graziano predicted a Holmes victory but was concerned that Gerry could score an early knockout. Jose Torres initially thought Gerry would become the champion but later altered his prediction, referencing seeing Gerry at the East Side's Magique disco.

The sports world—and many more outside of it—was anticipating and predicting the fight, taking sides, and feeling the natural excitement generated from a huge heavyweight battle.

* * *

The weigh-in was conducted in an unusual manner. Normally, the fighters weigh in consecutively and then pose in the classic standoff, with both fighters staring each other down. But the animosity between the camps was too primal. The fighters' respective entourages were sparring verbally enough. Even the venerable Eddie Futch insinuated that Gerry fought dishonorably at times. This, despite his immense respect for Victor Valle

Unlike perhaps any other sport outside of soccer, boxing thrives on ethnic and national identification. Why is anyone's guess. And how those who identify with multiple categories choose allegiances when said categories conflict is also anyone's guess. A prominent example occurred in 1938. White America's nationalism overcame racial allegiances as Joe Louis became America's first crossover American superstar athlete. Louis was a hero to most, whereas Jack Johnson was vilified by the masses years earlier.

In the late thirties, though racial divides remained terribly prominent, the evilness of Hitler's Nazi Germany united Americans in accepting the great Louis as their champion. Although Louis's foe, Max Schmeling, was unfairly characterized as Hitler's puppet (Schmeling was not a Nazi; he had a Jewish manager named Joe Jacobs), that wasn't how many everyday citizens viewed it. Americans of all backgrounds supported Louis as their champion. Ironically, this African American fighter would be "defending" his country in an arena that would not permit African American baseball players to compete against their Caucasian counterparts. Yet in this battle, he was an American hero.

Louis knew that although he wanted to win for his country, he was simply battling another fighter—not another nation, not solely a representative of another race. This reality is shared by all fighters come fight night. One human being competes against—fights—another one. The competitive warrior in Louis wanted to avenge his only loss (up to that point of his career) two years earlier. The entire world, outside those two men, had the luxury of assigning various meanings to the event. Yet the fighters were simply courageously battling for survival as much as for victory. These two dynamics might be synonymous in terms of combat sports. Ring warriors of any era need to simplify their focus on employing all their skills when the time calls for them, when the fight occurs.

The reality that boxing spectators strongly consider ethnic and national alliances remains valid to this day. Throughout generations, the sport thrives on the energy associated with identification with a larger group. Ethnic combat—right or wrong—appeals to fight fans. With relatively few Caucasian fighters in the sport, Gerry was inherently an outstanding marketing prize. Other people had time and focus to think about such things. Gerry was proud of his Irish roots, but he was not motivated by his skin tone. He just wanted to fight, to test his skills against the best in the world. This warrior's mind-set is known to only the few who engage in combat sports, enlist in the military, or place their lives on the line to protect others.

After all the hype and preparation, Gerry would be the only one in that ring opposing a focused and motivated champion.

* * *

As the giant heavyweight stood on the scales at 225.5 pounds, Gerry was simply a man on course to battle the most talented and proven heavyweight fighter alive. Holmes, an eight-to-five favorite to retain his title, weighed in at a trim 212.5 pounds. On the surface, both seemed physically primed for battle. Gerry weighed only a quarter pound more than he did for the Norton destruction thirteen months prior, which was actually detrimental, given the hot fighting conditions. Holmes's body had matured as he entered the latter stages of what are traditionally considered a fighter's prime years. He was three-and-a-half pounds heavier than he was when he put forth perhaps his greatest performance, a split-decision win against Norton for the title in 1978. This also could have been strategic, since the intense heat on fight night would produce much more sweat than normal conditions.

The prolonged quest toward the historic title shot was complete. The complications, controversies, disciplined preparations, emotional conflicts, and excessive partying with the world's most adored entertainers was all over. Only two warriors remained. There was nothing left to do but to wait out the hours until the richest bout in boxing history commenced.

On June 11, 1982, "Gentleman" Gerry Cooney was to fight arguably the best version of the legendary pugilist and all-time-great champion, "the Easton Assassin" Larry Holmes.

THE WRITING PROCESS
A Heightened Sense of Urgency

Not having watched TV for several months, I found myself captivated by the unfolding events on the diner's expansive screen. It was a strange sensation. My doctoral studies didn't leave much recreational time and losing myself in the video images was soothing. For a few moments, at least, my brain quieted down.

The diner was one of my favorites—a bit aged, perhaps, but comfortable and safe—and more crowded than usual for the late hour. The rising noise level forced me to read the slow scrawling words at the screen's bottom rather than hearing them. I felt a flash of annoyance as my ears caught just enough to make reading the delayed words a little confusing. Still, the views expressed were ones I had heard plenty of times.

"This is just another example of a celebrity who isn't ashamed that he is an addict, but frustrated that he got caught running around on his wife," the unnamed talking head spewed on some cable news channel. The man's energy level suggested that a state of mania was not far from emerging. "It's a way to distance himself, you see—from taking responsibility for his choices. He wants sympathy and forgiveness so that his career can continue—and you know something, it usually works. He'll go through his obligatory trip to rehab for public relations, and you know what, he'll go right back to doing what he's been doing."

The celebrity to whom the talking head referred, Oscar de la Hoya, was a future Hall of Fame boxer who had encountered challenges and glories similar to those that Gerry experienced. The processes were alike, though the specifics were different. Every life journey is unique, but feelings are universal. De la Hoya had just hit rock bottom and decided to deal with his addictions, he said, and was off to get the treatment he needed.

I suppressed the need to call my new famous friend to discuss the similarities and to get his take on the situation—after all, Gerry was a busy person, and I didn't want to burden him with too many communications. However, I added the topic to the growing list to discuss over coffee or dinner. Doing so instigated an anxious energy inside me, one that blatantly alerted me to the need for helping the public understand the adversities of substance abuse, the biological dynamics fueling their manifestation, and the amazing courage it takes to face it.

Sure, avoidance and manipulation tactics—including lying and stealing—make it challenging to have compassion for the addict, but I was feeling an ardent desire to help others balance contradictory but equally valuable dynamics. These include harboring compassion for the suffering addict's symptoms while holding them accountable for their recovery efforts and chosen actions, valuing explanations for harmful actions (to self and others) but distancing oneself from excusing them, and somehow comprehending that the shame alcoholics have for their addiction is, quite paradoxically, actually a primary determinant for their unwanted drinking episodes. At the end of the day, brains produce thoughts, feelings, and behaviors—compromised brains produce compromised thoughts, feelings, and behaviors and are symptoms of ailments, not poor character.

So complicated is the awful, persistently changing puzzle that is addiction, and I was feeling a heightened sense of urgency to offer some help explaining it.

Shaking my head, I returned focus to the soothing matzo ball soup in front of me. Still, I began to admire Gerry's journey even more after learning of de la Hoya's troubles. The former heavyweight contender had been sober for more than a quarter century, an absolutely remarkable achievement considering the extent of his traumas and power of his addictions. What makes him able to overcome his demons, to live fully and embrace life's blessings and challenges with equal levels of acceptance and determination? How can we communicate these inspiring processes in a way to connect with readers and potentially help them find their own paths to sobriety, health, and meaning?

Taking a deep breath, I trusted that the answers would present themselves one manageable day at a time.

Part Six

The Championship Quest

Boxers need to hit and not get hit. You can hit the hardest, but if you keep taking punches, your heart gets taken. You have to learn to miss the punches, then punch, and you become a balanced fighter. It took me a long time to really learn that, in the ring and outside of it. I had the greatest trainer who taught me what I needed to know, but with all the outside stuff, I couldn't really see everything that he wanted to teach me. But now, as a man, those lessons are with me in everyday life. It took me time to instill it in me because of the stuff that was going on, but I have it now, and I try to give it to others, especially the kids that I work with today.—Gerry Cooney

16

FIGHT NIGHT

The eyes of the sports world focused intensely on a boxing ring in Las Vegas, Nevada.

The brutally hot, sweltering evening—103 degrees before the fight, according to some estimates—was unusual even by desert standards. It was the hottest day of the year in Las Vegas. For the elite fighters taking center stage under the overwhelming power of the national spotlight, the heat was even more profound. The elevated temperatures did not prevent 29,314 fans from attending the event live, nor could they dissuade the Hollywood elite from attending the monumental event. Michael Landon, Farrah Fawcett, Ryan O'Neal, and Jack Nicholson were among the notables sitting ringside, ensuring their names and faces would be reported by the untold number of media personnel. Sports royalty, such as Joe DiMaggio and Wayne Gretzky, also attended. There were an estimated seventy-eight sellouts in closed-circuit locations in the tristate area alone—one location, New Jersey's Meadowlands racetrack, generated almost fifty-three thousand fight fans.

President Ronald Reagan had a direct phone line installed in Gerry's Caesar Palace's dressing room so that he could congratulate the new champion, should Gerry win. No such line was installed in the reigning champion's dressing room. This reality could be viewed as another slight against Holmes or perhaps the consequence of his combative personality and difficulty connecting to the masses in the manner achieved by the likes of "Sugar" Ray Leonard, Muhammed Ali, and his rival for the evening, Gerry.

Fans stood throughout the Caesars Palace parking lot, anxious for the warriors to enter the ring. Dramatics unfolded backstage as the champ insisted upon making his entrance second. This act of gamesmanship also was played before Holmes's challenge of Norton for the World Boxing Council (WBC) title. When the spotlight shines so brightly and the pressure so directly, it is only natural to employ any and all possible psychological edges. With Gerry being so young and relatively inexperienced—the fighter had fought only sixty-four complete professional rounds and parts of twenty-two others—Holmes no doubt wanted to extend the prefight moments. The extra time would, perhaps, encourage his thoughtful foe to feed into the natural anxieties associated with entering his first championship stage as a professional.

Gerry and his entourage were the first to the ring. The giant heavyweight was clad in a gray and white robe, his face mostly hidden by its huge hood, as he strode down what seemed to be a hundred miles to the combat zone. Upon walking up the four steps to the boxing ring, perhaps the most courageous act in modern sports, Gerry entered the ring and danced around its confines, getting a feel for the environment. The crowd responded favorably.

He really wanted to fight right away.

The anticipation was rising to a new height as the *Rocky* theme revved up fans of the fighter who had shared a *Time* magazine cover with Sylvester Stallone. Holmes entered next. It is customary for the champion to approach the ring last—a sign of respect for his status as titleholder. The primed, thirty-two-year-old pugilist jogged to the ring, maintaining his sweat and looseness—a necessity, given his opponent's proven ability to hurt and finish opponents in the early rounds—while a member of his team held the WBC belt high. The act was akin to a soldier holding his country's flag on the battlegrounds. "Ain't No Stopping Us Now," the 1979 disco hit from R&B duo McFadden & Whitehead, had replaced the *Rocky* theme on the speakers. The champion entered the ring, danced around, and shadowboxed, looking sharp and poised. Don King, clad in stylish white and black garb, stood prominently in the ring and clapped.

It was almost time for the big fight.

* * *

Standing in the ring surrounded by his team, the focus of millions of fans around the world, twenty-five-year-old Gerry Cooney was, nevertheless, alone. The dozen or so people in—or surrounding—the battleground may as well have been miles away. The young contender, less than ten years after his inaugural steps into the boxing world, stood opposing the undefeated heavyweight champion of the world—one whose professionalism, skill sets, and accomplishments would one day earn him status as an all-time-great heavyweight boxer.

Holmes stood imposingly in his corner, his face serious but softer than the intense scowl he employed prior to his confrontation with Norton. His sleek white and red robe covered an exceptionally prepared body that, according to Holmes's estranged former trainer, Rich Giachetti, was at his perfect fighting weight of 212.5 pounds. In the unusual position of being three inches shorter than his opponent—it would be the first time that the champion would be looking up to a foe—Holmes possessed the same eighty-one-inch reach as Gerry.

Of great controversy was the order of ring introductions. Holmes, the champion, was announced first. Understandably, this proved abhorrent to boxing purists and historians, as champions are traditionally presented last. This custom is viewed as an act of respect. Holmes had been introduced appropriately against the most decorated heavyweight in history, Muhammad Ali, but not against a young fighter in his first championship bout? Holmes's struggle for respect and adulation was likely never more evident than in that moment.

However, the patient eyes of history are objective and often quell excessive emotions to more rational levels. Although defying ring tradition, the order of introduction was nevertheless not unprecedented. Ironically, Holmes himself was introduced last while challenging for the heavyweight championship. Almost four years before to the day, Holmes had contended for future Hall of Famer Ken Norton's WBC world title. Although the combatants engaged in a legendary battle, few recall the unconventional order of introduction. In fact, sports announcer Howard Cosell did not bother to mention it during the broadcast. Years later, HBO's *Legendary Nights* documentary series featured the Holmes-Cooney clash but failed to mention that Holmes received the same preferential treatment when he challenged champion Ken Norton.

As the fighters strode to the ring's center, the crowd's indescribable energy could be felt by live and television viewers alike. The tension was palpable, creating the exceedingly rare buzz that occurs only when a magnificent moment commands unadulterated attention from a massive collection of people. For the moment, the world ceased to move for a great majority of sports fans. Worries, hopes, plans, and responsibilities were pushed aside so that the championship event could be most fully embraced. Immersed in the moment, fans were simultaneously anticipating a historic bout.

The contentious and often ugly fight promotions encouraged fans to wonder how the fighters would act during their first true face-off. What transpired was a portent of the healing, uniting dynamics that would signify their postfight friendship. Holmes stared serenely at Gerry's forehead, a contrast to the baleful glare he employed prior to his conquest of Norton. At six-feet, three-inches tall, Holmes normally looked down at his foes, but Gerry's six-foot, six-inch stature required the champ to gaze upward. Gerry, as was his way, lowered his head and stared at his rival's midsection. At the referee's prompt to touch gloves, Holmes offered unexpected words: "Let's have a good fight."

The words symbolized the transition from the hysteria of the fight promoters' greed-fueled, race-focused efforts to appeal to the worst aspects of America's character to the honorable, fundamental partnership of two human beings preparing to reveal their souls in front of the world through artful combat. The bond that would solidify the two men likely began at that moment. A level of respect known by only an elite few—competitors with the courage to put themselves in harm's way—was fostered. The moment reflected the best of the two fighters and symbolized the human capacity to transcend even the most challenging of realities, racial strife. A heartbeat or two after Holmes's classy words were communicated, Gerry spun back to his corner. He squatted briefly as he rested his long arms on the ropes. Springing upright, Gerry calmly made the sign of the cross before acknowledging his cornermen's supportive words.

The fans cheered wildly as they awaited the bout's commencement.

* * *

Serenely punching his fists together, Gerry turned to face his opponent. He rocked forward and backward, his left leg leading his right, arms swinging in unison. Holmes also actively waited in his corner, bouncing fluidly on the ring's opposite side. The bell chimed loudly, encouraging the combatants to wage war. The champion quickly met his challenger, trading jabs with the bigger man. Holmes circled expertly around his massive rival, who was relatively stationary in the fight's inaugural moments. "Sugar" Ray Leonard, who—along with Barry Tomkins—served as the fight's commentators, offered his expert analysis on the fighters' mental states. Well acquainted with the championship stage, Leonard noted that both fighters appeared "a little tight." Even so, the warriors appeared focused—if somewhat deliberate—in the opening moments.

Holmes's legendary jab began snapping freely, crisply targeting Gerry's face and body. Though not as powerful as Gerry's jab, Holmes's version stunned opponents and connected meaningfully—and seemingly at will. Feinting, circling, and jabbing, Holmes quickly moved within and outside of Gerry's range. He appeared sleek, fast, and strong. The primed technician was masterfully introducing his young challenger to the championship stage. Gerry, experiencing his first moments against a primed all-time-great talent, was providing Holmes with a great deal of respect.

Holmes transcended any negative emotions that may have existed and concentrated on executing his game plan. Watching his advanced skills displayed with focus and precision, one hardly would recognize the emotional, resentful man who created scenes and voiced unadulterated anger toward Gerry, his supporters, and those who refused to respect Holmes's accomplishments. It was clear, early on, that the future Hall of Famer had harnessed all of his potential for his career's most important contest.

It wasn't long before Gerry began adapting to the championship stage. Lacking the champion's speed and accuracy, Gerry featured blunt, heavy power. He methodically stalked his steadily moving target, absorbing multiple jabs while doing so. Gerry also caught some fire. His nose, which had a cut on its bridge from a training camp mishap, became red before the bout's second minute passed.

Gerry's first solid left to the body seemed to catch the champion's attention. The resourceful Holmes resumed his circling of Gerry, albeit with a noticeable decrease in speed and energy. His foe's movement more predictable, Gerry began firing his arsenal of punches, trying to locate his optimal range. Both warriors threw a greater number of punches as the seconds evaporated. Holmes's boxing intelligence and legendary jab prevented his larger foe from imposing his will or sustaining an attack. The Holmes jab was a perfect weapon. Offensively, it created damage and set up meaningful combinations. Defensively, it could halt steadied attacks by snapping foes' heads back, throwing them off balance.

Still, Gerry kept moving forward—into and through adversity.

Gerry was acutely aware of the bout's fifteen-round length. He kept telling himself to move slowly so as to avoid burning himself out. Few feelings are as difficult as those residing in a tired athlete's heart when ample time is left on the clock. Experiencing it with a primed legend like Holmes would be a horrific experience. Nevertheless, Gerry kept punching purposefully and with bad intentions. Eventually, Gerry's double jabs connected more often. They were slower than the ultraquick jabs of his counterpart, but the heavy "thuds" they produced indicated blunt power.

The fighters' respect for one another was solidified before the first round's termination.

* * *

When the bell signified round one's end, both fighters immediately dropped their arms and dutifully returned to their corners. As Gerry rested on his stool, his head trainer quickly began offering insights and directions. The boxing wizard was fiery and blunt with his number-one contender. Valle advised that "the single jab is no good" and encouraged Gerry to "throw double—not single—jabs"; to "move your head, so he can miss with that jab"; and to "relax." Valle emphasized his instructions and motivation techniques with expletives. Trying to break down the enormous task of defeating the great Holmes into manageable pieces, Valle repeated that "this guy's shit" to the young giant. He also advised Gerry to maintain his composure. "When he goes wild, don't go wild with him! Just take your goddamn time!"

Valle wanted Gerry to center entirely on his game plan, not to exchange with the champ on grounds favorable to Holmes. Professional fighters utilize their emotions, but their greatest attributes can be their disciplined minds. This includes having realistic faith in their own abilities. Valle, no doubt, sensed Gerry's periodic inclination to devalue his self-worth, both as a fighter and personally, and wanted to assert his own belief in Gerry.

Throughout Valle's impassioned motivational and instructional talk, Gerry nodded as he rested on his stool. His eyes wandered, looking toward his foe, around the ring, and at his trainer. Rappaport, too, encouraged Gerry to be calm as the fighters' reprieve came to an end. Like many members of a boxer's management team, Rappaport found it difficult to restrain himself from offering advice, even though his voice conflicted with parts of Valle's speech. When one's fortunes are invested in another person, it is difficult to refrain from giving advice. However, a fighter's team needs to have one voice in the corner. The boxer must come to terms with managing his emotions, calming—and sometimes battling—

his thought cycles, while capturing the wisdom of his trainer's instructions. Having two or more people speaking at once can ensure that the resting warrior receives no message.

* * *

The bell chimed, signaling the second round's commencement. As before, the fighters eagerly met at ring's center, albeit with more restraint. Gerry and Holmes resumed and maintained a steady offensive pace, mixing feints with jabs, power punches, and combinations. Gerry, however, struggled with accuracy. Although intensely focused, Gerry was in the midst of shaking off pounds of ring rust. The thirteen-month layoff since the Norton fight had been Gerry's longest. In contrast, the champion was remarkably accurate, given the respect he was paying his powerful challenger. Holmes slipped in and out of danger zones as he delivered his blows with unusual precision.

Gerry remained methodically tenacious. His timing was compromised, leading him to realize relatively limited offensive success, but Gerry's body language and facial expression exhibited almost serene focus. To ancient Eastern warriors, such a state is most esteemed. It permits one to respond to environmental demands without being burdened by concern for outcomes—even the most severe of consequences. By letting go, warriors actualize their fighting abilities to maximize body wisdom (bred from years of training), emotional control, and psychological strength. The same mentality can help one actualize potential in other arenas of life, including work output, personal relationships, or weekend sports. On this night, Gerry was periodically entering the "zone" when it mattered most, even while acclimating to fight conditions.

The challenger was striving to find opportunities to change Holmes's facial expression, trying to figure out his way in to land that big punch. Fighting is a science and an art. Gerry was figuring out what Holmes was offering. It was a chess match. Valle had given Gerry a great game plan, and he was doing what he could to employ it in the moment, which is much easier said than done, since actual fight conditions are always fluid.

Gerry's youthful exuberance and faith in his power led him to seek landing his big punch. One can understand this mentality. Gerry was used to hurting foes far more readily than most boxers. One punch could literally change the course of any fight. Most other fighters required an accumulation of punches or one extremely well-placed and well-timed blow to enjoy similar success. Gerry had an expansive window to inflict bout-changing punches. One-punch knockout power was intoxicating, and a youthful fighter with the opportunity to realize his dream was certainly prone to overemphasize his unusual gift. Almost each time he employed his arsenal, however, Gerry's ring rust and the superior skill displayed by the champ prevented the challenger from meaningfully connecting with and damaging his foe.

Holmes's advanced ring intelligence and elevated levels of concentration kept him largely in command of the round. Avoiding Gerry's bombs and rolling with those that partially connected with their target, Holmes kept pushing his challenger's head back with crisp jabs. Although there was a sense that Gerry was on the verge of landing a phenomenal blow, one that would punish the undefeated champion enough to devastate him, Holmes's actions kept Gerry's skills at bay. Yet the monstrous challenger kept pursuing.

Like many warriors who found success with their punching power— particularly those who have never been seriously stunned in the ring— Gerry was willing to absorb punishment in order to find Holmes. The reward was worth the relatively temporary angst. Brushing aside the frustration and mounting pain, Gerry kept after his opponent with the understanding that when he found Holmes, the outcome would be serious damage.

Then, it happened.

* * *

With roughly forty seconds remaining in the bout's second stanza, Holmes jabbed to Gerry's body and then threw a punishing right to the contender's chin. The punch was almost too quick to view in real-time action. Holmes's whole body seemed invested in the blow, which instantly wobbled Gerry's knees. The giant heavyweight was in serious trouble for the first time in his career—a stunning sight never before witnessed by his legions of fans.

Effective punches whip the head around, particularly in a rotational way. Neurons are then significantly stressed. To protect itself, the brain temporarily "shuts down." Many boxers believe that building shoulder and neck muscles can minimize head movement in response to powerful punches, but anticipation is key to diminishing a blow's impact. The punches that fighters don't see cause the most damage. This one from Holmes capitalized on surprise.

Having never been seriously hurt before, Gerry was enduring his first crisis—and the first opportunity to truly explore his resolve in the ring. In combat sports, encountering, enduring, and fighting through adversity is the essential intangible of a warrior's constitution. This attribute differentiates the all-time-great heavyweight champions from their near-all-time-great counterparts. Sometimes, the extent of a dominant fighter's courage is never truly tested until he is past his prime and his skills diminish enough for opponents to present true challenges. Other times, it occurs just prior to one's prime, when encountering a rival who provides skill sets that were never before encountered. Whatever the case, one's championship heart is never understood without facing true adversity.

Gerry was certainly encountering true adversity.

* * *

Recovering persons, particularly those who experience activating events as a result of past traumas, often encounter adversity. Sometimes, it occurs on a daily—almost constant—basis. Relapses, metaphorically similar to boxing's knockdowns, can occur. Life's punches can be as precise and expertly placed as the one that hurt Gerry. Others threaten to knock one completely unconscious, even if he or she sees it coming. Regardless of the level of the punch's consequence, how one responds to setbacks—both during and in the wake of its occurrence—reveals the true value of his or her championship heart.

The harsh smacking sound of Holmes's right hand was seemingly still resonating as Gerry strove to remain upright. Gerry was operating on his instincts. Bred from genetics and honed through years of absorbing emotional and physical abuse, Gerry's reaction was to struggle, fight, and persevere—the mind-set of a warrior—one with benefits that both include and transcend the ring's boundaries. Upright for a brief moment, Gerry's rubbery legs struggled to balance his massive frame. His boxing intellect advised him to retreat, temporarily, outside his foe's range to recover. Stumbling, his legs giving way and unable to properly understand his brain's instructions, Gerry briefly strode away from Holmes before collapsing to his knees. Almost sliding on the canvas, Gerry's momentum led him to the ropes.

Although only seconds, the knockdown appeared to last longer in Gerry's reality. Evolutionarily speaking, times of crisis force the mind to become more attuned to the moment, with senses primed to and selective of what information reaches conscious consideration. If normal life is viewed like a movie, with thousands of still images running so seamlessly that the unfolding dramas seem continuous, times of crisis slow information intake by eliminating every other still image. This allows for more attention to detail and a manageable view of the unfolding life process, which can be the difference between effective survival reactions and sudden death. Boxing, unlike other sports, features authentic threats to one's health—and sometimes even to one's life.

Entering this very rare life state, inner dialogue commenced beyond Gerry's awareness. His father's voice, or the doubts that unquestionably accepted his emotional abuse, asked Gerry what he was doing on this stage, fighting for the heavyweight championship. He didn't belong there; he was nothing, no good, and would never amount to anything. The war between his need to prove his father right and his ardent desire to prove him wrong resumed with great vigor.

What in the hell am I doing here?

And, as the lifelong internal war commenced, Gerry simply acted. He stood, facing the external world with resolve and courage, intent on fighting even harder.

* * *

The great "Sugar" Ray Leonard, caught in the moment and trusting his phenomenal boxing wisdom and instincts, quickly predicted that Holmes would stop Gerry before the round's end. The future Hall of Famer's words were expressed with a certainty that can only be developed through advanced experience. Gerry simply persevered through adversity and resumed his work. His legs appeared unsteady, but his heart and mind displayed poise, determination, and focus. Seemingly unaffected emotionally or psychologically from his first taste of true adversity, the giant contender methodically stalked forward, throwing jabs, hooks, and two-punch combinations.

He fought back and fought harder.

* * *

Leonard's perceptions were well justified. Younger, dominant fighters who are confronted with true adversity for the first time often falter. There are many dynamics that have nothing to do with one's courage. For example, being stunned and unable to fully control one's body is a confusing and surreal experience; working through this while avoiding physical attacks designed to inflict more severe damage is an incredible task.

Many fighters understandably do not survive. Those who survive learn how to maintain stability amid the storms of adversity long enough to recover physically and psychologically.

Holmes apparently disagreed with Leonard's assessment that Gerry was in position to be finished. The champion consistently had displayed tenaciousness and controlled fury whenever he was severely hurt in previous fights. Coming too close to a compromised Gerry, whose power remained and likely would be instinctively and aggressively unleashed in response to continued pursuit, would be to invite an upset knockout loss.

Holmes was a wise, patient fighter who accentuated his strengths and compensated for his few shortcomings. He was not a power puncher, but he was a tactician whose accumulated damage set up adversaries for late-round knockouts or one-sided decision losses. Additionally, Gerry had never fought beyond eight rounds, and logic dictated that the challenger would exhaust himself long before the scheduled fifteen rounds. Holmes decided to maintain his conservative but action-oriented game plan and not allow himself to be caught by Gerry's powerful offense.

Holmes continued with his masterful strategy of pumping out his brilliant jab to Gerry's face and large torso, moving inside and quickly outside of Gerry's range and sidestepping blows or rolling with them. An expert craftsman, Holmes's punches were efficient and effective, almost all of them meaningful. Despite the majesty of his offense and of hurting Gerry only moments before, Holmes respected his foe's enormous punching power enough to emphasize his defense.

As both Gerry and Holmes would observe later, the challenger responded to severe adversity by fighting his heart out. The champion was in position to sense the warrior's heart inside of Gerry more acutely than any observer possibly could, even an expert like the all-time-great Leonard. In the ring, as in life, Gerry fought and persevered.

* * *

The bell rang, beginning a much-needed reprieve for the young warrior. Before heading back to their respective corners, the fighters briefly stared at one another. There was no evidence of malice or of any particular emotion. Champion and challenger—the two greatest heavyweight talents on the planet—were simply sending nonverbal confirmations of respect.

Walking steadily toward his corner, Gerry rested on the large blue stool a cornerman provided. Valle rushed into the ring, eager to talk with his charge.

While Valle employed words meant to both inspire and guide Gerry, Rappaport attempted to motivate the challenger by declaring, "It's the changing of the guard. America needs you!" To some, this phrase was saturated with the same detrimental racial dynamics that had plagued the event for months. Rappaport denied that his comment was racist. Instead, he was simply consumed by the energy and emotion of the moment and hoping to find the right combination of words to inspire Gerry. At various points during the fight, Rappaport reportedly also implored Gerry to win for children suffering from leukemia or for his father—anything to motivate his fighter.

Some boxing historians, as well as those for other disciplines, would consider Rappaport's motivational plea regarding America needing Gerry as similar to those expressed in the early twentieth century. Jack Johnson had emerged as the first African American heavyweight champion of the world in 1908. His skills were incomparable in the ring, and his behaviors outside of it infuriated the dominant white culture. With no one seemingly capable of stopping the "Galveston Giant," the public and media encouraged the undefeated Jim Jeffries to emerge from his six-year retirement and defeat the boisterous Johnson.

Jeffries, who had never lost his world heavyweight title in the ring, heard messages of "America needs you!" "America is depending on you!" and "The honor of the white race is at stake." The racial motivations behind these words were decidedly clear—the most prestigious title in sports "needed" to be returned to the correct race. For white America, only the indestructible Jeffries could wrest the championship from the despised Johnson. The bout finally happened in 1910 and ended with a beaten Jeffries succumbing to Johnson's brilliance via technical knockout in fifteen.

As Rappaport was injecting himself into the event with his words, Gerry was quickly recovering from his first knockdown—and preparing to fight on.

17

I BELONG HERE

As round three commenced, fight fans were on the edges of their seats wondering how the giant challenger would respond to adversity. Holmes, predictably, resumed his patient, methodical approach, maintaining a solid offense that helped prevent Gerry from cornering him. The champion feinted and traded jabs with his challenger and absorbed a good body blow. Gerry maintained his composure as he consistently missed blows and absorbed sharp counters from the champ. He persistently quested to change Holmes's expression with his fists. His connect rate was rising to such a degree that combinations were launched and found their target.

Although Holmes was clearly more skilled and experienced, Gerry was physically stronger and commanded a more dominating presence. Both possessed powerful wills and even stronger hearts. Holmes's punches were fast and sharp, whereas Gerry's took longer to deliver. This made it easier for Holmes to elude or minimize the effect of many of Gerry's punches, but when they landed, damage was produced.

As the round drew to a close, the challenger's nose appeared red. Gerry took another solid right from the champion and responded by landing heavy jabs. Right before the bell, Gerry missed with a vicious left uppercut, momentum carrying his long arms well above Holmes's head. The round then ended with Holmes pointedly following Gerry with his eyes. Gerry, who characteristically put his head down as he began toward his corner, didn't seem to notice.

* * *

Between rounds, the fighters' respective trainers appeared to emit a strong sense of urgency. In the champion's corner, the guiding voice appeared to be the legendary Eddie Futch, who advised his fighter to keep moving, double up on the jab, and then look for the right. Eighty-three-year-old Ray Arcel, another legendary boxing trainer, tended to the champion's body as Futch issued his instructions.

Valle, trying to infuse his wisdom and energy into his fighter, implored Gerry to attack the body. "Listen, Gerry—you have to . . . you have to get that funny bone. You gotta get the funny bone. Get the funny bone!" Valle was exhorting his charge to connect with the soft side of Holmes's body. For the converted southpaw Gerry, that meant Holmes's right side. The instruction was emphasized three times to underscore the importance of damaging Holmes's body to not only inflict pain, but to induce fatigue, slow Holmes's offense, and to take some steam out of the champion's punches. The sweltering night made endurance an even greater factor than usual, and Valle wanted to take advantage of it. Plus, by going to the body with the profound power of Gerry's now-legendary left hook, it was possible that the challenger could find Holmes's floating rib area, where the liver is housed. A near-perfect connection to the liver could end any fighter's evening, even one as great as Holmes.

The strategy was ingrained in Gerry's head: punch through the body (not at it), damage it enough to motivate his foe to lower his hands, and connect to the exposed head. Many boxers are not patient enough for the cumulative effects of body punching to take effect. Gerry, too, with his repeated experiences of knockout wins and youthful aggression was still prone to headhunting at times. Still, he heard Valle's words and intellectually knew it was the best way to fight. Before the intermission ended, Valle offered technical advice about how to better land with his right hand to Holmes's chin.

* * *

The fourth round featured Gerry connecting more with his adversary. The ring rust from the prolonged inactivity was increasingly negated. His focus peaked. Gerry's life had direct purpose in these moments of combat, which generated a sense of comfort that paradoxically existed along with the constant threat of harm. In the ring, the danger was clear—and Gerry could protect himself and directly face it. No one was helping him, but the rage that generated from a childhood of stifling his voice out of fear of sharp reprisal could now be outwardly channeled and expressed.

Gerry controlled his destiny; he was competing at the highest levels and testing his skills with a great champion.

The crafty Holmes was taking some hits, but the veteran minimized damage when possible. Three well-placed shots hurt Holmes at best and dazed him at a minimum. His recuperative skills and poker face made it difficult to tell how stunned he was, but he remained relatively stationary and flat-footed. Holmes's boxing intelligence, likely among the highest of his all-time-great counterparts, guided him away from the ropes. Failure to do so could have resulted in being pinned against them and suffering an overwhelming onslaught from his gigantic rival.

A powerful blow to the body punctuated the round for Gerry. Holmes was slow going to his corner. His advanced preparations didn't lead him to anticipate Gerry's punching power and skills. The champ knew—really *knew*—that he was in a legitimate fight. The final blow had hurt him badly enough to cherish the sound of the bell.

* * *

On his stool, Gerry listened to Valle's instructions to move his head and to double up on his jab. The message "If you jab once, you have to jab twice" was instilled in Gerry. During battle, simple messages that are repeated time and again are the ones most likely to be understood and employed. Keeping it simple was vital. As always, Valle encouraged his charge to keep his hands up at all times. The fundamentals were forever stressed by the boxing sage, as they were with every elite trainer. They are never more needed than in times of great challenge.

His success in round four instilled confidence in Gerry. Holmes, an increasingly stationary target as compared to the fight's first few rounds, was catching more blows in round five. Still, Gerry was unable to land enough to force Holmes into the serious troublesome moment that would permit Gerry's finishing, swarming attack. Gerry's heavy jab was more consistently finding its target, however, and seemed to be the battering ram used to maintain his aggressor status.

Holmes's legs began to regain some steam as he danced out of striking range of Gerry's vicious left hooks. A right hand that backed Gerry up was followed by another one, prompting him to verbalize a taunt or two. A Holmes combination punctuated a momentum turn, one that prompted Gerry to headhunt more than to attack the body. Several more overhand rights by Holmes proved that the challenger possessed a quality chin, something that some suspected was not the case.

The fifth round came to a close.

* * *

Between rounds, Holmes's corner was alive with shouts of encouragement from his entourage: "You're the boss, Champ! You're the boss!" In the shadow of the great Ali, Holmes's greatness was never fully appreciated. During his reign, such encouragement satisfied that need for recognition, and fueled his determination. He worked extremely hard for his title—Holmes wasn't going to give it away. He would fight with every ounce of skill and energy he possessed.

Valle shouted instructions to his fighter: "Get under! You're standing too straight—get under!" Gerry was getting away from his disciplined mind-set of positioning his body optimally to land thunderous blows to the body, so that he could tire Holmes out, lower his arms, and set him up for a knockout blow. He was pressuring Holmes but needed more of the same. The constant focus on Gerry's stamina, which had never been tested beyond a handful of eight rounders, had affected him. He had trained hard, of that he was confident intellectually, but he hadn't fought fifteen live-action rounds before. There was doubt planted in his mind, and its roots were strong.

Human beings tend to manifest what they focus upon, even if it is what they don't want. Gerry wanted to show everyone that he could go the distance, if need be, but the repeated doubt of the media connected perfectly with Gerry's powerful demons. By focusing on the concern that he couldn't fight a prolonged fight, Gerry was unconsciously sabotaging himself. Self-doubt mounted and diminished his power, which was already compromised due to Gerry's concern that aggression and fury would expend his energy reserves.

Such concerns sometimes shifted to extreme confidence. There was conflict between the sabotaging energies and the confident warrior that fed off the thrill of competition. Gerry subtly tapped into his idol Ali's arsenal of entertainment antics during fights and winked at "Sugar" Ray Leonard. Despite the layoff and the lack of experience fighting into the mid to late rounds, Gerry appeared far fresher than his critics predicted he would by the sixth round.

* * *

Not long into the sixth stanza, Gerry caught Holmes with a right hand that wobbled the champ. This was confirmed when Holmes grinned, generally a universal reaction by hurt fighters who wish to convey that they were not at all affected by the blow. Yet Holmes's recuperative abilities were already established and would eventually be renowned by boxing historians. Later, Gerry landed a right to the body that left Howard Cosell declaring it his best punch of the fight thus far. He then conveyed that Valle had thought that Gerry's right would be the dominating blow of the fight, astounding the champion. The right was followed up by Gerry's first official low blow warning of the night.

Another right to Holmes's cranium was met with resilience. Both fighters, to this point, had been hurt and appeared able to impose their will at times. A combination to the body underscored this perception for the challenger, who then would absorb punishment by the champion. A right to the head wobbled Gerry badly as the round marched toward its final stages. The final twenty-three seconds were an eternity for the giant heavyweight. He remained on his feet, determined not to fall, as he ate blow after blow.

The adversity triggered the fight response imbedded in Gerry. He fought back with heavy-handed punches of his own. Holmes's onslaught was stifled, too, by Gerry's smothering tactics. Keeping his chest close to Holmes's prevented additional blows from landing and permitted him time to recover. He survived despite nearly falling through the ropes. A cut had opened over Gerry's left eye. The round ended with Gerry throwing three powerful left hooks. He survived by fighting back.

Severe adversity was a metaphor for Gerry's life—the emotional tumult being played out on the athletic battleground that was the Holmes-Cooney title bout.

* * *

The final moments of round six had left Gerry's left eye badly swollen. A cut had developed alongside his eyebrow and on the bridge of his nose. This was a significant event for a young fighter. Fighting through cuts is not something that one can adequately prepare for—similar to a person driving through a torrential downpour or a blizzard for the first time.

Gerry's introduction to this degree of adversity was on the championship stage, one that was among the most illuminated in the sport's history. But he embraced the challenge with a championship heart and a fighter's mentality.

* * *

The seventh round featured Gerry attacking the body to slow the champ down, but the offense was not slowing Holmes enough. Gerry had regained much of his early fight energy. He danced, bounced, and boxed. Holmes's brilliant boxing skills were manifesting as he masterfully employed his pugilistic strategy of connecting power blows when the risks were minimized, gliding away from the ropes and toward the ring's center, and snapping his vaunted jab to slow Gerry's forward progress.

Gerry's jabs appeared to be increasingly deflected or deftly avoided. Holmes's reliable offense seemed to contribute mightily to his defense. Gerry's monstrous power punches were not as well timed as earlier in the bout, whereas Holmes's overhand rights almost always found their target. The rhythm associated with the "zone," a near spiritual reality experienced when one's focus is most pronounced, had shifted to engulf Holmes's body, mind, and soul. The champion landed his blows and circled left, away from Gerry's power, weaving expertly in and out of the danger zone to deliver his own offense to his courageous foe.

The challenger was tapping into his reserves of resiliency. These moments of adversity exposed this treasured attribute. Holmes was performing as though immune from the heat generated by the summer temperatures and expectations alike. Gerry was weathering severe storms of tribulation and fighting back with everything he had. He was surviving and fighting, courageously facing adversity head-on, while enjoying satisfying success doing so.

Nevertheless, Holmes seemed to reach new levels of confidence. As was the case throughout the fight, when in close range and not able to dance out of Gerry's power scope, the champion pulled Gerry's head down as he clinched, throwing off Gerry's timing. It was another veteran maneuver by the pugilistic genius that was Holmes, but it also set himself up for some pain—low blows. Gerry landed another one and received a warning from referee Mills Lane.

Announcer "Sugar" Ray Leonard immediately voiced his opinion that the blow was unintentional. Gerry's low blows were not the result of anxious energy or desire to escape the fight. Instead, Gerry's offenses were largely produced by the brilliant boxing mind of the champion. Holmes, as wily as he was intelligent, knew how to redirect his opponent's strengths and interrupt his timing. He also understood that, despite being the challenger, Gerry was likely to receive generous scores from the judges. So with that in mind, Holmes decided to put himself in position to sacrifice some pain—actually, a great deal of physical angst—for a couple of essential points. Gerry was unable to quickly adapt due to his relative inexperience. He was learning lessons on the championship stage that should have been taught with fights against lesser, more manageable opponents.

The cut over Gerry's right eye was also affecting his performance. It was the first time he had ever been taken into such deep waters. But Gerry persevered. That's what fighters do. The round ended without the fireworks of the previous stanza, although Gerry had absorbed more punishment, which accumulated like gentle snowfall after a blizzard.

* * *

Between rounds, Valle's energy was palpable. He said Gerry was standing too straight, essentially providing Holmes a more stationary and expansive target. Valle directed the challenger to move forward, to rough Holmes up, and to get into a crouch. The trainer sought to utilize Gerry's size without making it a hindrance and to impose Gerry's will on Holmes. The champion was getting too comfortable, too far into the zone. There was a sense of urgency to alter the course of the fight, as the young contender could not continue to bravely absorb such punishment and expect to win.

Holmes walked to the center of the ring before round eight's commencement, necessitating a retreat to his corner. Gerry's eye condition seemed to fuel Holmes's insistence to commence fighting. The challenger's eye was swelling closed. The sight must have alerted Holmes to act decisively upon an important and painful lesson learned seven months earlier against the undefeated Renaldo Snipes. He had avoided hitting Snipes in his left eye once it was cut—Holmes's compassion subdued his competitive edge and the tenacity and precision associated with it. Coasting to a relatively easy decision, Holmes suddenly found himself knocked down in the seventh round. His undefeated streak and proposed multimillion-dollar payday against Gerry were at serious risk of evaporating. The experience taught Holmes to be a coldhearted finisher when similar opportunities presented themselves.

Gerry steadied himself and maneuvered to crowd Holmes. The champion maintained his mobility, bouncing and frequently jabbing to keep Gerry off balance. Wounded warriors can fade, becoming overwhelmed, or use the adversity to activate greater levels of reserve and resiliency.

The challenger's determination matched that of his adversary's disciplined aggression. Gerry was throwing double jabs again and absorbing the champion's offense. His eye was swollen shut and his nose maintained a steady bloodstream, but Gerry kept fighting.

* * *

Between rounds, Holmes's corner shouted encouragement while the legendary Ray Arcel, perhaps sensing a shift in momentum to the challenger's side, encouraged Holmes to not let "this bum" steal the fight. Holmes's camp felt that he needed to decisively defeat Gerry in order to secure a decision victory, something that is usually incumbent upon the challenger in championship fights. But Gerry's popularity, enough to secure equal financial footing with the champion, informed Holmes that he likely needed to dominate his foe in order to win a decision.

The reality that a ninth round would be necessary shocked most fight experts. Gerry had never fought past the eighth round and certainly never against anyone nearing Holmes's elite stature. After a well-placed right to Holmes's nose, the champion found himself on the ropes. His expert footwork had kept him away from the ropes for most of the night. The champion tied Gerry up and maneuvered away from him. Gerry's left eye was bleeding heavily by now, swelling and closing. It compromised his ability to see—initiating a healthy sense of urgency to impose his will. Gerry kept marching forward—the bull—with Holmes circling—the matador. The champion scored with an overhand right. It had been a powerfully effective blow throughout the night. Gerry's long arms kept swinging, directed increasingly by intuition as his sight became more and more compromised.

Another right staggered Gerry. The blow triggered an automatic response to fight back. One of Gerry's punches earned a warning by referee Lane against any additional low blows. "Don't do it again," the legendary referee advised, "or it's going to cost you." Moments later, Gerry's punch landed below the waistline. Gerry shook his head slightly as he looked to Lane, who followed through on his warning by deducting a point. Later, an uppercut to Holmes's groin instigated another point deduction. Decades after the fight, the champ would quip in "The Tale of Holmes-Cooney" episode of the HBO documentary series *Legendary Nights*: "Twenty years later, I still feel it." The groans of the surrounding fans reflected Holmes's pain.

As his adversary took time to recover, Gerry stood stoically in the neutral corner. Breathing deeply to secure the oxygen needed to replenish his strained muscles and to calm his racing thoughts, Gerry prepared to reengage. The fighters resumed without much drama, since both knew that the blows were unintentional. Less than a half minute later, the bell rang.

* * *

Between rounds, the sense of urgency was becoming palpable.

"What are you putting in there?" Gerry asked as Valle worked on his wounds.

"Don't worry about it. You're all right," Valle replied. It was such reassurance that Gerry had never received from his own father but was readily applied by his trainer.

"You gotta weave; you gotta weave and come back with a hook to the chin," Valle said, switching to action steps. His fighter needed to focus on action, not concerns regarding his wounds or his overall ability to win the fight, but manageable, black-and-white directions. "Go with the right hand to the kidneys," Valle continued.

The champion's corner was replete with positive affirmations. "Four years it's been yours, Champ," preached an inspired member of Holmes's camp. "Ain't nobody deserves it more than you, Champ—you work every day for it!" The champion's energy seemed to elevate, and his eye swelling appeared to have been contained since the early rounds.

Valle was inches from Gerry's ear, seemingly trying to shut out the young fighter's racing thoughts. Gerry had never been this deep into a fight before. Nor was he ever this hurt and tired. His body, mind, and spirit were being directly challenged in a manner never before endured on a professional level. Gerry wanted to take everything Holmes had and prove that the champion couldn't hurt him.

* * *

The tenth round commenced with both fighters meeting in the ring's center. Holmes's jab seemed sharper and crisper than in previous rounds. He landed a good combo, even while remaining relatively flat-footed. Gerry danced briefly, mildly mocking Holmes as if to say that he was not hurt. The message did not seem to deter the veteran champion. The challenger threw a low blow amid combinations of punches. Gerry put pressure on the all-time great, attempting to impose his massive will. Holmes absorbed the heavy blows, backed into the ropes, then clinched to break Gerry's increasing momentum. There were only so many punches one can readily deflect, absorb, or roll with from such a powerful puncher. Recovery was so important that every second counted. The champ now seemed fatigued and on the verge of being in trouble.

Gerry continued to throw hard punches, wading in with combinations. The offense created openings, however, and Holmes landed rights to slow his foe's momentum. The two warriors traded punches. The challenger kept charging ahead, seemingly refreshed and inspired by a second or third wind. The champion, in contrast, had become a stationary target at many points during the round. He may have slipped into a state of fatigue—or perhaps he was baiting his younger rival to punch himself out. The hot ring was burdening both fighters and, if one or the other did not pace himself, the odds of physically faltering were probable.

Then Holmes unleashed a patented right hand that stunned his giant adversary. More blows followed, but Gerry kept lumbering forward. As in life, Gerry instinctively battled forward, toward the onslaught. Both fighters tapped into their warrior instincts. Big punches were employed and received. The pugilists started fighting at closer quarters. The bell rang as Gerry landed another left, emphatically placing a stamp on perhaps the fight's most competitive and spirited round. Walking back to their respective corners, the fighters passed one another. Holmes appeared to pat Gerry's arm in a token of respect. It likely had been Gerry's most brilliant round of his career, given the legendary skills of his opponent and Gerry's embattled state.

* * *

Between rounds ten and eleven, Valle ordered Gerry to drink some water. He then implored his fighter to tap into his rage. "Now get rough, goddamn it, get rough," Valle shouted. Although gentle by nature, the ferocious tiger forever dwelled in Gerry's core ready to protect, to attack. Valle's words and energy were designed to unleash those chains enough for Gerry to impose his power on Holmes. The contender's eye seemed to have stabilized, perhaps the result of Gerry's catching more of the champion's blows with his gloves in recent rounds.

As the fighters took advantage of their one-minute reprieve from battle, the crowd came alive between rounds. No one had predicted that the fight would endure so long. Both men were displaying their most advanced skills and heart, and the masses fed into that primal and inspiring energy.

* * *

The elevated energy levels employed in the previous round appeared to have slowed the champion down. Round ten's pace had been ferocious at times. Both fighters tapped into their deepest reserves and into the primal energies that are bred from fighting for one's own survival. At such levels of competition, a person's character is exposed or illuminated.

The bell rang and Gerry strode to the ring's center. A slight smirk may have unfolded on his face. There is an immense satisfaction that comes from tapping into the limits of one's available capabilities. It can be an exhilarating feeling. Few events permit such wondrous experiences. Round ten had been one such event for Gerry, and the new stanza witnessed an improvement in his hurt eye, a third point deducted for a low blow, and some sharpening of his timing. The competitive rounds seemed to have shaken off a massive amount of ring rust, allowing Gerry to embrace the severe challenge required for accessing his available potential.

Adversity continued as Holmes's educated blows eventually reopened Gerry's left eye. Gerry had to be mindful of the low blows now that three points were taken away, a significant factor given his prodigious body-punching capabilities. Even slight hesitation can dramatically affect a fighter's effectiveness. While painful, Holmes's maneuvers produced positive outcomes, both on the scorecard and off it. The round ended with both fighters squaring off against each other. Gerry's wounds, while a factor, were well treated, and he remained very much in the fight.

* * *

Later, there were reports that Holmes was given amyl nitrate between rounds eleven and twelve. Known as "poppers" on the streets, the medication is used to relax blood vessels to a degree that blood and oxygen supply to the heart is increased. It is a vasodilator drug that can revive athletes. It is legitimately used to relieve the pain of angina attacks or to revive those who have fainted. According to reports, the champion stated, "get the smeller" after the eleventh round. Amyl nitrate is administered via inhalation. It can have a psychoactive effect and produce euphoria and even act as an aphrodisiac.

Rappaport and Richard Barathy were the main voices pointing to Holmes's potential inappropriate use of the substance. Videotapes were produced to bolster this argument. Holmes vehemently denied the accusation. The timing of the videotapes was also suspicious to some—Gerry was about to fight George Chaplin more than two years later. After the situation unfolded, Rappaport seemed to acknowledge that the accusations were inspired by the public's underwhelming reception of the fight. He also might have hoped that the tapes would inspire talk of a Holmes rematch.

The champion threatened to sue. Postfight urinalysis did not produce positives, but it is unclear if it tested for this drug. If anything illegal was taken, most insiders suggested it was spirit of ammonia or smelling salts, which can infuse energy into fighters. Illegal but akin to jaywalking. The most legitimate source for this theory is sportscasting legend Sal Marchiano, who reported that Ray Arcel admitted Holmes took the substance.

* * *

The challenger appeared to be in good condition as round eleven began, but emotional energies were compromising his psyche. Doubts now manifested with each passing blow that Holmes survived and with each one that he landed on Gerry. The contender had never approached such a late round in his career—it was unexplored terrain. His father's condemnations of Gerry's lack of value became more intense as the fight's theme—Gerry pursuing and hurting the champ but not quite enough to set him down while absorbing more and more punishment himself—suggested that he couldn't win. Between rounds, Valle hydrated his fighter, who was breathing heavily but prepared to resume battle.

18

YOU CAN'T HURT ME, MAN

Both fighters walked steadily to the ring's center. Gerry's outward appearance betrayed the messages that assaulted his heart and mind.

I can't win.

At the same time, his warrior side came alive—but, although it supplied defiance and strength, it also carried a negative thought.

I can't win—but listen; you can't hurt me, man.

Gerry was determined to fall on his sword, to take everything that Holmes had—to go the distance. No one thought that he could.

Holmes came out with yet another "wind." He was back on his toes. The champ landed a right that made Gerry's legs rubbery for a heartbeat. This was Holmes at his best—on his toes with razor-sharp focus and accurate blows. The punches paradoxically both demoralized and generated resolve in Gerry's heart and mind. He was willing to take the shots. All of them. But though he didn't believe he could win, his training and heart implored him to attack. His legendary left hook was obviously his best weapon to pull out the victory. The challenger, perhaps, focused too much on hitting the home run shot: not only were opportunities fleeting, but the extreme fatigue slowed his already compromised reflexes.

But Gerry kept pursuing the champion. He was willing to take every shot, just so he could connect. Punchers like Gerry always have a shot. But Holmes's expert footwork seemed to direct the action. The top and side of Gerry's nose began to bleed. Then Gerry landed three solid blows. But unlike all his previous opponents, they didn't result in severe damage. Fatigue diminished the power behind both warriors' punches. Gerry's heavy jab, in particular, appeared to become somewhat lethargic rather than its thunderous norm. The champion landed two good rights.

The stanza concluded, and Gerry walked back toward the most supportive father figure that he had ever known.

* * *

Sitting on his stool, Gerry inhaled as deeply as his tiring body would permit. His corner immediately began working on his left eye. It had reopened in the latter half of round twelve, a result of the champion's precisely placed right hands. His cut man would have to replicate his magical efforts in order to preserve Gerry's ability to see Holmes's punches.

Gerry, slouching in his corner and breathing heavily, declared that he was fine. "I'm okay." Valle, in a manner not dissimilar to a caring father trying to simultaneously calm anxieties and fuel the fires of hope in his ailing son, agreed. "You're okay," he said, reassuringly. But the boxing wizard, wishing to motivate his charge and communicate the keys to victory, soon returned to direct criticism and direction. "Gerry, you got to rough this guy—you're not roughing him—you're standing too straight; you got to get low."

Meanwhile, the champion's Hall of Fame corner prompted a sense of urgency. Ray Arcel knew the fight was close. "We need these rounds," he said to the seated Holmes. "Take the lead. Don't back away. Take the lead." The veteran trainer of eighteen world champions, who would retire after this bout, had observed that Holmes was at his best when on his toes and active. Moreover, with Gerry's eyesight clearly diminished, a technical knockout was a distinct possibility. But the challenger remained dangerous. A good, sustained offense would minimize that danger and perhaps put him away.

Arcel knew that an astute mind was essential to ensure that the champion avoided complacency. Complacency could permit Gerry to land a meaningful shot. Power is the last attribute to diminish in a fighter. A pugilist with Gerry's titanic strength and finishing ability forever maintains a "puncher's chance" throughout any contest. The champion needed to stay on his toes, literally and figuratively, and keep Gerry at bay with precise jabs and well-timed rights. Gerry's body was failing enough to plant seeds of doubt in his young mind, but he was, nevertheless, committed to charging forward.

* * *

The temperature remained unbearably high in what would be the fight's final round. The uncompromising heat from the television lights and the presence of the cameras, which communicated the fight scenes to thousands at myriad sellout closed-circuit locations, remained even as the weather graciously softened. The tiring fighters may have been too centered upon the task at hand to notice, but their cornermen must have appreciated the decreased temperatures. After all, a boxer's seconds must do all they can to ensure their pugilist is in prime condition to operate effectively. This is not only due to the competitive desire for victory, but for the fighter's physical well-being. Dehydration becomes a legitimate possibility as boxers expend energy and sweat profusely throughout combat, particularly since fluid intake must be artfully managed lest the athletes cramp up. Moreover, if the body is compromised, fighters are more vulnerable to blows, which can remove them from consciousness—or even end their life.

Despite his competitiveness throughout the fight and the encouragement from his revered father figure and trainer, Gerry now was convinced that he couldn't win. Having lost three points, the contender knew a decision win was outside the realm of possibility. Even so, quitting wasn't an option. He was willing to take everything the champion had to offer. It was a compromise between the fury that demanded he charge forward and the belief that he couldn't win. It was also a strategy similar to the one he employed as a boy and early adolescent.

* * *

During those awful childhood and adolescent years when his father possessed overwhelming physical dominance over his body and mind, Gerry had no option but to absorb punishment "like a man." It was his sole form of protest, the only aspect of the chaotic environment over which he had control. Feeling as though he was slipping out of contention as he entered the championship rounds, Gerry's mind brought him back to that defiant mind-set. He decided with concrete certainty to take all that Holmes had to give.

"I wanted to show him that he wasn't better than me," Gerry acknowledges. "I had three points taken away from me. Mills Lane didn't see that Holmes was pulling my head down to protect his body from shots, that the punches were not intentional. I thought I was screwed. Three points was big, and the fight was close. I wasn't experienced enough to have the

right mind-set. So I let him start hitting me. Instead of focusing on landing the big shot, fighting my fight, I wanted to show that he couldn't hurt
me. That was a mistake."

Gerry's youthful mind resorted to his default fighting strategy, one he
hadn't utilized in some time. It had been years since Gerry was in this
situation—being physically beaten, exhausted, in front of a tormentor
who was hitting him almost at will. Once the scared child evolved into
the rebellious adolescent—one still incapable of defeating his tough and
physically mature father—Gerry protested the beatings by taking everything his father had to give him. The pounding might knock him unconscious, but he would take it. He wasn't going to let his antagonizer—his
father in yesteryear and the great Larry Holmes at the moment—enjoy the
satisfaction of seeing him quit.

He just wasn't designed to give up; he was designed to fight on.

* * *

The bell chimed amid the continuous energy generated by the crowd's
anticipation. The fighters were entering the vaunted championship
rounds—that is, rounds thirteen through fifteen. According to various
studies, these rounds were the sport's most dangerous. Dehydration, exhaustion, and even brain damage is most likely to occur in the championship rounds (today's fights are a maximum of twelve rounds). The conditions on this horrifically hot day may have been magnified.

Gerry had never fought beyond the eighth round, much less competed
in the championship rounds. In contrast, at this point of his career,
Holmes had fought ten or more rounds ten times. The champion was
entering the thirteenth round for the third time of his career. Holmes had
earned a dominant fifteen-round decision over Trevor Berbick, a former
Olympian whose career eventually would span nearly twenty-four years
over four different decades. The burgeoning legend had also battled Hall
of Famer Ken Norton in a terrifically competitive split-decision win in
their fifteen-round 1978 contest (ironically, the bout led to legend Roberto Duran agreeing to a cameo in the upcoming *Rocky II* movie as a
sparring partner—Duran and Sylvester Stallone were seated together at
ringside). Holmes's endurance was established already, and he would go
on to fight fifteen rounds four more times in his career before the sport's
sanctioning bodies gradually reduced championship fights to twelve
rounds. Interestingly, Holmes would fight the World Boxing Council's
first twelve-round championship fight (UD 12 vs. Lucien Rodriguez) and

participate in the sport's last fifteen-round title fight, his controversial split decision loss to Michael Spinks in their rematch for the International Boxing Federation championship.

Despite his advance preparation and conditioning, Holmes was somewhat slower to emerge from his stool. The effects of Gerry's consistent body attacks, while hard to appreciate from an observer's point of view, no doubt affected the champion. Nevertheless, Holmes summoned his heart and resolve and began throwing his vaunted jabs. Gerry avoided many of them, catching them with his gloves and moving his head from side to side. He retaliated with a standard left-right combination but missed when the champion glided out of range. The champ was able to see Gerry's punches far sooner than he had earlier in the bout, as fatigue contributed to Gerry telegraphing his fistic intentions.

A solid right by the champion failed to back Gerry up. Not long after eating a left hook, Gerry connected with a right that followed a double jab, just before Holmes escaped Gerry's firing range. However, the blow seemed to lack snap due to fatigue. It was becoming clear that Gerry was on the verge of fading. His punches, though still heavy, seemed to be pushed rather than thrown with his signature bad intentions.

In the meantime, Gerry's damaged left eye compromised his vision. This made him extremely susceptible to the same right hand that had caused the damage. For the first time during the fight, Holmes seemed to consider landing a knockout blow. The champion was no longer circling left to avoid Gerry's power and to control the fight's tempo but was increasingly willing to remain stationary and trade blows with his adversary. Gerry continued to deflect or capture Holmes's punches with his gloves, but too many were finding their mark.

Gerry fought against the stinging pain in his face, physical exhaustion, and the increasing delirium from Holmes's landed blows. He threw a five-punch head-body combination that included a low blow. Gerry looked at Lane, who responded with a meaningful stare, but did not issue a warning. Holmes resumed his work, throwing mostly left jabs and hooks. Another right hand landed against Gerry's skull, but the warrior simply strode forward, seeking to land his next punch.

The champion was now frequently within Gerry's firing range. A primed professional with tremendous experience, Holmes could sense many things that his relatively inexperienced challenger could not—especially in the championship rounds. Holmes knew that Gerry's physical fatigue greatly affected his punching power, which is the last attribute in a warrior's arsenal to diminish. Gerry's punches were not hurting his foe as they had earlier in the fight. This signified that the contender was finally nearing the end. Holmes's strategy was always to "make a guy drunk before you mug him"—that is, to gradually wear him down with sharp, strong blows before seeking the knockout punch. This strategy accentuated the champion's technical brilliance while compensating for his lack of one-punch knockout power.

The contender was eating solid punches but remained upright and continued to march forward. Then, late into the round, Holmes landed a right hand that did not seem to hurt Gerry. A heartbeat or two later, however, the contender's legs began to wobble. With roughly one minute remaining in the round, Holmes began placing his left hand atop Gerry's head. It was a maneuver reminiscent of the great Ali, Holmes's mentor and friend, and the man that many thought Holmes strove to emulate. Gerry twice pawed off the gloves. As Lane stepped in to warn Holmes against continuing the act, the champion landed another right. Though not as severe as many previous blows, it affected the fatigued giant. The challenger stumbled slightly but noticeably as Lane spoke to Holmes.

Despite his increasingly compromised status, Gerry literally kept moving forward but without the disciplined steps that he had employed throughout the battle. He lumbered toward Holmes and managed to land another combination. Gerry's punches, however, no longer contained the explosive power that had felled so many foes. His legs were failing noticeably. He was fighting with every ounce of his soul. Extreme fatigue and the accumulation of punches finally caught up with Gerry, who was out on his feet but intent on fighting until he had nothing left. After one of the few clinches in the fight, Holmes sought to punctuate his fantastic performance.

The champion began landing vicious combinations—lefts, rights, crosses, and jabs. As was the case throughout the fight, Holmes's rights—set up adeptly by his piston-like jabs—were the most consequential. Gerry was determined to absorb Holmes's entire arsenal. Gerry's left eye opened up in response to the onslaught, and he finally began backing up. The valiant contender fell backward into the ropes. His left hand touched the ground at the 2:43 mark, signifying a knockdown. Gerry's right arm hooked the top rope, and he used both arms to immediately pull himself upright. He simply was not going to fall.

To the end, Gerry was determined to stand up to the great champion.

* * *

Lane looked to the knockdown judge to pick up the count. He had looked quickly at Gerry's eyes and determined that the contender could continue. However, Valle was already in the ring, having stopped the bout. Technically, stepping inside the ring before the referee stopped the fight disqualified Gerry, but the records indicate a technical knockout victory for Holmes. The battle-hardened boxing master knew that Gerry had given all he had that night—and that he would continue to give unless someone saved him from his warrior's spirit. Once he arrived at this perspective, Valle wouldn't permit Gerry to be endangered an additional second.

Gerry initially didn't protest the stoppage outwardly as Valle walked forcefully toward him. The sixty-four-year-old trainer actually bumped into a solemn Holmes and brushed aside Lane to reach his beleaguered fighter. He hugged Gerry, whose legs were still rubbery, and guided him across the ring to his stool. "I'm okay," Gerry pleaded.

"That's enough, son," Valle responded. "That's enough."

* * *

The epic battle in the Caesar's Palace parking lot was over. The end came within eight seconds of the round's expiration but the cessation was necessary. Gerry's heart would not allow him to quit, but his body was spent. Sometimes, fighters need to be protected from themselves. The damage inflicted in the ring can become permanent. Courage, at times, places one in unnecessary danger. Although the scorecards signified that he was still very much in the fight, Gerry's deteriorating physical condition precluded reasonable hope for a comeback. His ardent refusal to give up would have led Gerry to suffer unnecessary damage. Gerry's will did not allow him to consider this reality—a fighter, in moments of combat, simply does not have the ability to perceive life in such an objective manner.

Holmes, upon the fight's stoppage, put his head down and walked to his corner. It was arguably the biggest win of his career and clearly on the brightest stage of his career, yet he barely responded outwardly to his cornermen's hugs and shouts of congratulations. His professionalism and respect for his defeated foe prevented the champion from a demonstrative celebration. Don King, perhaps the main instigator of the racial divide that preceded the fight, vigorously hugged Holmes, but the champion seemed intent on connecting with his former antagonist. He walked through his own entourage, security teams, and others to congratulate Gerry on a good fight. There was sincerity and respect in his eyes that was shared with the fallen challenger. These attributes would serve as the foundation for a remarkable friendship, one that easily would transcend the ugly racial divides that preceded the fight and that would endure decades after their competitive battle.

The ring was soon filled to capacity as the ring announcer identified Holmes as the victor. The champion raised his arms but lowered them quickly to leave the ring. This was his moment—another defining victory in what was a Hall of Fame career—but Holmes's behavior was indicative of the classy gentleman, which was always his true character. Holmes, in victory, acted like he'd been there before; the champ did his job and let his actions speak for themselves. He was no longer the aggressive young lion who glared balefully and nearly head-butted Ken Norton during the in-ring referee instructions of their classic bout. Holmes seemed more at peace with the realities of the day and, perhaps, with the expectation that future historians would better understand his greatness.

* * *

Ten minutes after the battle's conclusion, Gerry apologized to his loved ones, fans, and support network. Later, he would apologize even to strangers, despite fighting his heart out—and earning an incredible $10 million. Gerry couldn't express his own sadness for himself, so he focused on his fans and loved ones. He would go to the hospital to have his eye and nose assessed and treated, but his emotional wounds were far deeper. Tony Cooney's abusive words dominated Gerry's mind-set.

You're no good.

You'll never amount to anything.

The thoughts were pounding Gerry's head more acutely and mercilessly than the precision jabs of the all-time-great Holmes. The champion had been predicted to weather an early storm from his younger, more powerful challenger and to register a victory by many ring experts. Gerry didn't yet have the experience and wasn't thought to have the stamina necessary to last deep into the fight. Yet he had done so and given the champ all he could handle.

Gerry's codependent symptoms heightened his sense of responsibility for disappointing others. Many people loved him, believed in him. This reality compounded his irrational shame. The abusive nature of his child-hood and the natural consequences of alcoholism on family members manifested the intensity of the feeling. Other boxing legends, such as Archie Moore and Holmes himself, had been quoted as not feeling the need to apologize for any effort. Further, Holmes would soon say that Gerry was a great fighter with nothing to be ashamed of, even while also joking about the severity of Gerry's low blows. There is a strong bond among fighters, a certain trust and fellowship, especially after having done battle.

Many times, the sunshine of rationality shone, and Gerry was able to feel dejected without shaming himself. He was proud of his efforts, in these wonderful moments, and did not feel the need to explain the loss to anyone—including himself. These were the times when his ideal self was able to push aside feelings of disappointment, anger, and confusion. He would simply go back to the gym, work hard, and prepare for another title run.

Unfortunately, circumstances outside Gerry's control, along with de-pression and chemical dependence symptoms, would prevent his active exploration of his capabilities.

* * *

With his latest victory, Larry Holmes bolstered his record to a perfect 40–0, with twenty-nine knockouts. More impressively, Holmes's perfor-mances were improving on the championship stage. He was now 13–0 in title fights, with eleven knockouts. During this incredible streak, Holmes recorded eight straight knockouts in heavyweight championship bouts, one more than the great Joe Louis and the longest streak in history. Not known for being a traditional knockout fighter, Holmes's sharp punches accumulated to wear down and hurt opponents. His defense against Gerry was among his better performances, given the unique challenges offered by Gerry's long arms and immense power. The champion needed to figure the challenger out, something no one had done to that point. It was the most significant victory since his conquest of Norton.

The victory also enabled Holmes to earn the prestigious *The Ring* magazine Fighter of the Year award in 1982—in fact, it was likely the only reason. His other victory that year—a fifteen-round decision over Tex Cobb—was among the least competitive and least compelling fights in heavyweight championship history, at least as judged by the legendary Howard Cosell's reaction: he abruptly retired from covering the sport.

The champion was solidly in the prime of his illustrious career, and his résumé of dominance ranks among the very best ever to lace professional gloves.

Holmes then went on his historic run of victories that left him one win shy of matching Rocky Marciano's undefeated record, five title defenses short of Joe Louis's standard of twenty-five, and second only to the great Louis in achieving the longest heavyweight title reign in history. Holmes would later call his efforts against Gerry the best performance of his career—quite a declaration considering the multiple landmark victories in his all-time-great career. Holmes's PunchStat numbers indicated superior efficiency throughout the bout. The champion averaged a 50 percent connect rate per round in both jabs (13 of 26) and total punches (20 of 40). (In comparison, heavyweights average 6 of 19.5 jabs—30.6 percent—and 17.3 of 46 total punches—37.5 percent.) This offense empowered Holmes to chop down the oak tree that was his challenger.

The judges' scorecards reflected the bout's competitiveness. Were it not for the three points deducted for low blows, Gerry would have been winning the fight on two of the three scorecards. Two judges, Duane Ford and Dave Moretti, had the fight scored 113–111 in favor of the champion. Jerry Roth, the third judge, scored the bout 115–109 for Holmes. Although most pundits agreed with Roth, none could argue that Gerry did not fight like a legitimate number-one contender.

By demonstrating immense heart and in-ring discipline despite a relative lack of experience and a prolonged period of inactivity, Gerry appeared directly on course to succeeding Holmes as the next great heavyweight champion. His time wasn't now, but it most assuredly would be with a few fights. Gerry had demonstrated power, heart, and determination. Additionally, Gerry, at twenty-five, was still a few years away from what was traditionally considered a fighter's prime years. Now, having fought through adversity and into the championship rounds against the world's top heavyweight, Gerry was in position to maximize his vast potential, to begin a clear course to dominate the division, and eventually to supersede a thirty-two-year-old champion who likely would not be in prime condition the next time they battled.

At least, that was what logic clearly indicated.

THE WRITING PROCESS
Writing at the "Office"

The garden, flourishing in the warm New Jersey summer sun, was as fully developed as it was devoid of life a few months earlier. I noticed that a Buddhist meditation symbol resided only a few feet away from an aged African face. Later, when I pointed out the latter item to the former contender, I was shocked to hear that it was given to Gerry by his father. It was almost too symbolic to believe—on the left rested an artifact bestowed upon him by his abusive father; on the right was a near-universal symbol of peace and tranquility.

"Hey, big guy, how ya doin'?"

I turned to see Gerry emerging from his home's back door. He always greeted me like family. Each interaction naturally fueled me with positivity, regardless of whatever was occurring in my life. "Great, Gerry," I replied honestly. "How you been?"

The giant boxing legend playfully came at me with a combination before replying. "Great, busy, and it's all good. You ready to go?" he asked, pointing inside. Normally this meant sparring, but this time it meant writing.

"Let's do it."

* * *

The spacious home was well kept and inviting. The huge, comfortable sofa served as our office. Surrounding the large-screen TV were mementos from a lifetime of experiences—pictures of Gerry with James Gandolfini, a plaque of the Statue of Liberty for an honor he received along with Arnold Schwarzenegger, pictures of him happily embracing Larry Holmes, another of Gerry with Elton John. . . .

"He cancelled his flight to see the Holmes fight live, you know," Gerry said as I gazed at the picture. "He was performing in New York City, Elton John. Great guy. He invited me to Helmsley Palace for a party, sang, 'When Irish Eyes Are Smiling' as I came in the door. Awesome night."

"That's terrific," was all I could muster. Gerry had so many great stories, far too many for one book. I was always struck by his balance of humbly communicating these experiences while also conveying them with an authentic, almost childlike enthusiasm.

"We have to make sure that we get some guys in the book, guys who were important for my development."

Wary of the page limits, I wondered how we could get all the meaningful people who Gerry wanted to honor in the book. "Well, who are you thinking about?"

"You know, guys like Hilton Cohen. He was a great friend—*is* a great friend. I brought him to the gym. We got better together, went to the Gloves together. I remember when I knocked out Ron Lyle. Our eyes met after the fight—it made my night, you know what I mean? We came from similar backgrounds; he cared about me, helped me train. He's a very important person in my life. Been with me from the amateurs right through the best times in my career."

I nodded as I typed furiously to capture all the information. The emotion of pure appreciation and caring radiated from the former contender.

"Another guy, Georgie Munch, he's got to be in there. He was a big part of my training, starting with the Norton fight. Weight training, cable training—which was new to boxing and to me. I love that guy. He put me in position to win those big fights. He straightened me out the best anyone could. Trained with me every day. One of the few guys I could trust."

"Georgie's an inspirational story," Gerry continued. "He was really sick for a while, but he recovered. Always there with me. Really took me to another level of training, both he and Hilton. Some of the best people in my life—ever. They were in my corner, saw the world together, did a lot of stuff. I couldn't have done a lot of stuff without those guys."

"I got it, Gerry," I said as I struggled to keep up with his stories. Each was important to him, and I wanted desperately to capture all of the information. The book, after all, was a celebration of my friend's life, and I wanted to help author a great book.

A few moments later, we talked about the fighting process. "Boxing saved my life, fed me, kept me alive. It was a chess match in there. I loved changing the guy's expression, seeing the hope going out of his eyes—there was a tunnel vision in there—setting up a punch, finding an opening, landing a shot, and feeling the 'ping' of everything working together like it should."

I've heard athletes describing the "zone" many times, but Gerry articulated what it meant to him in unique ways. Unlike many fighters, inflicting damage in itself wasn't a thrill for Gerry; it was the success of carrying out his tasks that was most compelling to him. Boxing was the vehicle to feeling accomplished. The processes of boxing allowed Gerry to find mastery in himself. It was a magical outlet that so few can find.

The discussion continued as so many had before, and since each moment was a thrill, it was like being privy to a reservoir of information on boxing history through the mind of an elite athlete. Not for the first time, I wondered at how incredibly fortunate I was to not only work with this great person, but also to have found such an inspiring friend.

Part Seven

Encountering Severe Adversity

Boxers need to hit and not get hit. You can hit the hardest, but if you keep taking punches, your heart gets taken. You have to learn to miss the punches then punch, and you become a balanced fighter. It took me a long time to really learn that, in the ring and outside of it. I had the greatest trainer who taught me what I needed to know, but with all the outside stuff, I couldn't really see everything that he wanted to teach me. But now, as a man, those lessons are with me in everyday life. It took time to instill it in me because of the stuff that was going on, but I have it now, and I try to give it to others, especially the kids that I work with today.—Gerry Cooney

19

BREAKING APART

"I wish I would have won. Been away from home a long time. I think the people were great. I wanted to win for them as much as I wanted to win for me. I feel sorry for all the people who really wanted me to win. I just want to say I'm very sorry."

These words were repeated, with slight variations, scores of times in the weeks after the big fight. Each time they were uttered, Gerry meant them with his entire soul. All the while, a new conflict emerged on the battlefield that was Gerry's heart and mind. Gerry, the elite athlete, wanted to dismiss the negative aspects of his performance that were outside his control, to learn from his mistakes and then let go, and to get back to training. The other part, invested in his father's hurtful messages, wanted to penalize himself for letting down those who seemed disappointed by his loss. He didn't know how to feel, so he mostly focused on how others were impacted.

Gerry was also sick and tired of his codependency roles—he was always in the middle of family conflicts, issues between his managers—everything was coming to the surface in the fight's aftermath. He was breaking apart inside. With limited coping mechanisms, Gerry resorted to the bottle for solace. It was easy enough—for some reprieve, all he needed to do was party. Thousands of people wanted to party, opportunity was all around him, and Gerry dived into this life. It felt like it filled a hole in his heart at the time. Alcohol covered up the pain.

For each moment of substance-induced reprieve, however, Gerry's confusion grew.

* * *

Gerry needed to get away. He was tired of the professional life—the media, the difficulty getting fights, the drama with management hating one another. As an amateur, he just fought the next best guy. As a pro, Gerry was fighting just to get a fight, and he was tired of waiting. Tired of it all.

Months progressed into years as Gerry awaited his next professional fight. The formerly adoring media appeared resentful of Gerry's inactivity. Their reaction—bred from disappointment—was understandable. The heart Gerry displayed against Holmes, despite the bout's consequence, proved that Gerry had all the tools to become a great champion. Not yet in his physical prime, Gerry had the power, size, and raw ability—all could be refined with experience and perseverance through challenge and adversity. Now that he had displayed a championship heart, which is often the elusive piece that separates champions from contenders, and all-time greats from champions, it seemed like only a matter of time before Gerry would succeed Holmes as boxing's king.

The giant heavyweight did what he could to live life without his most positive and significant coping mechanism: boxing and meaningful training sessions. That is, to train with a specific opponent in mind, on a specific date. Anyone who has had difficulty completing tasks without deadlines and waiting until the last minute before finding the motivation to work might understand the difficulty Gerry was experiencing in finding meaning in opponent-less training.

Gerry was lost during this era—partying, hanging out, enjoying life, and getting away from his boxing life. Gerry was disillusioned and managing many family issues. It seemed like everyone and everything was a mess. Gerry wasn't dealing with the problems, not fully, and resorted to the welcoming embrace of good times. The problems would remain in the morning, but the partying would keep them at bay for at least a few hours.

It was a traumatic time in Gerry's life. Boxing, his outlet for meaning and self-worth, was compromised in his mind. His managers made him feel as though they were doing him a favor by getting him fights. Howard Davis Jr. would later agree with Gerry; he had felt the same way. But Gerry needed to fight. Preparing for and participating in meaningful boxing events was needed for him to live, but fights were not predictably available to him anymore.

Without meaningful work, Gerry's alcoholism expanded to fill the void.

* * *

"My managers were supposed to help me; they knew about my problems," Gerry reflected decades later. "I was a young guy, directionless. If I'm a manager, I would help them with it or get someone to help them with it. We're supposed to be a team—I was young and suffering. No one took me aside and said, 'What's wrong with you? Let's figure this out.' They had their issues, and I was in the middle. I should have been guided, though. In a business, if something is messing with the product, it gets addressed. They didn't do that for me. Maybe because they were dealing with their own stuff, like we all do. I don't know. It's unfortunate."

Alcoholism leads one's life to spiral out of control. No one signs up to sacrifice opportunities to realize one's potential, to push away loved ones, to deplete finances, or to hurt those who love them the most. Like a cold produces a cough, addiction creates behavioral symptoms. Brains produce thoughts, feelings, and behaviors. Compromised brains, such as those suffering from addiction, produced compromised thoughts, feelings, and behaviors. It generally takes heartache and negative consequences for addicts to seek help. Gerry hadn't yet accumulated enough pain to pierce the convincing manipulations of his addictions. Combined with his self-sabotaging part that felt he didn't deserve success, the addiction symptoms and influences became uncontrollable.

Still, despite the challenges and pitfalls, the seeds of growth were being planted for Gerry's future self. He worked through life the best way that his current skills permitted. Such is the resilience developed—and demonstrated—by depressed persons each day. They find a way to live through the day. Sometimes, rising from bed is a major victory, as is going to work. For Gerry, work meant putting in gym time.

The sparring exhibitions did not replace preparing for an actual fight, but they were a productive way of finding Gerry work. There was purpose to be found in the ring. Still, limiting the risk of losses may have been a good strategy for protecting Gerry's marketability, but it was also horrific for the fighter's development. Gerry's skills needed the fires of adversity, which can only be found in authentic combat, to properly develop. Instead, his skills were atrophying.

Gerry's life quality was also impacted. Without the outlet of meaningful training and the validation from his boxing exploits, the iron will that drove him through the horrific rigors of trauma could guide Gerry only so far. He not only needed to box frequently against quality foes in order to maintain and expand his skills, but also to keep his body and mind healthy.

Gerry needed to risk fighting contenders, but management did not seem to want to risk a loss. Gerry was a big name, and each fight would generate millions, so attaining the biggest fight seemed to be the best way to minimize risks while maximizing rewards. But Don King's stranglehold on the division's fighters made securing good bouts very difficult, so Gerry's development was relegated to gym work and exhibitions.

Exclusively fighting exhibitions was far from ideal for any fighter. It was akin to sending a healthy major league baseball MVP candidate to play in the minors. Worse, the exhibitions often broadcast the carnival atmosphere that embarrassed Gerry. He occasionally set healthy boundaries with his managers, but he was also intrinsically compelled toward what he knew: chaos. Although it was not optimal, the unhealthy, dependent scenario was what Gerry was used to. Like most people, Gerry continued to replicate what was normal to him, even when it was not in his best interests.

Gerry had the talent and power to compete against any heavyweight on the planet. However, Gerry didn't have the experience necessary to beat Holmes. He had been the legitimate number-one contender, but with more than a year of inactivity and less than a decade of formal boxing experience, Gerry simply wasn't ready then. With a few fights, he would be.

Unfortunately, these opportunities were not possible. Promoter Don King's monopoly of the heavyweight division kept Gerry from being a top contender. He couldn't get fights unless he signed with King. The Twins understandably wouldn't deal with the famously money-hungry promoter. Also, Gerry's managers maintained their low-risk, high-reward business strategy that had worked so well in their businesses and in Gerry's early career. Economically smart, it resulted in the underdevelopment of a young, gifted fighter.

Another result was long periods of idleness, among the worst statuses for alcoholics.

* * *

Gerry's self-sabotaging activities, although certainly inspired by the conflict raging both to prove his father right and to disprove his awful messages, were also deleterious attempts to protect his ego. By digging himself a hole, Gerry had created built-in excuses for not succeeding. The reasons for any losses would have been under his control and so within his ability to correct. This responsibility can be hard for many people to accept because any setback would indicate character flaws or insufficient skills, if the person chose to interpret them as such.

The lack of meaningful training impacted Gerry on many levels. Fighting legitimate contenders was essential to not only provide Gerry the opportunity to develop his still-burgeoning skill sets but also to offer the work necessary to productively focus his energies. Instead, his mind was forced to fill idle time. When Gerry was not around other people, the extra time also created opportunities for despair—and for escape through alcohol.

Despite depressive thoughts, Gerry naturally became attuned to moments when interacting with fans. During these moments, Gerry's comical self would emerge, shielding him from the negative energies and replacing them with authentic joy. Communicating with people kept the fighter alive. Connections made with others were always healing, soothing. Laughing, too, was such a relief. Seeing the joy in other people's eyes was what he lived for—witnessing the happiness that he couldn't permit himself to fully feel served as an escape from the conflict within.

"How is the hand injury, Gerry?" was a common question that Gerry fielded during these times.

"It's okay. Come up here and I'll show you."

Laughter. For the young fighter, it was like water to a parched man stranded on unfamiliar desert lands. Laughing hard was a way to let go of the negative energies inside, if only for a moment before his demons regenerated them.

"When will you fight Holmes again?" was likely the most frequent query, particularly from his fans.

"It'll be on the first—the first chance I get!" Gerry would reply. Again, the laughter helped the giant cope with the sadness bred from falling short of his dream and from the increasing awareness that he might not have another opportunity to win the championship.

When the laughter stopped and his energy diminished, however, Gerry would recite standard "athlete-speak" responses. The contender would adopt the tone of a tired, almost disconnected man whose mind was miles away—and he was at times. Gerry tried to distance himself from the realization that he was not actively working toward the championship. This reality was made all the more difficult to accept when Gerry's rational side prevailed, the side that objectively estimated that he had the tools to win the title.

I can do it!

Just give me the shot. Please, just give me the shot!

Gerry wanted to shout his thoughts from the rooftop of Madison Square Garden; instead, he campaigned to justify his time off to reporters, fans, and likely himself, too. The routine would go something like this: "Well, I just needed some time off to get my head together, figure things out. You know what I mean? Things are better, now, and I'm getting back in shape, ready to fight. Exhibitions help me with that. Gettin' in front of people, in the ring, working the rust out. Then I'll train for a real fight so that all the people who lost money on me can win it back!"

The expressed hope was authentic. But when the crowds dispersed, proposed fights continued to fall through, and Gerry was alone, the fear of failure and of success would capture his attention. Each question regarding his inactivity again would assault him, reminding him on multiple levels that his time was running out. But he knew he could still do it.

Just give me one more shot!

* * *

It was a dark time for the former number-one contender. He wasn't the savior, the fixer of all that afflicted his loved ones, management, or relationships—it was all hitting him at once, and Gerry was angry that he couldn't be the savior and fixer. It was a hard reality; all he wanted to do was get away with some safe friends. Food, travel, drinking, bad relationships—he kept escaping. But the drinking was no longer working well, trying to fix problems for loved ones was no longer working; he was positive and expected good results, but the outcomes just weren't very positive anymore.

Now twenty-eight, Gerry was no longer the prodigy who challenged the future Hall of Famer Holmes. Instead, he was well into his physical prime and losing precious time. Ultimately, it would be twenty-seven months before Gerry returned to action after the Holmes bout. He fought twice within three months, earning two convincing technical knockouts against Philipp Brown and George Chaplin. His work with Richie Barathy—the famed karate black belt who owned the record for breaking granite slabs with a single karate chop—had enhanced the strength and speed of Gerry's punches. It also lengthened his muscles and bolstered the cumulative power and muscle dexterity. The frequency of fighting was optimal and revitalized Gerry's mind-set. Boxing, his cherished outlet for meaning and self-worth, had been reestablished.

However, still years away from actively employing self-care activities that would change his life, Gerry's brain gravitated toward chaos and self-destructive activities. His brain was simply bred for it, given his life conditions and lack of self-care. It was wired to maintain what it knew: living in chaotic environments, investing in unhealthy relationships, and trusting fears while minimizing strengths. Still, he had the physical tools and talent to make one last run at his cherished championship dreams, if only he was managed optimally to develop his boxing skills.

*　*　*

The danger of the combat sport of boxing activates primitive regions of the brain associated with fundamental survival. Cocaine and illicit drugs like it manipulate an equally basic portion of the brain associated with rewards. Many boxers seeking to replace the rush of fighting do so with drugs. Addiction becomes more likely when users have time to use, resources to secure the substance, and a predisposition for the ailment. Gerry possessed all of these.

Excessive time between fights, along with his fortune and lack of support, formed a perfect storm for Gerry's addictions to progress. The months following the Chaplin victory eroded Gerry's enthusiasm dramatically. After fighting twice during a period of nine weeks, Gerry had been hopeful that his career had reestablished itself. Fighting with this frequency would sharpen his previously dormant skills and add dimension to his professional character. New combat experiences would compound the wisdom derived from earlier ones, most notably Gerry's efforts against the great Holmes. He would do things right this time.

But as quickly as Gerry settled into the frequency of fighting that had served his development so well in the amateurs and his early professional career, his career stagnated again. Eight months later, Rappaport and Jones announced Gerry's retirement. The frustrated fighter—who at twenty-nine was in his physical prime—simply wanted to fight. But he wasn't fighting. Addictions had taken control over his life, and Gerry's codependency and compassionate heart made dealing with his family members' issues a primary focus. This took a great deal of time and energy, two precious commodities for athletes whose careers are far more finite than more traditional work paths.

It was all so draining. Authentic depression symptoms, too, made even routine life activities major efforts at times. Gerry's experience of these symptoms was a consequence of legitimate unhealed wounds of trauma and the aftereffects of the drugs and alcohol. After all, whatever the drug's effects that makes it so appealing to users, the aftereffects are the opposite as the chemical is processed. For example, cocaine produces euphoria, so when the body and brain rebound, depression results. Hand surgery and a shoulder injury slowed down Gerry's progress even further, as did fruitless attempts by his managers to secure a coveted rematch with Holmes. One of Gerry's loved ones was also enduring drug problems and mental health issues that prompted the fighter to pay thousands for rehabilitation stints.

Life began to crumble further for the giant heavyweight. The press had turned against him, as had several friends. It seemed that, as money accumulated, issues arose proportionally in the Cooney camp—and outside of it. Money solves many problems, but it also generates new ones.

Since million-dollar purses manifested and the prospects of negotiating future ones became a distinct possibility, rifts began to unfold. Gerry recalls a time when Jones hired an accountant who gave himself raises without asking the fighter. It was an awkward position for a young man with limited coping mechanisms. Gerry's people-pleasing tendencies and quest to maintain a stable, happy environment made it difficult for him to confront others at times—or at least to do so while calm. Gerry's "protector" side would take over when circumstances warranted boundaries to be set, but it was more easily manifested in the ring. Moreover, this version of himself was confrontational in a direct and threatening manner, but this was not the manner that Gerry wished to conduct himself in everyday life. Gerry was finding his own way through such extremes.

It was a challenging era.

* * *

Management's desire to secure the most lucrative fight overwhelmed the need to provide in-ring challenges in order to best develop their boxer. Gerry couldn't develop without live challenges. Worse, without a clear focus, Gerry was left without a purpose to train. Without meaningful work to conduct, Gerry's alcoholism, drug abuse, and depression symptoms had both the time and opportunity to grow in severity. He was learning how to manage them when they got bad, but he needed to eradicate and properly address them. His management did not display any concern about Gerry's well-being, which obviously impacted his career.

In many ways, the business strategy employed by the Twins—minimizing risks while maximizing reward opportunities—was extremely effective. Yet one may argue that by taking the educated risk of allowing Gerry to realize his potential, his management team set itself up for a great number of paydays. The risk of a loss, however, always seemed too great once Gerry made it to elite status. Anything could happen. Holmes's near loss to the unheralded Snipes in 1981 testified to that reality.

Eventually, the fighter offering the highest reward and lowest risk was former light-heavyweight champion Michael Spinks. The 1976 Summer Olympics middleweight gold medalist generated one of the greatest careers at light-heavyweight before upsetting Larry Holmes for the International Boxing Federation (IBF) heavyweight championship. Spinks's victory prevented Holmes from matching Rocky Marciano's legendary undefeated record of 49–0. Spinks would again defeat Holmes in a controversial decision seven months later.

The conditions were perfect for Gerry to again become a major player in the heavyweight division.

* * *

The fight with Spinks involved prolonged negotiation, much of it outside Rappaport's control. A broader perspective might have featured Gerry in several real fights—not exhibitions—during the complicated process of setting up the Spinks fight. The complications were due, in large part, to the HBO–Don King heavyweight title unification series that commanded the boxing world's attention. Both parties had courted one another, each offering the other the promise of enhanced revenue: HBO could provide increased exposure and higher paydays to King and his fighters, while the promoter could help HBO carve its sports niche by providing most of the top champions and contenders.

King, in the mid-1980s, was perhaps nearing the peak of his influence. He boasted contracts with the most prominent heavyweights, including two of the three heavyweight champions. Along with Pinklon "Pink" Thomas (World Boxing Council champ) and Tony "TNT" Tubbs (World Boxing Association titlist), King's stable was replete with most of the leading contenders. Unfortunately for King, Ronald Everett "Butch"

Lewis, a charismatic and strong personality, controlled the business fortunes of the third champion, the recently crowned IBF heavyweight champion, Michael Spinks.

* * *

Butch Lewis was born in Woodbury, New Jersey, but grew up in Philadelphia. Life was challenging for the young Lewis. After high school, he hustled cheap jewelry. Later, Lewis's father employed his son at his used car dealership. The elder Lewis had boxing ties—he had been one of the original stockholders in the agency that supported a young Joe Frazier.

Butch Lewis soon would be traveling with the future legend, seeing how mega-fights were made and establishing strong connections in the industry. Eventually, Lewis became a co-promoter for Frazier's rival, Muhammad Ali, for a fight (a 1976 World Boxing Association/World Boxing Council defense against Richard Dunn). The event was a significant one—fought in Munich, Germany, the experience earned Lewis employment with famed promoter Bob Arum. The position was an illustrious one—vice president of the firm Top Rank—that armed Lewis with the reputation he needed to carve out his own identity as a promoter.

Lewis was known for his shrewdness, tenacity, and ability to employ showmanship to the benefit of his fighter's—and his own—financial fortunes. The former street hustler and used car salesman's career as a boxing promoter catapulted when he signed two 1976 Olympic gold medalists, Michael and Leon Spinks. Still employed by Top Rank at the time, Leon Spinks's upset of Ali empowered Lewis to form his own promotional company. Eventually, Lewis would form Butch Lewis Productions, an entity that broadened its representation to entertainment figures. Most clients would be of ethnic minority backgrounds, which enabled Lewis to help others attain the same opportunities he had earned.

In the 1980s, Lewis's confidence in his abilities and influence was broadcast in his dress, words, and actions. His stunning flamboyance was in stark contrast to Michael Spinks's decidedly quiet demeanor. The promoter would attend fights wearing magnificent rings, pristine bracelets, and garb that usually consisted of a tuxedo and bow tie without shirt. In a sport full of personalities, Lewis proved to be a unique one.

Lewis's persistence altered the course of boxing history. Michael Spinks had publicly stated that he was reluctant to fight professionally after his incredible amateur career. Toiling as a St. Louis chemical plant's maintenance man working the graveyard shift, Spinks was eventually persuaded by Lewis to turn pro after months of encouragement. The decision ultimately led to a historically significant light-heavyweight career and, by the mid-80s, an improbable run as the lineal heavyweight champion.

Spinks boasted profound negotiation leverage as HBO and King worked to create the heavyweight unification tournament. Not only did he hold a major organizational title, but he also held the only one that really mattered to fans: the lineal heavyweight championship. Manager Lewis, ever the shrewd businessperson, was aware of his fighter's strong negotiating position and the many options that it offered. There were many methods of securing the best deal and many types of deals. Spinks was a relatively active fighter. Save for a 363-day period between 1984 and 1985 and an eleven-month respite early in his professional career, Spinks fought several times a year. Lewis needed to maintain his fighter's schedule while securing the best deal.

Now, with his once expansive future rapidly diminishing, hope returned to the still-dangerous "Gentleman." Spinks, while a highly skilled pugilist with a boxing intelligence among the sport's elite, was a blown-up light heavyweight who couldn't possibly contend with Gerry's power. A victory over a manageable contender like Eddie Gregg would instigate talks of another championship shot. Even though Gerry's latest extended streak of inactivity led some boxing enthusiasts to question his right to challenge Spinks, the fighter's power still captured fans' imagination. He still offered amazing marketing potential.

From a business standpoint, Gerry's management team had preserved their fighter's earning potential by limiting exposure to significant challenge—and the accompanying possibility of loss—while maintaining the public's interest in paying for a Cooney fight. Gerry, for his part, had faith that he could immediately make up for lost time against the ultra-talented but slightly built Spinks. He just needed a shot, one that would certainly be justified with an explosive knockout of the light-heavyweight legend turned unlikely heavyweight champ.

It would be a gift from the boxing gods, but first Gerry needed to defeat a contender in spectacular fashion.

20

A BRIEF RETURN TO COMBAT

Phil Berger's magnificent book, *Blood Season: Tyson and the World of Boxing*, offers some insights into just how cutthroat and Machiavellian boxing negotiations can be. In early 1986, Rappaport and his attorney negotiated with Butch Lewis's attorney throughout the night. The discussions ended the following morning despite unfavorable environmental conditions (there was no heat in the negotiating rooms). The deal was essentially complete save for Lewis's insistence that he be paid $500,000, nonrefundable, in the event that Gerry canceled the fight. Rappaport seemed to have secured Gerry a favorable championship shot against the lineal champion. And, with Mike Tyson not yet champion—he would fight thirteen times in 1986, the last bout resulting in his historic title win against Trevor Berbick—the fight was also the most marketable possible for all parties.

Lewis's adamant insistence that the check be certified, however, delayed finalization of the deal. The demand seemed unusual given the multimillions involved in the proposed bout. Later, evidence surfaced that Lewis might have been dealing with Don King while his attorney and business associate worked with Gerry's management team. The efforts might have been a tactic to drive up the offer made by HBO to secure Spinks's involvement in their heavyweight tournament. Indeed, shortly thereafter, King and Lewis announced a co-promotion of seven fights, which included HBO paying an astounding $17 million for television rights.

As the politics, business alliances, and wars unfolded behind the curtain that shielded fans from the myriad intricacies of matchmaking, Gerry split with Mike Jones in 1986. The two would battle in court, which culminated in a settlement to Jones's widow several years later. Gerry felt that it was unnecessary but he was tired of being in court. Rappaport continued as his manager until, years later, it was revealed that he—when he formed Tiffany Promotions along with Sam Glass and Mike Jones— was also taking more of the financial pie than the fighter had realized. Rappaport had been partners with Glass, the promoter, in real estate. Gerry suspected that they had some type of agreement during his career, but he hadn't realized the particulars of their co-promoting the Holmes fight with Don King until afterward.

The offenses were most damaging when Gerry's fights began to generate millions. However, it was not as destructive as the extended time away from fighting during Gerry's prime. The years unfolded and Gerry remained idle, accepting Rappaport's explanations. The manager made it seem like he was doing Gerry a favor by getting him fights.

Eventually, the puzzle pieces began to fall into place. Gerry hadn't been completely unaware of the mishandling over the years—after the Holmes fight, Gerry started to see what was unfolding. The excessive spending, including a team of bodyguards for $1,000 each week, seemed to benefit others, which, in turn, seemed to benefit Rappaport. Ultimately, Gerry sought to get out of his contract with the remaining Twin. It was a tough time that fed into Gerry's trust difficulties and expanding alcoholism symptoms.

Eventually, 1986 would witness Spinks's technical knockout of Steffen Tangstad in four rounds. Gerry did, eventually, find work—his first live bout in nearly eighteen months.

* * *

By the mid-1980s, "Iron" Mike Tyson's rise as both a contender and celebrity was approaching extraordinary status. He appeared on his second cover of *The Ring*, one of the nation's oldest sports publication. Tyson was just entering his second decade of life, in the midst of securing thirteen victories that year alone, and on the treasured precipice of earning his first heavyweight title. Like Gerry did more than a half-decade earlier, the young man was capturing the public's imagination.

About a decade Tyson's senior, Gerry was solidly in his physical prime. Time had progressed far too quickly for the aspiring champion.

The promotional wars with Don King and his management's philosophy had relegated Gerry mostly to training sessions for years. Since his epic contest with Holmes four years earlier, Gerry had fought only three times. This was an astonishing lack of activity given Gerry's marketing and boxing potential. But Don King's control of the heavyweight division was one of iron. The fights Gerry needed would not be available unless he signed with the legendary but controversial promoter. Though money was the primary motivating factor in the eyes of King—and most of the industry's power players—so too was control. If Gerry became a champion, King would lose a substantial piece of his kingdom. That would soon translate into lost profits, as King and his fighters would have to share more of the riches from championship bouts.

Despite having fought only seven professional rounds in four years, Gerry's power was still explosive and generated extreme interest. His size and personality, too, were equally compelling. Further, Gerry's life story was of interest to myriad casual and serious fans alike. It was reported that he was dealing with loved ones with substance abuse challenges, although the extent was largely unknown. The media often portrayed him as an enigma whose talent, potential, and championship heart were evident, but he was perceived as too lazy or greedy to fully explore the limits of his abilities. Such was never the case. Fighting fueled him as much as his interactions with the fans. He needed it, but the fights were not happening.

The fighter inside Gerry wanted to challenge himself in the ring as frequently and intelligently as possible. But idleness was a breeding ground for poor self-care. His constant efforts to help others often left him with no energy or time to heal his own wounds. Gerry's sense of responsibility for the needs and well-being of others constantly drained his own reserves. At that point of his life, of course, Gerry didn't have many tools to manage his powerful emotions and the chaos that being a celebrity entails. Gerry's need to help others to realize a modicum and fleeting sense of self-worth led him to find reprieve in alcohol. Lots of it.

It was all coming to a head. Circumstances led Gerry to contend with difficulties related to family, friends, and management, as well as people asking questions regarding his career, for which he had no answers— even a *Saturday Night Live* skit poked fun at Gerry's not fighting. It was disheartening. The press didn't understand. Gerry contributed to the problem; he was distracted, lost, sinking deeper into alcoholism, and wanted to be away from it all. At times, no one seemed trustworthy. Although there were factors outside his control that contributed to not getting fights, Gerry's worsening symptoms, which evolved in part due to not having a meaningful fight for which to train, were both a product and a cause of his inactivity.

But like any power puncher, Gerry was always in the fight as long as he remained conscious. The same was true of his career. Despite the inactivity and personal challenges, it would take only one dominating victory for Gerry's status to rise to the top of the division. His name again would be associated with the division's best fighters. But the public was largely unaware of how powerful King's influence was over the division. It would take a great deal to secure fights against the names that Gerry needed to get back on track to harnessing his potential. Still, that didn't stop the media and public from imagining how Gerry would fare against the sport's best—including Mike Tyson.

Gerry just needed some fights.

* * *

Gerry ultimately returned to fight Eddie Gregg, a St. John's University master's degree student who was studying both athletic administration and the heavyweight division. He had earned two New York Golden Gloves championships in the late '70s and was the first person to knock down the famously rugged Randall "Tex" Cobb en route to a unanimous decision victory. Cobb was in the midst of a four-fight losing streak and would taste the canvas multiple times in his next loss (a first-round knockout by unheralded Dee Collier), but Tex's chin had held out against greats such as Holmes, Norton, and arguably the heaviest hitter in history, Earnie Shavers.

The bout against Gregg was billed "Earthquake II," as it was being fought on the sixtieth anniversary of the San Francisco earthquake. The Cow Palace housed the contest. The combatants would generate $350,000 in purses, with Gerry commanding the lion's share. Gregg boasted a near-flawless record (24–1–1, 18 KOs) that led to his being ranked by all three major organizations. This included a number-three ranking by the World Boxing Association and number nine by the World Boxing Council (WBC). Defeating a ranked contender would eliminate any procedural obstacle to a championship fight.

But Gerry needed to win first.

* * *

Gerry began the fight night ritual with a trip to morning mass. His mother and three brothers were also present. The family had become more cohesive in recent months. This reality provided Gerry with profound strength and comfort. A nice breakfast of waffles and orange juice preceded a few hours of downtime. Around midday, Gerry made the trip to the Cow Palace in Daly City, California. It was to be his first professional fight in California.

Victor Valle passionately—as was his personality—reviewed the strategy with his charge as they were transported to the arena: set him up, be careful, and take advantage of openings by throwing short punches. The last was important given Gerry's long limbs and the enormous openings that wide punches can produce.

As it turned out, Gerry's power found its mark early on, and Gregg was unable to recover. The slightly smaller man had come out fighting, but less than twenty seconds into the first round, Gregg was affected by a left. Both fighters remained active. Gregg seemed intent on bringing the fight to the bigger man, perhaps trying to stifle Gerry's resolve or to work him over before Gerry's rusted skills could sharpen. Gerry was wild at times, missing with his vaunted left hook on occasion. The two warriors traded valiantly, but only one had all-time-great power. An enormous left uppercut had Gregg out on his feet before a follow-up left hook sent him to the canvas. Gregg rose but referee Rudy Ortega called the fight off.

A broad smile broke on Gerry's face. The fans were cheering, he had done his job, and those around him were happy. The thrill of victory, not felt for some time, was nonetheless familiar and intoxicating. Gerry's brothers, along with his professional family, mobbed him in the ring. The victory was a good one. It was only the second time in twenty-seven fights that Gregg had been knocked out. He had been confident and was eager to fight, which ultimately benefitted Gerry. With Gregg in firing range and charging forward, Gerry was able to find his target rather than being overwhelmed by the onslaught. The strategy may have been educated—after all, Gerry was not used to fighting such large men, he had a great deal of ring rust, and he likely would have needed time to become acclimated to live action—but this was simply Gerry's night.

The results catapulted Gerry to national recognition once again. Rappaport would maximize this reality to the greatest extent possible. Gerry had generated more than $13 million in his career thus far and was in his physical prime. He had felt great during the fight and had displayed his prodigious power once again. Gerry seemed to have put his angst regarding the Holmes defeat in the past and finally to have healed from a myriad of injuries from muscle tears to crushed knuckles. Unfortunately, the success also created the illusion of control over his drinking, drugging, and smoking, all of which had been conducted during the course of training. The joke to the Ohio reporter years before—that Gerry employed an all-alcohol diet prior to fights—was now somewhat true.

Still, the contender miraculously overcame his inner demons and remained among the planet's greatest heavyweight fighters.

* * *

Gerry's size and power—and, unfortunately, his skin tone—made him an instantly marketable fighter. So, too, was Gerry's charisma and ability to connect with others of all ages and ethnic backgrounds. Defeating Gregg in such a devastating fashion empowered Rappaport to demand premium dollars. These financial demands naturally stalled negotiations to fight. Like a fighter looking to land the knockout punch or a batter seeking to knock the ball out of the park with each swing, Rappaport wanted optimal economic rewards for Gerry and himself. This dedication resulted in another prolonged, year-plus hiatus from the ring.

Rappaport publicly proclaimed that Don King controlled all the fighters and wanted to control Gerry, too. This was reportedly accurate. Rappaport understandably did not want to share rights to his fighter. But there were still fights to be made, even if they were not optimal. This certainly was better than another period of idleness.

One can understand a manager's concern regarding placing fighters in the best position to secure victory—or, more accurately, to minimize the risk of loss. Rappaport's strategy was to maximize profit while minimizing risk, but this strategy sometimes was akin to playing a game not to lose rather than playing to win. Mike Jones was quoted in a June 8, 1987, *Sports Illustrated* article that Rappaport's strategy was employed to such a degree that Gerry never fought—that Rappaport was frightened to put his fighter in the ring. "He minimized the risk so much, Gerry never fought," said Jones. By this time, Gerry and Jones had parted ways. (Many years later, Gerry would applaud Jones as the better of his two managers, due largely to Jones's increased willingness to let him fight.)

This perception was not possessed by many in the boxing world at the time. Instead, some focused on the fighter as being responsible for his idleness. "Cooney went for money instead of development," said Eddie Futch, the esteemed trainer of four of the five men (Joe Frazier, Ken Norton, Larry Holmes, and Trevor Berbick) to defeat Ali. He also guided Frazier, Riddick Bowe, and Montell Griffin to end the undefeated streaks of all-time greats: Ali, Evander Holyfield, and Roy Jones Jr., respectively. "A boxer needs to face adversity." Few would argue that observation.

It was understandable that the fight world wanted to see Gerry test his skills far more frequently. The fighter did, as well. Being an active fighter would be good for the sport, too. Gerry had transcended boxing earlier in the decade and was still young enough to do so again. It was also understandable that Rappaport preferred to secure a big-money fight against a stylistically favorable champion like Spinks, rather than a good but lesser payday against a bigger heavyweight with a greater puncher's chance of victory. But the result was a persistent state of idleness.

Some quotes of the day suggested that Gerry supported Rappaport's conservative strategy. After a while, he sometimes began to buy into others' perceptions. Gerry had even stated that he should be pursuing only the biggest fight rather than accepting lesser ones in order to stay active. This was a rationalization that helped make sense of his lack of fights. Gerry wanted—needed—to apply rationale and meaning to his suffering. Rappaport, confident and charismatic, was a good foil for Gerry, with his background of codependency and a chaotic family life.

"You lose your heart if you're not put before the public in stressful situations, when it's just you and him and God," said Irishman Jerry Quarry in a June 1987 *Sports Illustrated* article. "I would've demanded tougher fights if my manager wasn't giving them to me." Looking back through the healthy eyes of sobriety and perfect vision of hindsight, Gerry would agree. However, his emotional status resulting from unhealed wounds and substance abuse virtually eliminated Gerry's ability to assert himself in such a manner. He simply wasn't aware of the situation with the escape of alcohol continually available, and he trusted his manager to his own detriment.

"Why risk losing to Page or Dokes or Witherspoon for $1 million when you can wait and fight someone for $5 or $10 million?" said Richard Barathy, the martial arts genius who also served as Gerry's trainer and physical therapist. "Shouldn't there be a greater desire than money?" asked eighty-seven-year-old Ray Arcel, esteemed trainer of eighteen world champions, including Larry Holmes during his championship victory over Gerry, after which Arcel retired. "It's more important for a man to learn his trade, and Gerry Cooney's only had one fight in his life. I think he fought my grandfather."

Even when Gerry signed on to fight, his fighting spirit was sometimes questioned. In the same *Sports Illustrated* article, future Hall of Fame reporter Mike Katz asked: "Why wasn't he fighting heavyweights like Michael Dokes, Greg Page, and Tim Witherspoon when they had the title? Then when a light heavyweight [Spinks] becomes heavyweight champ, he comes out of retirement and says he's ready?" It should be noted that at his Hall of Fame induction speech, Katz acknowledged that he did not have the whole story about Gerry and labeled him a great ambassador for the sport.

Like many fighters before and since, Gerry focused on his job—fighting and preparing to fight—and let his management team conduct the negotiations. He wanted to fight. There were times when he expressed his frustration about being idle. Promises and explanations filled his days, stretching into weeks, which then evolved into months and years. Substances and the dramas associated with addiction, particularly those of his loved ones, helped the transition of time unfold faster and faster until Gerry's prime years were spent largely inactive. Gerry would pour his heart, soul, and wallet into helping others secure the help that they needed—and that he unknowingly needed himself.

Meanwhile, time kept moving by.

* * *

Spinks was not the only fighter that the Cooney camp was targeting. WBC champ Mike Tyson, the knockout sensation, was also in talks to fight Gerry. Tyson's co-manager, Bill Cayton, reported that Gerry was offered $10 million to battle Tyson—as long as Gerry did not fight Spinks. A Spinks fight, after all, would undermine HBO's unification series. Rappaport confirmed that the two power punchers would have a roughly fair split of the purses, but he was not willing to wait long for a matchup. Gerry shared a *Ring* magazine cover with Tyson. Despite his sporadic fighting schedule, Gerry's popularity and the promise of his overwhelming power easily had captured the boxing world's interest.

A matchup with Tyson was compelling. The prodigy was knocking out one contender after another at an alarming rate, but he was still learning. Plus, the few who had given Tyson trouble were cagey fighters with extended reaches of eighty inches or more. Gerry's size advantage included a prominent reach disparity of more than ten inches. A properly trained and prepared Gerry could employ enough boxing skills to complement his already established power threat. Gerry had already demonstrated the ability to shock boxing pundits when he displayed massive heart in his loss to Holmes. A victory over Tyson would empower Gerry to reclaim much of what he considered to be lost time, unrealized potential, and unclaimed status as the top heavyweight in the world.

Holmes did not offer the same type of knockout power that Tyson possessed—nor did any of Gerry's previous foes. It would be interesting to see how Gerry would react to the inevitable pressure and adversity that Tyson could apply, particularly since Gerry had yet to display superior defensive skills. The questions were myriad, and fans and experts alike could debate the outcome at length. This was a favorite pastime of boxing enthusiasts, and the Gregg victory had them centering on the possible Cooney-Tyson showdown.

Interestingly, Gerry and Tyson had much in common, though paradoxically for different reasons. Both fighters had troubled childhoods that left them unprepared for the riches and stardom that their physical skills would provide. It would take many years for both men to harness the wisdom associated with enduring and surviving challenging life adversities. Their symptoms were also similar. Behind the public personas and smiles, Gerry and Tyson had difficulty trusting others and would go on to construct chaotic environments in their adult lives. The fighters also were extremely generous to those around them, often taking care of many others financially and, to the degree that they could, emotionally.

In short, the young men shared many demons and personal attributes.

There were also contrasts between Gerry and Tyson. The latter benefitted from living in a stable, nurturing environment in early adolescence. Cus D'Amato was profoundly and unconditionally dedicated to training the young Tyson, whose number of criminal behaviors at such a young age suggested authentic mental health challenges sparked by a difficult childhood. Tyson lived in what was a boxing paradise with extremely skilled mentors dedicated to his development. The legendary trainer eventually became Tyson's legal guardian.

After D'Amato's passing, Jim Jacobs would continue offering the young Tyson the authentic caring of a father. Jacobs would pass far too young, leaving Tyson directionless and vulnerable to the influence of chaotic environments. His psychological and emotional scars remained, and although they would eventually serve as the foundation for incredible emotional insights, they wouldn't manifest more fully until his career was complete.

Gerry's teens, in contrast, were spent struggling to survive emotionally, psychologically, and even physically. His father's abuses continued, and Gerry eventually struggled to make ends meet on his own. Even when management professionals offered promises of riches through a professional career, Gerry had no wise father figure to advise him. No boxing legend to guide him. Gerry would go on to meet quality mentors but not until his formative years had passed.

Gerry also began organized boxing a bit later than Tyson. Still, both would fight for the championship only nine to ten years after their first structured training session and endure the fast-paced lifestyle of stardom without the fundamental tools for managing emotions, relationships, and the unhealed scars of traumatic experiences. The two men, so different physically in terms of body type, size, and race nevertheless shared a great deal on the most significant levels of human existence.

The two, unfortunately, would never fight in the ring.

* * *

Gerry was kept in limbo once again. With no one to trust in his life, he was forced to believe management was capable of securing the best deal. Explanations regarding how outside powers were preventing them from securing a fight were largely accurate, even though other options to find Gerry live action remained. Spinks was the primary target for multiple understandable and intelligent reasons. He was the lineal champion—a victory would place Gerry in perhaps the best position possible in negotiations with future foes. If the "Gentleman" was a titleholder and lineal champion, his popularity would soar. The power puncher with a murderous ability to attack the body was in his physical prime—even if his inactivity left him off his peak form. However, he matched up well against the awkward but talented Spinks.

A loss to Spinks would be catastrophic from both a business perspective and a career vantage point. It was viewed as an acceptable risk—not only would it generate a quality multimillion-dollar payday and allow Gerry to recapture the marketing prestige and associated financial rewards described earlier, but a victory would catapult Gerry's confidence and bolster his résumé. It was a good risk with a high reward. After all, Spinks was an undefeated lineal champion who, albeit a light heavyweight for most of his career, had improbably (if controversially) defeated the great Holmes. A conquest in the best money bout available might also help Gerry exorcise some of the demons associated with losing to Holmes. Even if the International Boxing Federation (IBF) followed through by stripping its champion if he refused a mandatory defense (ultimately identified as Tony Tucker) in order to fight Gerry, Spinks would maintain his "People's Champion" status.

Gerry's team had some negotiation leverage. Gerry represented the biggest money-making fight to Spinks—but the champion had options. Worse, if Spinks did enter the HBO unification tourney, he would not be able to fight Gerry for another year or so. Fighting on HBO's ever-growing television screen was also an appealing factor to Spinks's marketability. With complicated negotiations looming, HBO demanded that Gerry's team provide assurances that he would engage in the HBO unification bout if he defeated Spinks. Ever the shrewd businessperson, Gerry's manager wanted to retain all of the fighter's rights from the promoters and to maximize their options, particularly since a victorious Gerry would be in the driver's seat in any subsequent negotiations. Gerry was simply worth more than what HBO would pay him. Plus, Rappaport and company must have understood that HBO's urgent need to produce a real unified champion, one that could not be disputed, left them somewhat vulnerable.

HBO could "only" offer Gerry $2 or $3 million for a battle with Spinks. The contender was worth more than that amount for a championship fight. Yet a victory over Spinks would make Gerry even more marketable. From a business perspective, it was understandable that Gerry's team would not sacrifice finances to make the bout happen despite the potential long-term benefits. However, in what had become a theme since he became a marketable superstar, the financial shrewdness sacrificed Gerry's development—both psychologically and in terms of developing his fighting skills.

The complex negotiations produced myriad false starts, enough to make Gerry question the legitimacy of promises that a bout would be produced. Lewis wanted to secure a provision for Spinks to fight Gerry, but HBO was not enamored with the threat of losing a champion in its unification series (since Gerry would not fight under its banner). Finances and politics prevented the fight from being signed. Although explanations do not devolve into excuses until one ceases to develop solutions and act upon them, Gerry's brain remained wired to maintain chaos and to delve deeper into his already substantial alcohol dependence. His intuition had similar tones as his fears, and in his condition, Gerry was compelled to sabotage his efforts rather than to take control of his career. And so he continued to allow his management to conduct their matchmaking strategies despite their recent lack of success.

Many contemporary writers assumed that Gerry saw himself as entitled and not needing to reclaim his number-one contender status by beating other top heavyweights. Such perspectives tore at the gentle giant's heart—Gerry was desperate to fight. Boxing was the only healthy outlet for the powerful emotional energies he contained. His emotional and psychological health required a strong purpose, one found through meaningful ring challenges. Gerry longed for the days of the amateurs, when matchmaking was far more efficient and predictable, when the time that lapsed between purposeful training aligned with the period necessary for him to heal from his wounds and to optimally prepare.

Times were very different.

Butch Lewis's keen business mind was alert to all possible advantageous outcomes, but it also sought to construct safety nets should fortunes not favor his fighter. He understandably insisted on a provision that, in the event of a Cooney victory, he would have promotional interests in the "Gentleman's" next two fights. Lewis also considered the possibility that, if Gerry's perceived hero's complex led him to cease boxing to pursue other entertainment endeavors—such as commercials, movies, charity events, interviews—Lewis would earn a percentage of subsidiary incomes. Rappaport and company would not agree to such demands.

Meanwhile, Don King offered Lewis a deal to co-promote Spinks with the understanding that Lewis, should his fighter be defeated by another contender, would co-promote with King for the rest of the HBO series. The complicated dealings and offerings were numerous, but at the end of the day, Rappaport offered Lewis a much bigger single payday. Gerry and Spinks needed one another. As the biggest names in the heavyweight hierarchy outside of King's sphere of influence, a compelling battle could upset the power structure of boxing. At least, it would wrest some control from the phenomenally powerful grip of King and perhaps provide them both with more opportunities in the future.

With all the stops and starts, the reality was that Gerry was finished with boxing. He didn't care anymore. The continual failed negotiations and media scrutiny was just not working. Gerry wanted to fight and it wasn't happening. And it hadn't for a long time. The fight game was now full of snakes, lowlifes, and thieves who used him. He was sick of it. Idleness was not what Gerry wanted from boxing—he just wanted to fight the next best guy, just like in the amateurs. It was the most embarrassing era of his life. To get away from it all, he would drink. The drinking itself became a part of the problem as it led Gerry to passively let it all happen because he was numb to it all. He did not trust his management, but at the same time, there was no one else to trust.

No one was there to help him into the next phase of his career. He didn't know how to say no to boxing; all he knew was boxing. No one was helping him to find his own way, which now included finding him a new career avenue. Something meaningful. Something to fill the void of the sport that had consumed his life for so many years.

Gerry was going through the motions. The only fight that would have reignited his passion was a Holmes rematch. Gerry thought that his performance merited a rematch. But alcohol had now completely taken hold of him. It was an escape from reality that numbed Gerry's mistrust and heartache. It was his only coping skill at this point of his life.

* * *

As negotiations among multiple dominant power players unfolded, Gerry remained without purpose to train. With only actions and outcomes to formulate their conclusions and the assumption that Gerry directed his team's actions, the boxing media viewed Gerry as a jittery fighter unable to fully resume his promising career. But Gerry was not strategically backing out of fights. Some were respectful of the psychological and emotional challenges that result from loved ones with addiction challenges, but many were frustrated with what they viewed as frequent injuries and postponed fights.

Family challenges increasingly plagued Gerry during this era. His loved ones were continuously asked questions about him and thus were themselves feeling marginalized because of their famous sibling. Gerry's compassionate heart and codependency symptoms left him feeling responsible for his family members' pain. A loved one's heroin addiction once required hospitalization. Gerry did all he could to be supportive. He coped with the pressures, pain, and lack of career purpose with recreational drugs and alcohol. His young life had been replete with challenges that left Gerry struggling to survive emotionally but suffering through the powerlessness of loved ones' painful addictions was among the most difficult.

As Gerry endeavored to caretake those around him and govern situations far outside his control, his management team continued to encounter the myriad business obstacles to producing a championship fight.

* * *

The dimly lit bar was a place of comfort for the bored contender. The promoters had, once again, backed out of the Spinks fight. The IBF had threated to strip the champion of the title should he fight Gerry, insisting that Spinks combat their mandatory challenger, Tony Tucker. Giving up the title would affect Spinks's earning potential—a serious obstacle to setting up a fight with the Irish heavyweight. Moreover, it gave Spinks more leverage in negotiations.

Aside from Holmes, who was unlikely to receive a third bout with Spinks after two defeats, there were no legitimate number-one contenders, Tucker included. Gerry no longer qualified due to his inactivity, but two or three quality fights against capable foes would no doubt put him in the same lofty position as when he ended Norton's career. Tucker likely would qualify as one of those opponents. In fact, fighting him for the right to combat Spinks was an entertaining thought.

Tucker was a promising young fighter with an unblemished record. The fact that his best win had been over a seriously aged Jimmy Young who had lost four straight fights would not affect ticket sales. Tucker likely hadn't reached his prime but fighting Gerry—and securing the lofty payday that would no doubt accompany the bout—could prove to be a smart career move. Even if a loss eliminated a championship shot, Tucker's public exposure would soar.

Something can happen, Gerry concluded with the hint of an inspired smile arising on his face.

My guys can make something happen; I'll take care the rest.

Such thoughts, while capturing Gerry's imagination and instigating hope, eventually illuminated the despair of his uncertain situation.

Nothing's gonna happen, anyway. Never does, he lamented.

Business and politics were driving the sport, as always, and Gerry's hope for another shot was diminishing. No longer in his mid-twenties, Gerry's prime years were spent waiting for fights. He was an able warrior who was refused combat. With nothing to train for and in a near-constant state of career limbo, Gerry's confusion and anger reached new depths. It was only among other people—as well as the numbing powers of the limitless supply of alcohol and other spoils of his celebrity status—that Gerry could find some solace. The brief window of respite would shut harshly in a few hours and compound the amount and intensity of his anguish. But for alcoholics, feeling good and avoiding pain is all that matters, even when they know better. Let the next moment take care of itself, their addiction advises, but right now it is time to feel good.

Strung along yet again, waiting for a shot that would materialize then vanish within days, Gerry lost hope. His management team often told him not to trust anyone else except them—similar words to those of his father, who implored Gerry not to tell anyone his business. Gerry really couldn't trust anyone's word. Even if the Spinks fight materialized, something would happen to take it away.

So why bother?

21

DEAD MAN FIGHTING

Ultimately, the fight with Holmes's conqueror, Michael Spinks, was secured. Spinks was universally regarded as among the best light heavy-weights in history. In its September 2002 issue, *The Ring* ranked him third in this category, with only the legends Ezzard Charles and Archie Moore ahead of him. Spinks was the 1976 middleweight gold medal Olympian who became the first reigning light heavyweight champion to win the heavyweight championship. Now he was set to fight the power-punching Gerry, who was attempting a comeback.

Spinks, still the lineal champion and the champion in most fan's eyes, was no longer a titleholder. The International Boxing Federation (IBF) title that Spinks had won from—and defended against—Larry Holmes in two controversial bouts was stripped from Spinks when he passed up a mandatory defense against Tony "TNT" Tucker. The undefeated would-be challenger was a quality fighter who boasted a stellar amateur (115–6) and unblemished professional record (34–0–0). He would go on to defeat James "Buster" Douglas for the vacant title before losing it to "Iron" Mike Tyson less than nine weeks later.

Spinks's decision was a smart economic one. According to his Box-Rec.com biography, Spinks was set to earn 75 percent of promoter Don King's purse bid of $711,000 to fight Tucker. This translated into a $533,250 payday. Fighting Gerry would generate nearly eight times that amount—$4 million. Such was the marketing power that Gerry boasted. *The Ring*, along with more than twelve state commissions, viewed the bout as a world title fight.

The implications associated with a Cooney-Spinks match were linked directly to the division's immediate future. Tucker's technical-knockout (round ten) victory over Douglas was to occur around two weeks before Gerry's bout with Spinks. Since Spinks had never lost the title in the ring, that naturally generated interest in the winner facing Tucker for the championship. Or, even more inspiringly, a little patience following a victory over Spinks would have put Gerry in line to fight Tyson—the sport's biggest attraction.

A dominating victory over Spinks likely would set up a mega-fight with the young phenom, one that would eclipse Gerry's battle with Holmes in terms of public interest, money generated, and possibly even historical significance. Tyson was a compelling figure who appealed to the masses in a way that Holmes did not. He had been named *The Ring*'s Prospect of the Year in 1985 and was the publication's Fighter of the Year in 1986 (and, after his destruction of Spinks, again in 1988). His second-round conquest of Trevor Berbick earned him recognition as the youngest heavyweight titlist in history. Tyson's decision victory over Tucker made him, a little more than a month after his twenty-first birthday, the youngest unified heavyweight titlist in history.

A clash between Gerry Cooney—the richest non-title-holding boxer in history at the time—and the dominating prodigy Mike Tyson easily would transcend the sport and capture the masses' imagination. It would be the "Gentleman" against the man of "Iron" and arguably the most powerful left hook in history against what was becoming the most balanced blend of overall power and speed ever witnessed in the ring. Only one man stood in the way of such an event.

Michael Spinks.

Spinks's reputation as a heavyweight was something akin to that of a masterful baseball pitcher who only can throw eighty-five miles an hour: everyone thinks they can hit him, even after going zero-for-four with four contact outs. They feel like they just missed. For Spinks, his slender athletic frame and history as a light heavyweight made most heavyweights salivate to fight him. They felt that success was very much within their grasp.

Despite fighting the majority of his career under the 175-pound light heavyweight limit, Spinks steadily had added size as he rose in the heavyweight division. By the time he fought Gerry, Spinks weighed 208.75 pounds—still undersized for the era but not small. He had hovered around

200 pounds for almost two years and three heavyweight title fights. Spinks's advanced skill sets, superior hand speed, undefeated streak, and successes on the championship stage made him a formidable foe.

Spinks's pedigree, too, was absolutely superb. As the generations pass, the Spinks family seems to become more and more like boxing royalty. His older brother, Leon, won the light heavyweight gold medal at the 1976 Olympics and defeated the great (if also aged at the time) Muhammad Ali in just his eighth pro fight. Michael Spinks's nephew would earn the undisputed world welterweight championship and, later, two IBF light middleweight championships. Currently, Leon Spinks's grandson and namesake, Leon Spinks III, is authoring what he hopes to be another historically significant career for the family.

The soft-spoken Spinks boasted a standout boxing career and according to most historians is among the very best light heavyweights of all time. His gold medal win at the 1976 Olympics (middleweight division) resulted in Michael and Leon Spinks becoming the first brothers to earn gold at the same Olympic Games. Overall, Michael compiled an outstanding 97–3 record during his amateur career. Interestingly, Michael—like his brother, Leon—won the heavyweight championship in a bout that *The Ring* would honor as Upset of the Year.

* * *

As life was lived, Gerry tuned out the critics. Some were among his own brotherhood—active or retired pugilists. Jerry Quarry once remarked that Gerry was cheating the fans and too complacent after such a huge payday against Holmes. The historically gifted Archie Moore insinuated that Gerry enjoyed a privileged life. Joe Frazier suggested that Gerry didn't pay his dues. It appeared that all believed that Gerry was his own career strategist, demanding profound paydays and refusing to fight unless granted rich rewards.

In regard to Gerry's status as contender and star attraction, the theme of privilege was pervasive. Racial overtones persisted. Many bemoaned that African American fighters needed to pay more dues for mega-paydays and title shots than did Gerry. For example, Pinklon Thomas, a contemporary of Gerry's, cited his need to reestablish himself for a title fight against Mike Tyson despite being a former champion.

Such critics were often unfair in the standards they used to evaluate Gerry's career. Thomas's foes between his championship loss to Trevor Berbick and his title shot against Tyson combined for a record of

43–19–1. A journeyman record did not justify outrage over mistreatment, nor the contention that the former champ needed to fight wars simply to secure another shot at the title. Additionally, title shots were provided to countless fighters with lesser credentials than Gerry prior to his fight with Holmes. Thomas was granted a title shot in his twenty-sixth fight against Tim Witherspoon. This was the same number of fights as Gerry had going into his epic battle with Holmes. Witherspoon earned his shot against Holmes in just his sixteenth fight. Other fighters were granted shots with fewer fights and with less success: Randell Cobb (20–2), Scott Frank (20–0–1), Marvis Frazier (10–0), James Smith (14–1), and on and on it goes.

Even in the days before he took on the division's legitimate kingpin, Michael Spinks, Gerry was criticized for not combatting heavyweights like Witherspoon, Michael Dokes, and Greg Page when they boasted title belts. The criticism would have been more valid had it been directed at a perfect storm of boxing politics and Gerry's management team's philosophy of minimizing risks and maximizing rewards. Gerry wanted to fight—needed to, in fact, as boxing was his sole tie to feelings of self-worth and accomplishment. His addiction, codependency, and mental health challenges produced acceptance—an explanation, not an excuse—for not being more forceful in satisfying his needs to fight.

No one seemed to understand that Gerry was a pawn in the power games associated with the intense politics of mega-money boxing industry. His brain, though wired for peacemaking, trusting, and supporting manipulators, gravitated toward chaotic relationships. Gerry's eagerness to see others happy was authentic, a way for him to experience joy in a more complete manner than he could solely for himself. But the multitude of clown figurines and mime masks that decorated his home reflected the darker aspects of Gerry's existence: their expressions almost universally revealed his inner pain and sadness.

Except for one: an unknowing symbol of hope to the pugilist entering the final stages of his fighting career. Like a ray of sunshine on an otherwise cloudy day or a realistically positive thought among hundreds of irrationally negative ones that race through one's mind, the happy clown unknowingly predicted the path Gerry would ultimately—and eternally gratefully—travel upon. But not without research regarding his relationship to drugs and alcohol and how they affected his life in general and his career in particular.

Gerry's substance abuse issues continued, but the seeds of change that had been planted throughout his adult life had begun to sprout. The awareness that he was a slave to chemicals had become apparent. The thought was an abysmal one that produced a bevy of negative emotions, each of which connected to Gerry's developing resolve to construct a new life somehow.

The partying wasn't producing the temporary highs that they once had. Chasing those highs resulted in increasingly diminished success, but the negative consequences became more glaring and severe. Gerry's terrible views of himself became more prominent. Fears of not being enough—good enough, funny enough, or good-looking enough—magnified with each passing day. Ingesting alcohol and substances no longer assuaged this pain, even temporarily, but only amplified it. The onslaught of negative thoughts, including his views about himself, his career, and how he interacted with his family, was more vicious and destructively brutal than any blow employed by human hands.

It just wasn't working anymore.

* * *

The Spinks fight was finally secured, but still Gerry wondered if it really would occur. The lead-up to the "War at the Shore" had been despairingly unpredictable and disappointing to Gerry. The fighter had been so used to training without purpose that it was challenging to generate the intensity necessary for optimal preparation. Because of the fight's previous, near-continuous limbo, Gerry was conditioned to expect the fight to be called off, which led to a diminished desire to train. Meanwhile, his partying had reached an all-time high. With consistent, meaningful training camps for planned fights a thing of the distant past, Gerry's tools for handling his emotions consisted primarily of alcohol abuse.

As had been the case since he became a contender in the early eighties, Gerry's unwillingness to sign with Don King, along with his manager's strategy of minimizing risks while maximizing rewards, was the primary obstacle to his fighting. In the June 8, 1987, edition of *Sports Illustrated*, Dennis Rappaport summarized the first aspect of this conundrum while justifying Gerry's inactivity. "Listen, Holmes was the champion," said Rappaport. "Spinks beat him, so he became champion, no matter what the WBA [World Boxing Association] or WBC [World Boxing Council] or IBF say. Gerry isn't fighting just to fight. He's fighting to win the championship. Besides, Don King owns all those fighters, and he wanted options on Cooney if he beat them. No way we were going to do that. Maximize the profit and minimize the risk—I've always believed in that."

Gerry's career reflected Rappaport's expressed strategy. The effect was a legitimately marketable fighter who had become the richest non-champion fighter in history. Even with his stock far below what it once was (and still could be), Gerry generated enough interest to increase his bank account by a guaranteed $2.5 million (and to help bolster Spinks's, the champion's, account by $4 million). Some estimates raised that number to more than $5 million for Gerry, which would place his career earnings at about $18 million in twenty-nine fights.

Gerry wasn't prepared to break away from his chaotic surroundings nor was he in position to take control of his career. Albeit counterintuitive, without intervention and immense self-care practices, a brain trained to accept chaos and sabotage will seek out more of what it knows. Moreover, because of his diminished self-esteem, Gerry on some level doubted that he could break away from his current management and find one that would manage him more as a fighter than a cash cow.

Such insights were not privy to Gerry at the time. Life was so fast paced, his demons so powerful, and his conflicts so incredibly enduring that Gerry was driven in more directions than he could handle. It was impossible for him to be aware of his intrinsic battles, as drugs and alcohol numbed his insight and shielded him from his intuition, keeping his conflicts outside his conscious mind where they could heroically be challenged and methodically overcome.

No longer a young man, at least in sporting terms, Gerry's physical prime was ending and the window to his championship quest was closing. Despite the inactivity, idleness, and poor management, Gerry had a chance to win the lineal and *The Ring*'s championship. Further, the "War at the Shore" would be his opportunity to crush a great undefeated fighter in what was, for Gerry, an outstanding matchup.

* * *

About a month before the Spinks bout, Gerry had a realization—a deep, profound realization that was different than previous insights—that he needed help with his addiction. The conclusion was a resounding one but also somewhat fleeting. Such is the way of human change. Addiction produces the rationalizations and denials that are as much a hallmark of addiction as is shame, despair, and irrational behavior. So powerful was

Gerry's alcoholism and unhealthy desire to prove his father's harsh words correct that his brain justified poor preparation despite the opportunity to not only win the lineal championship and earn a mega-payday but also to stop the undefeated streak of Holmes's conqueror.

In fact, by not preparing optimally, a part of his mind reasoned that he would have a viable explanation if he lost. Spinks was a favorable opponent for Gerry. The lineal champion's lithe body, which fought below the heavyweight threshold for many years, was not designed to endure power-punching body shots from a pounder like Gerry. The stars were aligned for Gerry to exorcise stubborn demons, realize his championship dreams, enter the history books, and silence—if only for several meaningful moments—the angry condemnations that constituted a portion of his father's abusive tactics.

Yet the power of alcoholism fueled by unhealed trauma can be stronger than most can fathom.

* * *

The lineal champion Spinks entered the fight boasting a sterling 30–0 record (21 KOs). His lanky 208.75-pound frame was the heaviest of his competitive career. A heavyweight for only three fights leading into his bout with Gerry, Spinks had taken the historical ascension to the heavyweight championship while enjoying the status as reigning light heavyweight champion. His two controversial wins over Holmes had solidified his status as the lineal champion, even if the Mike Tyson phenomenon was beginning to take hold of the boxing world. Spinks's promoter, Butch Lewis, had a championship belt specially designed for his fighter. Although not affiliated with any alphabet organization, the lineal champion understandably and proudly boasted the title "People's Champion." Nearly sixteen thousand fans arrived at the event.

Arriving at the convention center, a small part of Gerry's mind still entertained the possibility that the fight would be called off. He was underprepared physically, as the drinking episodes eroded his reflexes and muscle memory even worse than the latest year-plus layoff. Against Spinks, the inactivity was far worse than the inactivity that preceded Gerry's shot against Larry Holmes. Essentially, Gerry had fought fewer than seven rounds in the half decade since that legendary clash with Holmes. The pressure associated with the fight—perhaps being Gerry's last opportunity to resurrect his career and to access his phenomenal potential—was immense.

To escape his emotions, Gerry had resorted to alcohol. The cycle was well established. It would take a Herculean and holistic effort to identify it and construct new life strategies. Sadly, this process wouldn't begin until after Gerry's battle with Spinks. But one must walk the valleys before finding paths toward the mountaintops.

Like a prodigy student underprepared for a test, Gerry sat in his locker room, a shell of his former self. Somehow the window of opportunity had closed dramatically before he could even partially explore his potential. Now a veteran after racing through his prospect and prime stages of career development, Gerry nevertheless began centering his attention on the upcoming battle. The substance abuse and belief that the fight would be canceled yet again had fueled one another to such a degree that Gerry's fire was stifled during preparation. Although he was arriving at a gun fight with larger guns, they were without bullets.

The biggest names in boxing joined other famous athletes and entertainers to witness the heavyweight clash, which, oddly, was held on a Monday evening. "Sugar" Ray Leonard, jockey Angel Cordero Jr., NFL quarterback Vinny Testaverde, future president Donald Trump, Jersey Joe Walcott, and cruiserweight king Evander Holyfield were a few of the notables at ringside, but perhaps the most intriguing figure was Mike Tyson. The reigning WBA and WBC champion joked with the celebrated Leonard at ringside. The young champion was scheduled to fight Tony "TNT" Tucker for the same IBF championship that Spinks never lost in the ring.

The battle between the two undefeated titlists, Tyson and Tucker, would generate a new undisputed champion—undisputed, that is, in terms of ownership of the title belts of boxing's three main governing bodies. The winner of Spinks-Cooney would own the cherished lineal championship, thus setting up the most anticipated fight since Gerry's challenge of the great Holmes six years earlier.

Much would be decided on this night.

* * *

The battle was an intriguing one. Spinks's unorthodox style would magnify Gerry's ring rust, keeping him safer from the heavy punches, particularly the left hook. An off-balance fighter's ability to set up his punches is compromised, further protecting Spinks from fully experiencing power punches. Spinks's plan was to frustrate the giant and take him into deep waters. Although Gerry had competed well against a primed

Holmes in the late rounds, that was many years earlier. By evading poundings and peppering Gerry with blows from strange angles, Spinks hoped to prevent Gerry from finding his rhythm, cutting off the ring, and imposing his will.

Walking to the ring, anxiety plagued Gerry. It had never occurred to this degree before in his career. He couldn't catch his breath. The realization that he wasn't prepared overwhelmed him for a few moments. Still, he kept moving forward—even though he was not himself, Gerry operated on the default mechanism to keep marching forward toward adversity. The feelings didn't fully pass until the fight began.

The pugilists strolled toward the ring's center for prefight instructions as two very different fighters with diametrically opposed paths to the title fight. Although the same age (thirty), Gerry outweighed Spinks by thirty pounds and enjoyed a five-inch height advantage along with six inches in reach. The ring activity was even more lopsided in Spinks's favor. During the five years since his fight with Holmes, Gerry fought three fighters and less than seven rounds. Spinks, in contrast, had fought ten times against good to championship-caliber competition. All of the contests were light heavyweight or heavyweight title fights and totaled almost ninety-seven rounds. Even so, the fight was simply a bad matchup that favored even a rusty Gerry Cooney, whose power should have slowed down—and ultimately knocked out—his foe.

Valle held Gerry throughout the referee's instructions. His left hand remained on Gerry's waist as his right hand massaged the back of Gerry's neck and upper back. If Valle could have willed his life energy into Gerry, he would have done so. Valle loved his fighter like a son, and that caring was reciprocated. On this night, Gerry was tasked with battling an undefeated and skilled foe in a bout that he was favored to win, and he wasn't prepared mentally, physically, or spiritually.

What the world didn't know was that the former number-one contender was a walking dead man on this particular night.

* * *

The first round commenced with the natural mix of concern and focus manifested from adrenaline. For some heartbeats, Gerry felt "normal," back in his habitat where the rules were simple and permitted his skills to be fully explored. His mind was centered on combat and survival, but his body would not respond to his mind's commands. It seemed to take years for his limbs to listen and obey the instructions from his fighting intuition. The muscle memory was simply not honed in enough. It was comparable to a person taking a written test years after last studying the material—there was a time when the knowledge easily was within his grasp—and still could be with some quality preparation—but for now it was long gone.

Spinks moved awkwardly around the ring, throwing Gerry's compromised timing off a bit more. Normally a slow starter, Spinks was also well aware of Gerry's power and tendency to be a fast starter. A brace supported Spinks's right knee so that old injuries wouldn't hinder his maneuverability. With Spinks's movements and unorthodox shifting, many knees would be vulnerable to faltering. It was a potentially prominent factor for Spinks, who had to hit and immediately move out of danger in order to win. Although Spinks had been knocked down only twice at this point in his amateur and professional careers—against Russian Rufat Reskiev in an amateur bout and a questionable knockdown against professional Dwight Muhammad Qawi—he was not a natural heavyweight and he was not used to absorbing punishment from much bigger men. Being elusive was required against a power puncher like Gerry, and he fought that way.

The second stanza commenced with Gerry tapping into what was left of his capabilities. He landed a nice combination that launched Spinks around the ring. Spinks's prolific output became less accurate briefly before he resumed his uncanny timing. The offense accumulated and kept the compromised but competitive giant from setting up his own punches. Spinks's jabs and overhand rights—an effective weapon throughout his Hall of Fame career that was often referred to as the "Spinks Jinx"—landed frequently enough to keep Gerry off balance.

As the round unfolded, Spinks became more stationary. His offense would halt Gerry's production enough for him to glide out of danger. The giant's timing and rhythm remained off. Gerry's heart kept him competitive, but his body was not well prepared. Spinks was experiencing success and it empowered the fighter.

Increased confidence and positive results permitted Spinks to be less elusive as he flurried and kept Gerry at bay and unable to connect. The strategy was a dangerous one for Spinks. Late in his second fight with Holmes, Spinks had been dazed by his rival's right hand. The experience highlighted his need to be evasive. Yet after some success in this fight, Spinks seemed to be fighting as he did against less powerful light heavyweights before he made defense a focus against slower but more powerful heavyweights.

The round ended with a Spinks flurry and an accidental head-butt, which led to a cut over Spinks's eyebrow near the bridge of his nose. Cutman Percy Richardson immediately went to work on the slash between rounds. Gerry was always a strong finisher, particularly when he saw blood and could impose his will and size. The cut was a major concern for Spinks and a source of legitimate hope for Cooney fans that their man would capitalize and change the course of the fight.

The early moments of round three witnessed Spinks pawing at the cut. Like a beleaguered shark sensing prey, Gerry felt a brief surge of invigoration, but the energy couldn't be sustained. Spinks was able to beat the bigger man to the punch, delaying Gerry's momentum enough to stifle any concentrated surge. The reality was horrific for the former contender—his mind knew what needed to be done, but his body just wouldn't respond. It was too fatigued, unresponsive, and underprepared. His body's muscle memory had dementia and was slow to take orders when it even had the energy to do so.

Gerry's skills were simply dormant, unavailable to be called upon.

* * *

The fight continued to unfold in unexpected fashion. Spinks maintained his scoring with multiple punches, largely the jab, along with quick inside left hooks. The overhand right, a quality counter against a left hook, was among Spinks's most effective weapons. In most ways, Spinks was at his masterful best. Gerry, in contrast, could employ only a watered-down version of his capabilities. He followed Spinks, rather than being the aggressor and effectively cutting off the ring as he normally would. He doubled up on left hooks, taking the wind out of Spinks, but did so relatively sparingly.

Still, by round four, Gerry's timing seemed to be evolving. After a brief warning to both fighters for holding, Gerry began blocking Spinks's rights for the first time in the fight. Not coincidentally, Spinks's activity dropped as Gerry began dictating the pace. But these moments passed. Spinks rebounded by throwing blows that did not land but prevented Gerry from accessing enough of his skills to land a flush power punch, which would make Spinks more stationary. Although round four seemed like Gerry was regaining his rhythm and timing, it would prove to be his final sustained attack. A shadow of his past in-ring performances, it was the best of which he was capable on this evening.

From the spectator's perspective, Gerry entered the fifth round with momentum. But the giant pugilist had spent what remained of his physical and emotional energies. Spinks's jab, surprisingly accurate all evening, was aided by the ring rust and the still-persistent demands and condemnations of Gerry's father. Each landed punch made Tony Cooney's admonitions that his son was a loser more and more real. By this point of the fight, Gerry's mind was polluted by diminished self-worth. As in the Holmes fight, Gerry bravely resolved to take as much punishment as his tormentor could deliver.

The punches came seemingly without pause. Those that were seen came too quick to avoid—Gerry's body no longer was responding to his brain's instructions to roll, slip, shift angles, or catch punches. The blows were individually manageable, but collectively the damage accumulated on Gerry's weary body. Spinks, himself meticulously prepared, was able to back up his larger foe. Like a woodsman chopping down an oak tree, Spinks kept hammering Gerry until the latter showed signs of being in trouble with one minute and twenty-five seconds left in the round. Nine seconds later, Gerry fell to the canvas. His eye swollen, Gerry stood up and resumed absorbing Spinks's ceaseless attack. Gerry fell again with fifty-three seconds left in the round and rose at the count of eight.

The end arrived only after a historically prolific collection of punches from the reigning lineal champion. Gerry was not defending himself or holding on, bravely taking the punches as he had Tony Cooney's assaults years before. He managed to land a solid blow that briefly interrupted the onslaught. He walked into Spinks's offense, taking the punishment until the referee called an end to the fight. Gerry remained defiantly upright, but the conclusion to the worst night of his athletic career had manifested. He had absorbed an inordinate amount of punches. Of the round's eighty-nine landed punches, Spinks connected with eighty-four. The defensive skills ingrained from years of training had become almost dormant on this night.

Perhaps most despairingly, despite being woefully underprepared mentally for the battle, Gerry was winning on one scorecard (Harold Lederman: 39–37), slightly behind on another (John Stewart: 39–37), and tied on the third (Tom Kaczmarek: 38–38). The result was demoralizing to Gerry, as well as disappointing to others. Kevin Rooney, Mike Tyson's trainer who was present for Cooney-Spinks, lamented that he had been rooting for Gerry because a Cooney victory would have generated more money in a bout against Tyson. The boxing world had to adjust to the unanticipated result.

Spinks's incredible skill sets took advantage of outside circumstances—this time, meeting a much larger power-punching opponent, one who matched up well against Spinks, at his career low point. The underdog had upset Holmes's quest to match Marciano's undefeated record, as well as the quest to regain the title, and now he thwarted plans for an especially intriguing fight between two historically powerful heavyweights that likely would have produced more profits than any fight in history.

As heartbreaking as the loss was for Gerry and as lonely and despairing as he experienced his rock bottom, it would serve as the powerful foundation upon which his eventual rise would be constructed.

THE WRITING PROCESS

God Hears All Prayers, but Sometimes the Answer Is No

Working with Gerry on his biography has led to profound personal and professional growth. The fighter's emotional intelligence and authentic caring for others, including me, was quite healing. His plight normalized my own. His big brotherly encouragement provided me strength and hope. It quickly was clear to me, upon our introduction, that Gerry was an unusually authentic man with an incredible heart. Our experiences led to great reflection on the challenges and benefits associated with being a superstar professional athlete. Surprisingly, the processes, emotions, and thoughts associated with these challenges mirrored my own "normal life" difficulties.

To me, there appear to be many paths to the mountaintop of success, and each person has his or her own unique constellation of "life answers." For many, a focus on the positive leads to manifestations of a good portion of one's success. Others believe that centering on anger and rage can lead to their definition of victory. Some rely on the cool calm of tranquil mind-sets, permitting them to be attuned to the moment's demands and alert to the wisdom found in their own intuition. Almost all approaches possess attributes of some of these. Each athlete must identify his or her own needs, strengths, and potential and develop his or her own strategy for success, however it is defined.

What makes this puzzle even more complicated is that the pieces continually evolve and shift. One's body and mind mature, experience offers opportunities to develop vital and treasured attributes, and sometimes insidious demons of doubt sabotage one's efforts and shorten one's prime years. Each athlete's career journey is unique. It is up to mentors to help encourage and guide the athlete to approach the limits of his or her potential through any number of strategies and approaches. There is no singular approach, no matter how many insights science uncovers.

Still, there are many commonalities, even among participants of different sports. For example, healthy levels of fear and concern can alert one to the need for better preparation. The notion that one's career is immeasurably shorter than those in other lines of work can also lead an athlete to appreciate the moments with vigor. One's sense of urgency can be a motivating factor—or a debilitating one.

Many athletes experience the emotional challenges that all those who live through career life cycles face. But their learning curve is far more truncated than the average citizen. There are pros and cons to this reality, but as evidenced by endless stories of depressed, retired stars striving to reproduce the emotional highs that used to be a daily part of life, the negatives can sometimes be life threatening. This is particularly true for boxers, whose line of work not only places them in absolute danger with each contest, but also threatens severe cognitive challenges bred from the accumulation of damage over a career.

* * *

"I look back and it's tough to think about what could have been—should have been, really," Gerry contemplated. His eyes appeared to be gazing into life chapters written long ago, even as he strolled among his well-manicured backyard gardens. "But then I think—I'm lucky as hell, you know what I mean? There are guys of my generation really walking on their heels. Not able to enjoy life. Maybe if I became champion of the world, who knows, maybe I'd be one of those guys?"

I nodded in agreement, even while appreciating the nature unfolding around us. The topic of dementia and cognitive decline had been an interest of mine for some time. It remains, also, a primary fear. Anyone who has witnessed a loved one battle dementia for any period of time likely shares this immense respect for the horrific consequences of neurological challenges.

Sidestepping a bee that was taking a distinct interest in me, I recalled an interview before the Holmes battle that Gerry conducted. The then-young man expressed an interest in fighting for as long as his passion and skills were maintained but noted that he would not be like many fighters who hang on too long. This is a tragically common ending for many fighters—the sport has to force them out. Something that Gerry side-stepped due to his recovery work filling the expansive void of a completed career.

In Gerry's perspective, I witnessed something more than pure authenticity. Clearly, the teachings of Victor Valle remained decades after their partnership ended. The tough but optimistic trainer would assume that disappointments were challenges that no doubt ultimately proved helpful by steering one clear of more serious consequences. Gerry, after his first few decades of fearing positive emotions due to the expectation that they would be ripped away from him, now embraced them and assumed that life's mysteries and perceived bad fortunes favored him somehow. His spiritual work had begun with the nurturing influence of Victor Valle.

"I've had a lot of great times, met a lot of great people. I'm very fortunate. That's the bottom line. And I'm able to appreciate all of it."

Part Eight

Lost Legacy Found

Walking out of the dressing room to the ring, right there, that's when the real man comes out. It takes courage to get up those four stairs into the ring, but before you know it, you can't wait for that bell to ring—to get in there, fight, figure the guy out, and change the expression on his face.—Gerry Cooney

22

PREPARING TO RISE

The aftermath of the Spinks debacle added dimensions to Gerry's disappointment and other negative emotions. Authentic depression symptoms make completing everyday functions as difficult as elite runners completing races while transporting a two-hundred-pound backpack. Or, for some sufferers, even more weight. What direction and support that others offered was unable to be truly absorbed. Career mortality was now imminent for Gerry—a confusing and difficult encounter for any person, let alone a championship fighter. The hidden gold in heartbreak was not yet discovered or even searched for—Gerry's addiction-damaged brain would not permit it.

At least, not yet.

* * *

The realities of his career status were more devastating than any physical assault—the future, once seemingly never-ending, suddenly became incredibly finite. The lineal championship had been within his grasp but it eluded Gerry.

How could this have happened?

How could the time, once so infinite, suddenly become so short?

Is it all over?

The questions pounded Gerry's mind with a ferocity that no fighter could replicate. Gerry could hear his father's shaming words, harsh criticisms, and acute admonishments. It was almost as if the words were a thin veil over everything he perceived, even when he compassionately interacted with supporters and fans—they kept him alive, hopeful, but only for the duration of their communications.

Some of Gerry's questions regarding life changes were legitimate—realistic and not bred from the irrational fears that enabled so many of his shaming thoughts. Athletes age far quicker than those in almost any other profession. With incredible speed, they experience career stages that are often described as:

- Growth: Four to thirteen years old
- Exploration: Teens through mid-twenties
- Establishment: Mid-twenties through mid-forties
- Maintenance: Mid-forties through mid-sixties
- Disengagement: Mid-sixties and beyond

* * *

Fighters race through these stages at a pace that others cannot fully appreciate. Their disengagement occurs when most others their age are in the establishment phase. The process can be disorienting. After all, the accumulation of life experiences can help one to accept the subtler evolutions of body, mind, and work capabilities. Athletes experience this cycle at double the pace.

Seeing others of lesser talents achieve what was within his grasp and the knowledge of what he could have done could be dispiriting for Gerry, particularly as the increasingly perfect vision of hindsight alerted the former contender of his true potential and established abilities. These moments of clarity regarding his skills began to replace Tony Cooney's original messages. Realistic hope began to occur and expand.

A powerful part of him was confident: somehow, Gerry would find his way.

* * *

Sometime during the aftermath of the Spinks debacle, Gerry found himself reflecting. Years before, Gerry invited his idol, Muhammed Ali, to his then-new East Hampton home. A bachelor who didn't really know how to entertain Ali and his large entourage, Gerry had to rethink the invite and ultimately cancelled. The two enjoyed one another's company, and the respect was mutual, too. As Gerry prepared for his title shot against Holmes, Ali had stated that the contender "was not the 'white hope' but the 'right hope.'" The endorsement was akin to receiving a direct blessing from the pope. It also counteracted Holmes's criticisms, as well as those from other boxing experts such as Steve Farhood, who once astutely suggested that Gerry's background would negate his ability to make it as an upper echelon fighter.

It seemed as though a generation had passed since then. Gerry was in the same place, but he wasn't the same man. Yet the environment was a healing one for the fighter. The state's easternmost town is surrounded by water on three sides. Little did Gerry know, but the gift of desperation—of simply being sick and tired of being sick and tired of living through booze and recreational drugs—was about to be unwrapped. Gerry's mind was coming to the point where change was more comfortable than maintaining what he knew. Since chemicals had hijacked Gerry's brain to think that they represented survival itself—a view aptly explained by addiction science—one can appreciate how difficult the decision to change may be for the addict.

But in the world of recovery, miracles happen every day.

* * *

Flipping through the channels, Gerry happened upon "Alcohol Awareness Week in the Hamptons." George Benedict was the presenter. The story depicted how the alcoholic's brain worked. George's story was crazy but made sense to Gerry—a process that he related to on a personal level. Although the specifics were different, Gerry connected to the insanity of the story. Gerry called the number and said that he thought he might have a problem. George invited Gerry over, introduced him to recovery principles, and provided a game plan for Gerry to employ. George provided self-care options to Gerry, which included going to George's rehab center, where Gerry worked a few years later.

Gerry wasn't alone. There were others who had endured similar plights, emotions, and adversities. The stories didn't include fights with all-time-great heavyweights, but they did include battles that included stress, uncertainty, pressure, and emotional angst. Others were also powerless against the chemicals, haunted by abuse inflicted decades prior that remained fully present in the form of memories, negative belief systems about themselves and the world, and the difficult feelings that arise from those memories and beliefs.

Gerry wasn't alone, and that reality was remarkably encouraging.

* * *

Some realizations began to manifest in the fighter's mind. Gerry had to start being an adult—a true adult—and work on himself. He committed himself to recovery for six months; if it didn't work, he'd try something else. But it did work. Gerry had been attracting sick people because he was sick himself. But now he started to take good chances, healthy risks (in terms of inviting others deeply into his life). Gerry began to see people for what they were, to let go of the built-up residue from years of being lied to, neglected, abused—he could now let people in and trust them. Most importantly, the question, "Can you help me?" was formulating in his mind, and it was a query that required—absolutely needed—an affirmative answer.

Endless feelings welled within—finally, Gerry sensed an answer to his most powerful foe, alcoholism. It explained his issues, such as why emotions were so difficult to feel. Through substances, he had avoided them since before his adult years began, so he remained a teenager in terms of his emotional constitution and maturity. But he had found his resolve. He also found realistic hope: others not only encountered similar challenges and overcame them, but also used their setbacks to improve the quality of their lives.

Gerry wanted what those recovery folks possessed.

* * *

The fighter felt his determination to transcend his addictions swell. His authentic commitment to God was leading him to shift gears, wake up, appreciate life, and unite with healthy people with similar challenges and similar desires to evolve. He had a great life in most ways, but it was no longer working. Too much of his life had been dark, doing the same thing over and over again, and devoid of pure feeling. Recovery was placing Gerry on the road to feeling—the good and the bad and everything in between—and to accepting it all on life's terms.

The journey was magical. It also included challenging moments that placed Gerry in position to grow. However strong the challenge, faith provided him a lifeline and foundation to grow. Gerry's connection to God felt more powerful at the moments of pure desperation than at any time. Those moments were filled with pleas for the Lord's help. Compulsions to use and drink went away as Gerry connected to an aspect of his soul that he didn't before realize existed. Gerry was ready to authentically commit to something with all his heart, soul, and mind: recovery.

The next few months featured Gerry connecting with new people, going to new places, and doing new things. The fighter needed a change from the people, places, and things that were associated with alcohol—which accounted for a large portion of his life. Through novel experiences, Gerry found realistic hope. He learned that he could use his fighter's mentality from the ring and apply it to his quest for recovery. The former contender found the vehicle to face his reality, to look at his life and understand why he was hiding behind alcohol and self-sabotaging to avoid the pain. He was now forced to look by compassionate guides and angels who comprised his increasingly expanding recovery community.

Three months after beginning his abstinence from alcohol, Gerry was alerted by a wise peer that he was in danger of drinking again. Gerry thought she was crazy because he felt so great. Complacency and excessive confidence left the door open for Gerry's addiction to impose its irrational logic. Gerry had been warned by recovery peers that after the "pink cloud" of recovery evaporated, he could be vulnerable to returning to drugs and alcohol. For alcoholics, all it takes is a stray thought left unchecked to lead to a relapse. Like a small spark, it can be stifled and extinguished or catch fire and generate a raging inferno. "Alcohol thoughts" can be managed or can dominate the sufferer's mind completely. The types of environment that lead to the latter include stressful conditions, facing unfinished business with loved ones, or experiencing emotional difficulties. Oftentimes, long-term abusers might be encountering elevated levels of negative emotions for the first time in years, perhaps even the first time in their adult lives.

Like an overconfident fighter whose relaxed guard allows a punch to land, Gerry relapsed. The two-month-long return to active addiction included all his old behaviors and symptoms: drinking all night long, verbal disputes, avoiding loved ones and those looking out for him, excessively focusing on the negative views of life, and lamenting his career, his father's abuses, and his mother's inability to protect him.

The run would end, however, as suddenly as a perfectly executed left hook to a foe's jaw would terminate a boxing contest. One day, Gerry went into a breakfast joint—it seemed as though he was being guided there—and ran into his old bodyguard, Jack B. Gerry's old friend invited him to sit down and told Gerry that he had three years clean and sober and that Gerry never needed to drink again. Those words resonated.

The date—April 21, 1988—would prove to be vitally important in Gerry's life. At 10:40 am, the realization that he was in trouble truly connected to his heart. The relapse led Gerry to realize that he was a grain of sand on a beach, not anything special, and that he needed to be vigilant in his recovery efforts just like everyone else. Gratitude for his blessings, including a loving family and property, generated a healthy sense of urgency to get well. Now that he realized—truly realized—there was an issue, he could get on the path to getting better. He had become authentically committed to recovery.

Thus began Gerry's extended sobriety, now more than three decades long, a remarkable achievement that has been realized one single, manageable day at a time.

23

THE PREACHER AND THE PUNCHER

Immersing himself in sobriety, Gerry began to experience life very differently. Colors seemed brighter and more distinct. Driving to his home in the Hamptons, he noticed that he had been seeing the world in all gray. The damage inflicted by years of substance abuse still was being worked upon—it can take a year or more before the biology positively alters enough for dynamic changes to be experienced methodically—but Gerry was cognizant that his life was evolving. He was thinking things through and increasingly choosing his actions, not simply living on autopilot and reacting to life.

The reality of alcohol's devastation of his career became increasingly apparent. The old guy at the gym who told Gerry so many years ago that his career would go by quickly was right. It seemed like yesterday that he was in his early twenties with all the time in the world; age thirty-five was a century away. Now, it seemed like hours away. If he had the tools that he was now developing back then, where could Gerry have gone? How much of his potential would he have realized? Would he have been able to alter the course of his career, convince the Twins to secure him more fights, or hire managers who would have done so?

Still, each preceding moment was necessary to make Gerry the man he had evolved into, and for that, he was grateful. The valleys of despair needed to be traveled so that he could appreciate the heights of sobriety. Plus, he was not far removed from his physical prime. Perhaps he could make that comeback? Legendary heavyweight George Foreman, himself constructing what would become a historic comeback, seemed like an interesting challenge.

* * *

George Foreman's previous top name in his comeback—the esteemed Dwight Muhammad Qawi—was a battle-hardened cruiserweight at the time of their fight. Ring wear was showing on the proud warrior. Roughly three-and-a-half months before losing to Foreman (TKO by 7), Qawi had been knocked out on the championship stage by Evander Holyfield in four rounds. These would be the only knockout losses in the durable Qawi's Hall of Fame career, but Foreman's victory was dismissed for being against a far smaller foe. Moreover, Qawi's weight (222 pounds) suggested that he was very much out of shape. Even so, he had won multiple rounds. A Foreman fight against Gerry—a fellow giant with enormous punching power—would largely validate Foreman's comeback.

Although not seen as such by many at the time, Foreman's revived career was simply astounding and gaining increased legitimacy as his foes faltered under his own historically significant power. After defeating Everett "Bigfoot" Martin, Foreman boasted an unbelievable sixty knockouts in his sixty-four wins. His first professional career, which spanned from 1969 to 1977, produced forty-five wins (42 KOs) against only two losses. Foreman's comeback bolstered those numbers significantly: nineteen dominating wins, all but one resulting from a knockout. In fact, Foreman's first eighteen bouts had ended inside the distance. His knockout streak had ended about a half year earlier in his last bout, a ten-round unanimous decision win over Martin. Seeking a bigger name to produce a legitimate event—one that would take his second championship quest to the next level—Foreman sought out his fellow power-punching heavyweight. A defeat of Gerry on a big stage likely would add volume to Foreman's shot at Mike Tyson's championships.

Gerry's two-year, seven-month-long layoff since the Spinks fight roughly coincided with Foreman's comeback, which began on March 9, 1987. Gerry's last fight—the worst experience of his boxing career—had occurred a little more than three months later. Again, Gerry was placed in the position of shaking off ring rust against an established foe whose own activity had been at or near optimal levels. Against manageable opponents, the more than forty-year-old Foreman had fought consistently and often: nineteen fights during the thirty-four months leading into his fight with Gerry.

For Gerry, it would be another opportunity for him to go the distance and to get the most out of himself and his abilities.

* * *

Tom Mara was Gerry's new manager and a Long Island construction tycoon. He was acutely attuned to Gerry's mind-set and would not entertain talks of a comeback until he felt Gerry was invested fully. One day, Gerry's enthusiasm to commit to a comeback convinced Mara to set up a fight. Finding a new trainer for Gerry would be a key task for Mara. In July 1989, happenstance led Mara to secure a perfect replacement for Gerry's beloved trainer and surrogate father, Victor Valle. In fact, this man was the only trainer Gerry wanted at that point in his career.

Mara attended a wedding at which the legendary Gil Clancy was also present. Closer to seventy years old than sixty-five, Clancy had not trained a fighter since 1977. He had joined CBS as a part-time analyst and, beginning in late 1978, would also serve as matchmaker for Madison Square Garden (assuming responsibilities from Teddy Brenner). In 1981, Clancy's role at CBS expanded enough for him to cease matchmaking responsibilities, and he continued to respectfully decline myriad invitations to resume the role of trainer. Clancy simply loved working in front of the camera. Many attempted to lure the boxing sage out of retirement but no opportunity was compelling enough for Clancy to cease his beloved television duties. Clancy didn't really consider the offers.

Yet Clancy always had felt that Gerry had vast potential ever since seeing him as a seventeen-year-old amateur. That potential was never fulfilled, but, as Clancy sometimes joked, Irishmen matured late, with pugilists particularly slow to evolve. At thirty-three years old, Gerry was possibly still in the last stages of his physical prime, given his relative lack of ring wear.

Clancy's résumé was profoundly impressive. His wisdom had been established by his work with multiple champions, such as two-time middleweight and three-time welterweight kingpin Emile Griffith, lightweight titlist Ken Buchanan, 1970s stalwart heavyweight contender Jerry Quarry, legends Muhammad Ali and Joe Frazier, and even George Foreman.

Mara asked if Clancy would look at Gerry in the gym. Clancy, who had earned a master's degree in education from New York University, thought about the situation. Gerry always intrigued Clancy. If properly motivated, even an older Gerry Cooney could compete favorably given that powerful left hand. The time off from the ring likely saved Gerry from the damage usually assumed by fighters in their mid-thirties. Never an elusive fighter, the natural rigors of age wouldn't be as prominent for a fighter like Gerry. Changes would have to be made to adjust to age and other factors, but not significant ones.

However, Gerry needed to be serious about his latest comeback. Mara assured the esteemed trainer that Gerry was completely dedicated. Clancy stated that he would see the former contender but that he would train him only if he sensed that Gerry had something left. Otherwise, Gerry would have to quit and Clancy would continue his thirteen-year retirement from training. Gerry's workout demonstrated not only that he maintained quality skills, but that he was fervently dedicated to displaying and improving them.

After a career being led by Victor Valle, Gerry now won Clancy's imagination—and enlisted a new trainer.

* * *

Everyone has a constellation of gifts. It takes mentors, nurturers, and guides to help us become aware of them and encourage us to explore the limits of our potential. Victor Valle had served those roles with passion and authentic caring for Gerry. Like the sun's nurturing rays shining through on cloudy days, Valle's efforts penetrated through Gerry's substance abuse issues whenever humanly possible. And like the sun empowering seeds to grow, Valle's training and love ultimately resulted in Gerry becoming more than just a better fighter: he became a better man. It just took time for those seeds to grow enough to be seen.

Clancy took the baton from Valle to guide Gerry's next career chapter, a battle against the incredibly powerful George Foreman. The fight's announcement occurred in the summer of 1989, a time when Mike Tyson was at the peak of his historic first championship reign. It was to be held in Atlantic City Convention Center on January 15, 1990.

The bout was intriguing for fight fans. Gerry's chronic inactivity and advancing age suggested that his days as a contender were over. However, his punching power remained, and a convincing victory would reignite legitimate hope that he finally would fulfill his vast potential. Moreover, Gerry remained a legitimate heavyweight and former top contender with the power to hurt Foreman—something none of the former champion's previous rivals conceivably could do.

An interesting note was Clancy's previous involvement with Foreman. The duo worked together after Foreman's unforgettable championship loss, as 3–1 favorite, to Muhammad Ali until "Big George" retired for the first time on March 17, 1977. That night, Foreman had a spiritual awakening following his upset loss to Jimmy Young. Clancy interpreted the event as Foreman being severely dehydrated and hallucinating. Whatever occurred, Foreman would take a decade off before his return to the ring. Now, in 1989, the intriguing battle featured two fighters and one venerable trainer making comebacks. All were motivated for honorable reasons, ranging from love of the sport (Gerry and Clancy) to generating funds for a beloved community center (Foreman).

* * *

Gerry, persistently on the comeback trail due to long delays between fights, was enjoying his first training camp while sober. His camp was located in what is normally a romantic getaway, Caesars Brookdale, a 110-room resort located in the pristine Pocono Mountains. The wilderness limited distractions, but Gerry's insides were adjusting to his newfound sobriety. He was still in early recovery. His brain was adjusting to life without chemicals. The transition could take more than eighteen months for some addicts and alcoholics. His body and brain were changing for the good, but there were growing pains in the form of mental and emotional fatigue, mood swings, disturbed sleep, and other symptoms associated with post-acute withdrawals (PAWs). This, in addition to coping directly with emotions for the first time in his life without the numbing effects of various substances, was a remarkable but also challenging era for the fighter.

Clancy's memory of Gerry's debacle against Spinks was acute. He needed Gerry to be sharp, focused, and in the moment. Gerry's sobriety was an important indication that he could manifest a greater portion of his potential. Yet sustained sobriety is needed for the type of expectations that those outside of the recovery community can reasonably expect. Some in early recovery not only encounter PAW symptoms, but mental health symptoms, which can manifest with unprecedented intensity since emotions are felt directly for the first time. These are some of the reasons why addicts and alcoholics relapse so frequently.

Somehow, Gerry maintained his recovery. It was amazing that he abstained from alcohol, since he not only endured the biological challenges that come with early recovery from prolonged addiction, but he also struggled with managing his emotions. He never fully felt them before, yet he was doing so while training for a significant fight, which itself produced pressure and uncertainty. He was praying consistently for guidance, simply doing his best each day, and mindfully enjoying the outcomes to the best of his current capability. Increasingly, he balanced determined focus with authentic calm and was improving his ability to divorce himself from outcomes and instead to focus on the task at hand. Each action step, however large or small, compounded the progress of the previous one.

Gerry's new guide had constructed an educated plan. The goal was to simply carry it out while being alert to environmental cues that validated the guidelines or pragmatically suggested a modification. The same could be said for approaching life outside the ring. Essentially, Gerry was replacing destructive mind-sets and habits with empowering ones, which was fuel for greater wisdom and spiritual growth. Each previous adversity had meaning, as it elevated Gerry's appreciation for the moment and the opportunities found in those that remained. Clancy was seeing more of the magic he saw in the amateur all those years earlier, when the teenaged Gerry displayed all-time-great promise.

Without the anchor of substance abuse, Gerry now had a great deal of time on his hands. Freedom is difficult at times for the recovering alcoholic. Unoccupied time leaves recovering persons susceptible to filling it with well-established addictive behaviors. Change is hard. Human beings are often averse to even positive change. It can be confusing, too. Further, it isn't enough to cease unhealthy habits, including those related to thinking patterns, but they must be immediately replaced by meaningful and productive substitutes. Thankfully, meaningful work and a strong support network can fill the gaps left by abstaining from chemicals—and as Gerry's work was growing rapidly so was his new circle.

A training camp without substance abuse was beyond rewarding for the former contender. Once again faced with a prolonged layoff and unsharpened skills, Gerry was empowered to work toward his dreams, to implement the plans to realize them, and to begin embracing setbacks as opportunities to evolve (rather than as evidence of being a "failure").

Gerry had entered a new world—a brilliant one—but as with any change, there were adjustments to be made.

After all, it takes time to evolve.

* * *

In what was likely one of the more difficult fights to predict, Foreman emerged as the oddsmakers' favorite. But a significant minority contended that Gerry would thwart Foreman's quest to regain the championship. There were too many intangibles to consider. Foreman's advanced age may have been misleading considering his extended time off. Also, the frequency of his fights during the past few years was nearly ideal to hone his skills. Gerry was younger chronologically, but he was also past his physical prime and his ring rust was profound. Not only had he not fought in two and a half years, but Gerry had competed in only thirteen professional rounds during the past seven and a half years. Foreman would be twenty pounds heavier than Gerry's 230-pound frame, but he would also need to punch upward at the six-foot, six-inch Irish giant. This was unusual for the six-foot, four-inch Foreman. The "punching preacher" must have felt like a lightweight after losing approximately sixty-five pounds since he first began training with vigor.

Meanwhile thirty-three-year-old Gerry was embarking on a new chapter in his development. Balance was a key focus throughout camp, particularly after throwing his vaunted left hook. The old-school Clancy had put an eye patch on Gerry's left eye each time he worked the bag. This helped the huge heavyweight square up to the target. Clancy's camp featured a more laid-back feel as compared to Valle's leadership. This approach seemed ideal to a veteran fighter. Gerry's workload remained the same. His days were broken up into morning runs, late morning exercises, afternoon ring work, and evening weight training with George Munch. The "Gentleman" was modifying his body through disciplined action, his sobriety was changing his brain, and the two combined were reconnecting Gerry with his compassionate warrior's soul.

A few weeks prior to fighting Foreman, Gerry fought an exhibition against Wesley Watson (15–2, 11 KOs). Both combatants had January 15, 1990, dates against two formidable foes: Watson was to confront the rising undefeated prospect, "Merciless" Ray Mercer (12–0, 9 KOs), while Gerry was scheduled to headline the card against Foreman. Mercer had been Watson's army teammate and the Olympic gold medalist in 1988. Watson boasted an impressive amateur résumé of his own. He had been the 1985 National Amateur Athletic Union super heavyweight champion while boxing for the U.S. Army and a runner-up a year later to Alex Garcia. He had also battled some quality names in the professional ranks. Watson had recently lost to Michael Dokes (38–2–2), who two fights and five months earlier had fought what *The Ring* cited as "the best heavyweight fight of the 1980s" against undefeated Evander Holyfield.

With Foreman fighting earlier in the night, Gerry tested his skills against Watson amid a smaller but supportive crowd. At six feet, four inches, with striking power (eleven of his fifteen wins had come via knockout), the army-tough Watson was a good test for the former contender. Watson and Gerry had worked together often in the past and put on a good exhibition. Gil Clancy looked on as his charge moved as fluidly as could be expected from such a prolonged period away from live combat. Clancy's participation negated many of the upcoming fight's cynical critics, who had dismissed the bout as an event featuring two aged fighters whose ability to become relevant contenders had long since evaporated.

The two warriors had much left in their tanks and were readying for battle.

* * *

The fight was staged in the same location as Gerry's match against Spinks—Atlantic City, New Jersey. It was hosted by Caesars Atlantic City at the convention center. It was the first significant heavyweight fight of the new decade. The cold January air did not prevent fans from packing the center to its capacity. Foreman—no longer the surly warrior whose ability to intimidate was equally as destructive as the TNT in his fists—was finding that his popularity had transcended the sport. The marketing of his comeback as a happy preacher—whose success was evidence that middle age can be as productive as young adulthood—was an inspiration for many whose age-related physical changes signified the finality of important life chapters. Gerry, although the recipient of many negative words regarding his inactivity, still connected to the masses. The public viewed the fighters as two good men whose prodigious power could serve as a time machine, resurrecting their former contender statuses and instantly reinserting them into the heavyweight picture.

It was the first time Gerry was outweighed by an opponent. Foreman's 253.25-pound frame was considered a liability to many, but it would take the 231-pound Gerry some getting used to, since Foreman was a huge, powerful man who knew how to use his size for maximum advantage. Gerry entered the ring with almost twenty months of recovery, and he was also coming off a two-and-a-half-year layoff. The former top contender also had been nursing an Achilles' heel issue. Foreman was not an elusive target but Gerry's defensive timing needed to be honed, lest one of Foreman's massive fists lands flush.

The famed ring announcer, Michael Buffer, introduced the two giant heavyweights to an excited and intrigued crowd. Power sells and compels, and Foreman-Cooney boasted more power than any fight in heavyweight history, as evidenced by their combined eighty-four knockouts in ninety-two victories (a 92 percent knockout rate). Economically, the fight was also lucrative enough to guarantee each fighter $1 million, despite no title being at stake, but below the market value of the day for such huge names. The boxing world just didn't know what to expect from the fighters.

The fight, billed as the "Preacher and the Puncher," was promoted by Bob Arum. Critics of both Foreman and Gerry labeled the fight the "Geezers at Caesars." Approximately 12,581 fans filed into the arena and thousands of others viewed the battle through pay-per-view and closed-circuit television. Referee Joe Cortez was assigned the responsibility of managing the battle between two of the largest fighters in history. The contestants would compete in a bout that would have serious implications for the heavyweight division's hierarchy.

The first round witnessed Foreman methodically employing his offensive skills and cross-arm defense. Outdated by some standards, Foreman utilized the defense that famed trainer Archie Moore taught him to negate Gerry's powerful blows. Foreman would later say that Gerry's punches, even the blocked ones, vibrated his body. Such was the inherent power in Gerry's fists, something with which he was naturally blessed and that he honed through a lifetime of athletic training. His frame was well-crafted by his first sober training camp in his career, contributing to sharper and more educated punches than one might expect from a rusty fighter.

Gerry focused on his game plan, his legs permitting him to be elusive enough to offset Foreman's timing. Gerry was the lighter man, allowing him to use his movement effectively against the heavier Foreman. His heavy jab connected enough to keep Foreman at a safe distance. A chopping left to the jaw removed Gerry's mouthpiece. It took almost thirty seconds for Cortez to recognize that Gerry's teeth were unprotected and to call a time-out so that the equipment could be replaced.

Toward the end of the round, Gerry caught Foreman with his devastating left hook. It was the first real adversity of Foreman's comeback. He wobbled as his body fought to stabilize from the blow, leading viewers and spectators to wonder if the former champion would fall. After the bout, Foreman would identify Gerry as the hardest puncher he had fought, likening his left hooks to bombs. Perhaps instinctively, Foreman plodded forward and stifled any chance of Gerry fully capitalizing on his success.

Soon after, the bell sounded.

* * *

Between rounds, Clancy provided encouragement to Gerry. His gentle, strong, and calmly confident voice commanded his fighter's attention. The first round's closing moments witnessed Gerry's hitting power. Though always a ferocious finisher, Gerry may not have capitalized on the moment as thoroughly as possible—his timing was simply off. Gerry's ring rust negated his boxing instincts to some degree. The relatively few seconds that separated the opportunity to unload on a hurt Foreman and the end of the round was enough to separate Gerry from his best opportunity to win this battle.

Even so, the 20/20 vision of hindsight—that includes all the Foreman fights yet to come—indicates that Foreman's rugged chin likely would have withstood a swarming attack, perhaps leaving Gerry open to Foreman's one-punch knockout power. Moreover, Foreman had yet to demonstrate profound stamina, particularly against a fighter with Gerry's power. The wise decision was to be methodical, to continue attacking the body, and to move enough to stay out of range of direct Foreman blows. The evidence available at the time led to the logical conclusion that an overweight, forty-year-old Foreman would tire out when absorbing a sustained body attack. So it may have been prudent to be methodical.

Gerry would not secure the opportunity to employ his game plan. Clancy intended Gerry to take Foreman into deep waters, seven or so rounds, and to be content with moving and wearing the older fighter down with an accumulation of body punches delivered at a relatively safe range. One mistake against Foreman is enough to remove oneself from consciousness, but Gerry's finishing instincts had been activated. He trusted his power. Later, Foreman would admit that Gerry hurt him but that he made sure Gerry didn't know it. Foreman stated that one of Gerry's blows to his elbow was felt all the way up to his chin. But the former and future heavyweight champ kept his poker face and composure throughout the pain.

Gerry wasn't operating from his strategic mind, but from his primitive, predatory one, which had served him well throughout his career. Such is the nature of fighting. It is especially difficult to stick to a fight plan when one is punched—primitive survival instincts simply take over. This time, Gerry's ring rust negated the intuition presented by his warrior spirit. In boxing, as in most sports, the difference between winning and losing can come down to inches.

* * *

The fight's second installment witnessed Foreman's educated, steady, and accurate jab finding Gerry. Foreman cut off the ring—something that Gerry was accustomed to doing himself—as he intelligently maneuvered himself in position to land his thunderous blows. He began leading with power punches. Foreman caught Gerry with vicious blows, despite the former contender's improved guard. Gerry absorbed a Foreman heavy-handed combination before being forced to the canvas. Pure courage and warrior's instinct pulled Gerry to his feet, but he was only partially conscious as he righted his six-foot, six-inch frame.

Heartbeats after referee Joe Cortez determined Gerry was well enough to continue, Foreman masterfully positioned himself to unload a perfectly timed, brutal left uppercut that separated Gerry from consciousness. His accuracy was near perfect, perhaps the result of frequent fighting and disciplined training. Gerry fell and the fight was immediately stopped. Only three seconds remained before the round's expiration, but there was no possible way that any person could rise from such perfectly placed bombs by the powerful Foreman.

It took Gerry some time to get back to his feet. He had endured some of the heaviest punches that history's most prolific power-punching heavyweight was capable of throwing. The two warriors later embraced with mutual respect for each other's abilities. Later, Foreman referred to Gerry as his best friend and said that he loved Gerry.

Gerry, thoughtful and reflective, completed his postfight interview and calmly announced his retirement after joking that he would come back a few more times. He referred to "straightening out some things" and thanked his trainer and Caesar's Palace. Gerry's work was symbolic of his spiritual development—outcomes are often influenced by factors outside one's control, leading one's preparation and effort to be the truest, most pure measure of success. Against Foreman, Gerry completed a sober training camp, managed the pressures and life circumstances without the deleterious aid of substances, and did the best he could with what he had at the time.

This is success.

* * *

Foreman sat comfortably in late-night talk show host David Letterman's chair. He sported evidence of a black eye, declaring that Gerry's left hook was harder than the great Joe Frazier's version of the devastating punch. In fact, "Big" George stated that Gerry was the hardest hitter he had ever faced. This opinion has survived the test of time. Long after his career finally terminated, Foreman was interviewed and again stated that Gerry was the hardest hitter he ever faced. Foreman further relayed that fighting Gerry was one of his three most important fights (the others being against Ron Lyle and Muhammad Ali) and said that when Gerry hit him on his left side, he felt it on his right.

Fifteen months and four early-round knockouts later, Foreman would contest a primed Evander Holyfield for the heavyweight championship. Foreman lost the bout while going the distance, proving himself an authentic player in the heavyweight picture. After a loss to Tommy Morrison, Foreman would compete for the title again more than fifteen months later. Behind on the judges' scorecards—and perhaps losing every round—Foreman blasted champion Michael Moorer into unconsciousness to assume the title of the oldest heavyweight champion in history.

Although many would never have believed it at the time, the Foreman that Gerry fought was a future heavyweight kingpin.

* * *

"God hears all prayers, but sometimes the answer is no." These ten words, when truly understood, permit one to let go of resentment, heartache, and regret. As flawed human beings, we do not have all the puzzle pieces on the table of life. Life invariably includes adversity that challenges our trust in a higher power, a process that paradoxically can lead to a powerful faith that life is unfolding with perfect precision. Heartaches, setbacks, and changes are often a necessary part of the process.

Gerry's retirement after the Foreman clash was his last. Now in his mid-thirties, the future was a vast unknown. Unlike before, the prospect of returning to fighting—the only occupation that he treasured and fully understood—was no longer an option. For the first time, Gerry *knew* it was time to move on. He now would need to fill the expansive gulf created by disembarking from his cherished dream of earning the heavyweight championship of the world.

Retirement presented the adversity of freedom. Freedom is cherished, but it often can be a terrifying reality. With choices comes the responsibility for the outcomes and the possibility of unwanted consequences. There is loneliness, too. The closing of a career and a more direct focus on the unknown triggers an awareness of one's mortality. Such awareness is not usually conscious, but it can create anxious and depressive mindsets.

A person in early recovery can be particularly overwhelmed when confronting such awareness. The unknown can be intimidating and the absence of work can be fertile ground for relapses. The brief reprieve provided by drugs can be incredibly appealing, despite the intellectual understanding of its medium- and long-term consequences. The primitive brain, the one impacted by drugs, doesn't consider much beyond the immediacy of pleasure and pain. It takes remarkable efforts, a terrific support network, and phenomenal discipline to develop new norms and responses to life's difficulties, good fortunes, and uncertainties.

Through smiles and authentic efforts to help others, Gerry continued to instinctively tap into his resiliency, compassion, and courage as he found his way, one manageable day at a time. The human capacity for these treasured attributes is limitless but uncertain and inaccessible until severe adversity presents itself. The most difficult steps of the adversity journey occur when God's answer is "no," when every fiber in our being wants it to be "now"—such as Gerry's quest for the world title.

Yet with faith, patience, and the humility to accept that our own will is not the highest authority and is not based upon omnipotent awareness, the divine reasons for "no" can become understood and even welcomed.

24

DOING THE "NEXT RIGHT THING"

Although his battle against Foreman ended in a knockout loss, Gerry had advanced toward a far greater victory: he established the foundation of his recovery and was increasingly acquiring the tools appropriate to sustain it one day at a time. Practicing simplicity in a chaotic world demands acceptance of setbacks and commitment to resume good work. But, as in sports, life unfolds in moments. Nothing is permanent. Each moment leads to the next, but none occurs at the same time. Taken in such a way, the future is manageable. Emotions are manageable. Goals are possible because they are broken up into doable actions.

Going the distance, or realizing one's most inspired dreams, becomes more and more possible.

* * *

Gerry's life and professional career, once boxing politics and multi-millions of dollars became the prize for each contest, had been fixated on the future—as well as the consequences of victory and defeat. Recovery was teaching the fighter to focus on the moment, what was occurring now, and fully living it. He began to sharpen a here-and-now focus on gratitude, health, and opportunity. This mind-set created the conditions for greater access to Gerry's resiliency, self-acceptance, and forgiveness.

Unlike most elite pugilists, Gerry somehow evaded returning to the intense allure of combat. He had been finding meaning in his recovery to fill the void left by fighting. Recovery also healed the unnerving realization that his potential largely was left unexplored due to factors within his control and those outside of it. Gerry was increasingly living the magnificence of a spiritual life, connecting with others, and exploring his own capabilities. He was finding happiness, living life on its terms, and embracing whatever the moment brought.

Life outside the ropes was not only possible but wondrous; there were new and legitimate challenges to face and overcome in much the same manner of comparing talents against fellow pugilists. Exploring business endeavors, such as owning several minor league baseball teams (along with his business adviser, Ken Silver), was a quality use of his intellectual abilities. Dedicating his life to helping others realize and maintain recovery nurtured Gerry's spiritual self. Investing time and energy into good relationships and taking healthy risks of trusting others became the norm.

Gerry's recovery journey manifested at the time when most boxers falter into deeper stages of addiction: at the end of their careers, during the immediate aftermath of their retirement. The end of one's career usually generates a gulf of emptiness as a result of the removal of work, confusion about the future, and boredom that manifests from too much free time. The primal energies associated with fighting produce an incredible high that is frequently replaced by drugs and alcohol. Most human beings do not know the unique highs of combat nor of hearing thousands of people cheer their names. Once that feeling is experienced and known and then is no longer possible, it is challenging to avoid seeking such highs through other means.

Despite the normal challenges of transitioning to his post-career life, Gerry developed a sturdier trust in his intuition. Quieting his mind through connecting to his higher power, Gerry increasingly listened to his own inner wisdom. Like a quality jab, he didn't force or push it, he let it manifest naturally and according to all the spiritual practices that occupied him over the years. "I'm only scratching the surface," he humbly and consistently acknowledged. "I'm a work in progress."

* * *

Consistent recovery work results in progress on multiple levels. As life unfolded, Gerry came to find that the abuse from his father's huge hands was not his fault. The work is continuously evolving, growing positively with each accepted insight into what is—and what was. Such acceptance permits focus and energy to center on life's blessings, what is occurring in the moment, and what can be rather than excessively focusing on life's myriad challenges, what might happen, and what once occurred.

The process of change is a difficult and laborious one. The reality that is comfortable is not always healthy. Gerry's formative years were spent in a chaotic environment that produced feelings of insecurity and danger. People replicate what they know. That is, the same relationships seem to materialize with different people assuming the roles of paramour, friend, and so forth. As a result, the same issues arise. The same emotions, too.

The common denominator of each relationship, however, is the person. As Gerry worked more on himself, he found out who he was and wanted to become. The struggle to survive increasingly became a striving to flourish. Gerry found out that he needed to move on, make peace with the mistakes, feel all of the emotions, and change. The former contender also gave himself permission to be happy. Always having his faith as a resource, Gerry came to live it more completely and improved upon providing himself the compassion and support that he instinctively dispensed to others. For addicts, alcoholics, and children whose parents abused substances, easing up on self-shaming is extremely difficult. Accepting compliments without trying to convince others that the kind words are false and providing similar generous words to themselves is even more challenging.

His body may not be as responsive as it was yesteryear, but Gerry's acquired knowledge allows him to predict life's demands with more accuracy. In the ring, too, he strives to teach troubled youth and aspiring champions how best to learn not only from his experiences, but from their own. Boxing careers are too short not to act upon the lessons in the ring. Life also is too brief to persistently make the same mistakes. This reality is, perhaps, most acutely relatable to ingesting substances. Addiction can take advantage of complacency—that is, no longer working on one's recovery—or the belief that the person can drink normally or within predetermined limits. By repeatedly embracing the reality—confirmed through experience—that one cannot drink or use drugs "normally" (by stating that she or he is an alcoholic), the person stifles the addiction's attempts to reintroduce itself in the person's life.

This is much easier said than done, and it is all done one manageable day at a time.

* * *

According to Ashley Montagu, the famous anthropologist and humanist, the most profound human defeat is found in the disparity between what a person was capable of becoming and what he or she has become.

This realization often occurs after one's window of opportunity has closed. Athletes are confronted with this crisis far earlier than most, generally in their mid-thirties. There is wisdom to be derived from such heartbreaking realities.

As Gerry grew more accustomed to his promotional activities rather than being the one who is promoted, he sought out ways to help peers less fortunate than himself. One of Gerry's most prominent projects, the Fighters' Initiative for Support and Training (FIST), was created in 1998. Gerry and his wife, Jennifer, were moving and came across some paperwork regarding helping fighters. Jennifer brought it to Gerry's attention and worked with him to make it a reality. The duo worked with such boxing notables as Steve Farhood, major entities like Showtime, HBO, and Madison Square Garden, retired boxers, and others who loved boxing. It was an honorable and necessary endeavor. Fighters are rarely prepared for retirement challenges, such as accumulating sufficient savings, accepting the loss of one's career, and the need to transition to a new life stage, as well as finding viable work. FIST helped fighters make this transition.

The organization assisted fighters on innumerable life levels. Prominent was its focus on career development, mental health care, substance abuse evaluation, and education regarding available benefits. The void created by retirement can be a challenging transition for most. Fighters are often specially trained and do not have many established skill sets necessary for other occupations. Many attributes can be generalized to other jobs, but they may not be readily apparent. FIST helped to provide aptitude tests to explore occupational opportunities. The experience helped Gerry turn the page in his own life, empowering him to assist his peers in the small community that is combat sport athletes. As with most altruistic efforts, these undertakings helped Gerry develop even more meaning in his life, which had been evolving and expanding in correlation to the quality and quantity of his recovery efforts. In all, FIST supported more than three hundred fighters before ceasing operations in 2007 as the result of nonprofit certification issues with federal and state authorities.

* * *

Like dozens of bricks combine to constitute a strong wall of protection, Gerry's recovery has been founded upon positive acts that nurture his soul. Many of those involve service to others. In fact, such actions are the heart of his existence. Myriad charitable activities provide meaning to his life and permit opportunities to provide others with the encouragement and faith that were nonexistent during the first few decades of his life. By doing what he can to ease the suffering of others, Gerry heals himself: the wounds that he can't address physically are accessible through connecting meaningfully with children and helping them feel safe, special, and worthy of love.

Other bricks in the wall that help to prevent addiction thoughts from becoming addiction behaviors include self-care and surrounding oneself with like-minded individuals committed to utilizing resolve and courage to redirect suffering into wisdom, insight, acceptance, and peace. Interacting with other people who understood his struggles, in itself, was healing. Gerry wasn't alone. That is a powerfully healing realization. Other people shared his powerlessness over alcohol. There was an immediate fellowship with strangers bred from the shared courage of having walked through the valleys of despair only to emerge stronger and increasingly serene.

Adversity now served as opportunity for personal evolution. It is through the process of healing and helping others to do the same that wisdom is most readily generated. But the process can be a strained one if the survivor does not enjoy strong support. This is particularly true for those growing up in abusive families. The persistent activation of the child's fight, flight, or freeze stimulus leads to chronic stress. However, human brains can transcend such psychological damage—it requires awareness, insight, and quality daily work, but it can be done.

Somehow Gerry retired financially secure. He wasn't an enormous spender and, even at a young age, understood that he needed to protect himself for a rainy day. Such is a benefit of growing up without much money. Being self-sufficient financially permits Gerry the opportunity to assist others. It also empowers Gerry to satisfy the need for challenges—a vital dynamic that formerly was experienced during his fighting career—through healthy mediums. He has become a self-made entrepreneur many times over, owning minor league baseball teams, becoming involved in thoroughbred horse stables, promoting boxing legends like Roberto Duran, "Sugar" Ray Leonard, and George Foreman, among countless other small and large ventures.

As meaningful and exciting as the business world and its various opportunities can be, Gerry's greatest career passions are teaching others, training fighters and ordinary folks, and his highly successful SiriusXM radio show with Randy "Commish" Gordon, *At the Fights*. Gerry invests the same degree of focus and effort in training middle-aged business professionals as he does legitimate pugilistic prospects. Gerry highlights hard work and identifies shortcomings so that his charges are prepared for their fights. Whoever they are—businessman, teacher, professional fighter—Gerry wants them to leave with an understanding of the sport. His fighters may hear and intellectually understand, but they must experience a fight before they truly know what he is saying.

Just like in life.

* * *

As a trainer, Gerry acts upon his interests in other human beings' futures. When he is training multiple fighters simultaneously, he spends as much time with young national champions with legitimate hopes for stardom as he does with aged businesspeople who desire solely to improve their physical condition. Each moment is a treasured one that features Gerry imparting his enduring message to work hard, to keep punching, and to have fun doing so.

Technically, Gerry focuses on defense, defense, defense. Victor Valle's wisdom lives on in Gerry's training. As a young power puncher, Gerry's inclination was to go, go, go—to engage savage, raw power during the high emotions of present-moment combat. He couldn't absorb all of Valle's teachings amid the lightning fast pace of life, even though he loved the learning process. At the time, life was fast. Age and wisdom have slowed it down. The growth has helped Gerry to forget the setbacks while retaining the lessons.

Now, Gerry's comprehension has deepened exponentially, and he values the artistry of the sport: setting foes up, foiling opponents' attacks by making them miss, anticipating blows, and using well-honed muscle memory to employ ideal counterpunches. Learning to fight more than prepares one for future opponents; it sets one up to live life more fully. "If you can fight, you can do anything," the former contender frequently states. "Fighting is what life is about. You have to create the opening, have a plan, and you have to perform it. There is no better feeling than setting a guy up, creating an opening, and landing your shot. You can't wait, because the opportunity is going to pass in a minute. Just like in life."

Gerry's external battles, the famous ones that took place inside the boxing ring, are symbolic of Gerry's inner strife—and our own personal challenges. Boxing was a vehicle for the young Gerry to confront and overcome his fears. It fed him, keeping him alive and providing him confidence and self-worth. But realizing and maintaining sobriety—one moment at a time, one challenge at a time—was the mechanism that enabled Gerry to heal enough to not only survive, but to fight for his life, for a meaningful existence. Incredibly, Gerry's greatest achievements occurred far from the eyes of sports historians or boxing's innumerable fans, and they began just as his championship dreams definitively ended.

These accomplishments are within the grasp of a great many of us. They include actively experiencing and processing the powerful emotions bred from challenging experiences and life's confounding lessons. This is oftentimes a courageous and potentially overwhelming process that requires a solid therapeutic support network. Viewed from a productive and rational perspective, Gerry's life demonstrates how one's effort, bravery, and determination can be utilized to endure adversity and transform perceived defeat into a platform for future success. Most of us are far more capable than we allow ourselves to believe—adversity and setbacks are life's methods of helping us access our dormant skills, abilities, and potential. Our journeys are unique, but human emotions are universal. They allow us to connect with one another and our life stories. Each life journey is a solitary one, but we are all interconnected on a common voyage of existence.

* * *

"Boxing is life, you know what I mean? Just like life," Gerry proclaims enthusiastically. He recounts a story about a friend who had endured a difficult life challenge, fought through the issue and the depression that accompanied it, and how each life happening was like taking a punch in the ring. And although everyone is in the ring of life alone, we have support systems. The boxer has cornermen; a person has family, friends, and peers. Picking the right people with whom to surround ourselves elevates the odds of success. So, too, does embracing opportunities and challenges as they arise.

"I learned that you have to take the shot every time; take the shot and whatever happens, happens," Gerry often states. "Go the distance, no matter what. Get the information, and go for it. I hope the best for everyone. Move forward, have fun doing it—taking the punches that life throws and get up and fight harder. I don't want to be a survivor; I did that for too long. I want to live life to the fullest. And that's what I've been doing. The fans, the people—that's what it's all about, meeting people and giving back. Hopefully, I can help some people along the way, as much as I can."

Going the distance—the term once imprinted in Gerry's mind going into the Holmes fight—once created some doubt that he could do so. Now the term is an empowering one. The lessons of that fight and so many others—both inside and outside the ring—contribute to the happy, productive, and giving man that Gerry evolved into throughout the course of his life. Each moment was needed, even the tough ones—perhaps especially the tough ones—in order to come to the cognitive and spiritual awareness needed to joyfully author a meaningful existence. Go the distance and learn to live life fully, whatever that definition might mean for you. Take the chance, embrace what happens, keep fighting for happiness, and give more than you receive.

We, the authors, wish this for you.

BIBLIOGRAPHY

Anderson, Dave. "Boxing Opinions." Sports of the Times. *New York Times*, May 27, 1982.
———. "'Look Fierce, Fake It.'" Sports of the Times. *New York Times*, April 22, 1986.
AndersUnlimited. "Gerry Cooney vs. John Dino Denis, November 1979." Filmed November 1979. YouTube video, 13:24. Posted April 2013. www.youtube.com/watch?v=5GNFb3xodTY.
———. "Gerry Cooney vs. Tom Prater, June 1979." Filmed June 1979. YouTube video, 6.28. Posted May 2013. www.youtube.com/watch?v=pJDCM_zvRz8.
Associated Press. "Cooney Injury May Jeopardize Rich Title Fight." *Schenectady Gazette*, January 20, 1982.
———. "Cooney Victorious in Return to Ring." *Southeast Missourian*, September 30, 1984.
———. "Cooney Wastes No Time Punching Out." *Evening Independent*, May 12, 1981.
———. "Gerry Cooney, Brown to Try Again Tomorrow." *Vindicator*, September 28, 1984.
———. "Weaver Will Defend against Tillis, Not Cooney." *Star-News*, July 2, 1981.
Berger, Phil. *Blood Season: Tyson and the World of Boxing*. New York: William Morrow, 1989.
———. "New Problem for Troubled Witherspoon." Boxing Notebook. *New York Times*, December 18, 1986.
BoxingRoyalty. "Very Rare Larry Holmes vs. Gerry Cooney Buildup to Fight Part 1." DailyMotion, 43:20. Posted 2014. www.dailymotion.com/video/x26vgk9.
Conner, Vinny, and Kate Conner. "Gerry Cooney Former WBC World Title Contender Signed Photo." Champs UK. www.champsuk.com/i-2011/gerry-cooney-former-wbc-heavyweight-world-title-contender-signed-photo.html (accessed September 18, 2018).
"Cooney Getting Ready to Come out of Limbo." *New York Times*, March 15, 1982.
"Cooney Is Arrested in Bar Incident." *New York Times*, December 10, 1985. www.nytimes.com/1985/12/10/sports/cooney-is-arrested-in-bar-incident.html.
"Cooney Is 'Keeping Loose.'" Sports of the Times. *New York Times*, February 22, 1981.
Deegan, J. "Larry Holmes: Joe Frazier Was a Great Fighter and a Great Friend." Lehighvalleylive.com. www.lehighvalleylive.com/sports/index.ssf/2011/11/larry_holmes_joe_frazier_was_a.html (accessed October 11, 2013).
"Fight Promoter Ready to Purchase Yankees." *Deseret News*, September 4, 1988.
Gildea, William. "Cooney: Promises to Keep: He's Confident He'll Top Spinks, Challenge Tyson." *Los Angeles Times*, June 12, 1987.
Goodpaster, Michael. "Holmes-Cooney Prefight Show." YouTube video, 45:45. Posted September 2014. www.youtube.com/watch?v=-aYK4xzUh8E.
Grassley, Will. "Huntington Loves Gerry Cooney." *Ocala Star-Banner*, June 8, 1982.

Gray, Tom. "Hall of Fame Inductee Barry Tompkins Recalls 1980's Glory Days." Ringtv.com. www.ringtv.com/502074-hall-fame-inductee-barry-tompkins-recalls-1980s-glory-days (accessed December 12, 2017).

———. "Larry Holmes: Gerry Cooney Was 'a Helluva Fighter.'" Ringtv.com. www.ringtv.com/502457-larry-holmes-gerry-cooney-helluva-fighter (accessed October 20, 2017).

Hauser, Thomas. *A Beautiful Sickness: Reflections on the Sweet Science.* Fayetteville: University of Arkansas Press, 2001.

Heller, Peter. *Bad Intentions: The Mike Tyson Story.* New York: New American Library, 1989.

Кадры, Крутые . "1987 06 15 Michael Spinks Gerry Cooney." Filmed June 1987. YouTube video, 28:28. Posted January 2014. www.youtube.com/watch?v=mP_piqK5Q1I.

Katis999. "Larry Holmes vs. Gerry Cooney (High Quality)." YouTube video, 1:13. Posted August 2012. www.youtube.com/watch?v=6s2rOOocTXs.

Katz, Michael. "Cooney Hurt; L.I. Bout Off." *New York Times*, January 20, 1982.

———. "Racial Hype for a Title Fight." *New York Times*, June 9, 1982.

———. "Rappaport's Ploy Irks Holmes." *New York Times*, December 13, 1984.

Keidan, Bruce. "Foreman KO's Cooney in Second Round." *Pittsburgh Post-Gazette*, January 16, 1990.

Lindsey, Robert. "Boxing Case Figure Believed Aiding F.B.I." *New York Times*, February 10, 1981.

Marantz, Steve. "Time Running out for Gerry Cooney: Unbeaten Challenger No Mystery to Sparring Partners." *Spokane Chronicle*, June 1, 1982.

Matthews, Wallace. "Mike Jones Was Indeed a Good Manager, a Good Man." *Los Angeles Times*, July 1, 1990.

MrJr2b. "Gerry Cooney vs. Ken Norton 1981." Filmed May 1981. YouTube video, 9:26. Posted November 2010. www.youtube.com/watch?v=bRhsraJ4u8A&t=6s&frags=pl%2Cwn.

MyInnerEyeInterview2. "George Foreman @ The David Letterman Show." Filmed January 1990. YouTube video, 11:25. Posted March 2014. www.youtube.com/watch?v=QFEpL775faE&frags=pl%2Cwn.

Plummer, William. "Can Gerry Cooney Take a Punch? 'Tis Better, He Feels, to Give Than Receive." *People*, June 14, 1982.

———. "Cus D'Amato." *People*, July 15, 1985.

The Ring Magazine. "*The Ring* Magazine's Annual Ratings: 1980." BoxRec.com. http://boxrec.com/media/index.php/The_Ring_Magazine%27s_Annual_Ratings:_1980 (accessed March 3, 2016).

Robinson, Kym. "Gerry Cooney vs. Eddie Gregg 1986." Filmed May 1986. YouTube video, 11:48. Posted August 2010. www.youtube.com/watch?v=quJMLgWpE40&t=417s&frags=pl%2Cwn.

Rogers, Thomas. "Weaver, Tillis Set for Fall Bout." *New York Times*, July 5, 1981.

Schulian, John. "Marvelous Marvin Just a Regular Guy." *Lewiston Daily Sun*, November 9, 1983.

Scopitone2011. "George Foreman vs. Gerry Cooney (1/15/1990)." Filmed January 1990. DailyMotion, 33:28. Posted 2011. www.dailymotion.com/video/xp7b4s#.UQiUr0pFdF8.

Sheppard, John. "Fight:40266." BoxRec.com. http://boxrec.com/media/index.php?title=Fight:40266 (accessed August 10, 2013).

———. "George Foreman." BoxRec.com. http://boxrec.com/en/boxer/90 (accessed April 2, 2016).

———. "George Foreman." BoxRec.com. http://boxrec.com/media/index.php/George_Foreman (accessed April 5, 2016).

———. "Gerry Cooney." BoxRec.com. http://boxrec.com/en/boxer/2463 (accessed February 24, 2015).

———. "Gerry Cooney." BoxRec.com. http://boxrec.com/media/index.php/Gerry_Cooney (accessed March 27, 2015).

———. "Gil Clancy." BoxRec.com. http://boxrec.com/media/index.php/Gil_Clancy (accessed May 8, 2016).

———. "Ken Norton." BoxRec.com. http://boxrec.com/en/boxer/168 (accessed February 27, 2015).

———. "Ken Norton." BoxRec.com. http://boxrec.com/media/index.php/Ken_Norton (accessed March 16, 2015).

———. "Larry Holmes." BoxRec.com. http://boxrec.com/en/boxer/150 (accessed June 5, 2017).

———. "Larry Holmes." BoxRec.com. http://boxrec.com/media/index.php/Larry_Holmes (accessed June 10, 2017).

———. "Michael Spinks." BoxRec.com. http://boxrec.com/en/boxer/1286 (accessed January 18, 2018).

———. "Michael Spinks." BoxRec.com. http://boxrec.com/media/index.php/Michael_Spinks (accessed January 22, 2018).

———. "Packy East (Bob Hope)." BoxRec.com. http://boxrec.com/media/index.php/Michael_Spinks (accessed January 22, 2018).

Smith, Gary. "A Bout against Doubt: Will Gerry Cooney Ever Be Hungry Enough? Not Even He Seems to Know." *Sports Illustrated*, June 8, 1987.

United Press International. "Critics' Blows Toughen Cooney." *Sun Sentinel*, June 7, 1987.

———. "Title Shot the Prize for Norton, Cooney." *Pittsburgh Press*, May 10, 1987.

Wilner, Barry. "Don't Call Gerry Cooney Boxing's Great White Hope." *Daily News*, October 17, 1980.

Winderman, Ira. "Spinks Looks to Defense Won't Go Toe-to-Toe vs. Cooney Monday." *Sun Sentinel*, June 13, 1987.

INDEX

ABOUT THE AUTHORS

Gerry Cooney had a legendary boxing career that culminated with his challenging all-time-great Larry Holmes for the heavyweight championship of the world. The bout was one of the most viewed battles of all time and cemented Gerry's place in boxing history. Gerry currently works with Randy "Commish" Gordon on their popular SiriusXM radio show *At the Fights*. He actively participates in numerous charity events and lives in New Jersey with his wife, Jennifer, and two of his three children.

John Grady is dually licensed as a mental health and addictions counselor, teaches at Kean University's counselor education graduate program, and is completing his PhD in organizational leadership at the Chicago School of Professional Psychology. John lives in New Jersey, where he manages a private practice that specializes in performance enhancement for sports and non-sports professionals alike.